PRINTREADING
for RESIDENTIAL CONSTRUCTION

Sixth Edition

AMERICAN TECHNICAL PUBLISHERS
Orland Park, Illinois

Leonard P. Toenjes

Printreading for Residential Construction contains procedures commonly practiced in industry and the trade. Specific procedures vary with each task and must be performed by a qualified person. For maximum safety, always refer to specific manufacturer recommendations, insurance regulations, specific job site and plant procedures, applicable federal, state, and local regulations, and any authority having jurisdiction. The material contained is intended to be an educational resource for the user. American Technical Publishers assumes no responsibility or liability in connection with this material or its use by any individual or organization.

American Technical Publishers Editorial Staff

Editor in Chief:
    Jonathan F. Gosse
Vice President—Editorial:
    Peter A. Zurlis
Assistant Production Manager:
    Nicole D. Bigos
Digital Media Coordinator:
    Adam T. Shuldt
Art Supervisor:
    Sarah E. Kaducak
Technical Editor:
    Gregory M. DeLaLeurs

Copy Editor:
    Talia J. Lambarki
    Catherine A. Mini
Editorial Assistant:
    Alex C. Tulik
Cover Design:
    Robert M. McCarthy
Illustration/Layout:
    Robert M. McCarthy
    Nick W. Basham
Digital Resources:
    Robert E. Stickley

AutoCAD is a registered trademark of Autodesk, Inc. Dryvit is a registered trademark of Dryvit Systems, Inc. International Residential Code and IRC are registered trademarks of International Code Council, Inc. LEED is a registered trademark of the U.S. Green Building Council Non-Profit Corporation. NAHB is a registered trademark of the National Association of Home Builders of the United States. National Electrical Code and NEC are registered trademarks of the National Fire Protection Association, Inc. National Electrical Safety Code and NESC are registered trademarks of the Institute of Electrical and Electronics Engineers, Inc. Plyform is a registered trademark of APA–The Engineered Wood Association. Quick Quiz, Quick Quizzes, and Master Math are trademarks of American Technical Publishers. Romex is a registered trademark of General Cable Technologies Corporation.

© 2016 by American Technical Publishers
All rights reserved

6 7 8 9 – 16 – 9 8 7 6 5 4 3

Printed in the United States of America

ISBN 978-0-8269-0494-2

 This book is printed on recycled paper.

ACKNOWLEDGEMENTS

The authors and publisher are grateful to the following companies for providing technical information and assistance.

American Hardwood Export Council
APA—The Engineered Wood Association
Calculated Industries, Inc.
California Redwood Association
CertainTeed Corporation
David White Instruments
The Garlinghouse Company
Hilti, Inc.
ITW Ramset/Redhead
James Hardie Building Products
KIP America
Kohler Co.
Kolbe & Kolbe Millwork Co., Inc.
Leica Geosystems
Merillatt Industries
Plan Ahead, Inc.
Rodger A. Brooks, Architect
Southern Forest Products Association
Steel Framing Alliance
Topcon Laser Systems, Inc.
Trus Joist, A Weyerhaeuser Business
Tyco Fire Suppression & Building Products
Vico Software, Inc.

CONTENTS

LEARNER RESOURCES

- Quick Quizzes®
- Illustrated Glossary
- Flash Cards
- Print Sets
- Stewart Residence 3D Model
- Master Math® Problems
- Symbol/Abbreviation Tests
- Printreading Tests
- Media Library
- ATPeResources.com

INTRODUCTION

Printreading for Residential Construction presents printreading fundamentals and provides printreading activities related to residential construction. Topics presented include sketching, computer-aided design (CAD), trade math symbols and abbreviations, plot plans, floor plans, elevations, sections, and details. This new edition provides information on revised building codes, LEED for Homes, green building practices, advanced house framing techniques, insulation, and the whole-house systems approach.

Two sets of prints and a trade plan are included in the vinyl sleeve at the back of the textbook. Prints for the Wayne Residence are covered throughout the textbook. Prints for the Stewart Residence are used in chapter 12 for the final exam. In addition, the Campbell Residence trade plan is included for additional printreading activities. A list of the prints is included on the inside back cover of the book. Digital versions with interactive navigation can be found with the *Printreading for Residential Construction* online learner resources.

To obtain information about related training products, visit the American Technical Publishers website at www.atplearning.com.

Sketching Exercises, Review Questions, and Trade Competency Tests assess the student's comprehension of the subject matter covered in the text

Chapter introductions preview content to be covered

Tech Facts provide supplemental information to chapter topics

Photographs, technical illustrations, and print examples visually reinforce topics covered in the text

USING PRINTREADING FOR RESIDENTIAL CONSTRUCTION

To obtain maximum benefit from *Printreading for Residential Construction,* read each chapter carefully, noting the new terms introduced, elements detailed in the illustrations, and related information provided in the photographs. Identify and review the key concepts presented in the chapter before completing the Review Questions and Trade Competency Test included at the end of the chapter and the Quick Quiz® included on the online learner resources. Review Questions are based directly on the content included in the chapter. Trade Competency Tests are based on information and prints associated with particular chapters and other reference material such as the Appendix. Chapter 12, Final Review and Exams, comprehensively assesses mastery of information covered throughout the textbook, based on the Stewart Residence prints. The Review Questions and Quick Quizzes® should be reviewed prior to completing the Final Exam. Each of these learning activities provides an opportunity to reinforce and apply concepts presented in the chapter.

LEARNER RESOURCES

Printreading for Residential Construction also includes access to Learner Resources that reinforce textbook content and enhance learning. These online resources can be accessed using either of the following methods:

- Key ATPeResources.com/QuickLinks into a web browser and enter QuickLinks™ Access code **281467.**
- Use a Quick Response (QR) reader app to scan the QR code with a mobile device.

Printreading for Residential Construction includes access to online learner resources that reinforce textbook content and enhance learning. These learner resources include the following:

- **Quick Quizzes®** that provide interactive questions for each chapter, with links to highlighted content from the textbook and the illustrated glossary
- An **Illustrated Glossary** that serves as a helpful reference to commonly used terms, with selected terms linked to textbook illustrations
- **Flash Cards** that provide a self-study/review of common printreading symbols as well as key terms and definitions
- **Print Sets** that consist of digital versions of the prints used throughout the textbook
- The **Stewart Residence 3D Model,** which provides a three-dimensional representation of the Stewart Residence prints, with trade related review questions
- **Master Math® Problems** that provide self-study opportunities to apply trade-related math concepts
- **Symbol/Abbreviation Tests** that assess a learner's knowledge of symbols and abbreviations in an interactive format
- **Printreading Tests** based on sections of prints that provide a more in-depth assessment tool
- A **Media Library** that consists of videos and animations that reinforce textbook content
- **ATPeResources.com,** which provides access to additional online resources that support continued learning

CONSTRUCTION DOCUMENTS

CHAPTER 1

Working drawings contain the graphic information necessary to complete a construction job. All of the construction professionals involved in the building process utilize the working drawings and prints as a common reference throughout a project. Plot plans, floor plans, elevations, sections, and details comprise working drawings. Working drawings are most often made with computer-aided design (CAD) systems that use computers, plotters, printers, and specialized software, while some drawings are produced in a more traditional manner using T-squares, triangles, and other drafting instruments. Specifications provide the written information related to the drawings to completely build the project.

OBJECTIVES

1. List the different types of construction professionals.
2. Define working drawings, and list the types of working drawings.
3. Define and describe plot plans and floor plans.
4. Define and describe elevations.
5. Explain sections and details.
6. Explain title blocks.
7. List and describe the types of prints that are made from drawings.
8. Explain how drawings are produced using the traditional drafting method.
9. Describe the basic tools and instruments used in drawing.
10. Define computer-aided design (CAD) and explain how it functions.
11. Describe CAD input systems and output systems.

CONSTRUCTION PROFESSIONALS

Owners, architects, engineers, building officials, contractors, subcontractors, suppliers, and tradesworkers utilize working drawings and prints to coordinate their efforts in building a structure. **See Figure 1-1.** Accurate working drawings, prints, and specifications ensure that the final project is completed in direct accordance with the intentions of the owner and architect and in compliance with engineering and legal standards. Various parties involved in the project communicate throughout the process to ensure that they agree on the information contained in the prints and specifications.

Owners, Architects, and Engineers

A builder or prospective owner (client) meets an architect to discuss the design and planning of a house. The architect determines the parameters of the available building space based on items such as lot size, lot shape, desired living spaces, and available project budget. House styles are discussed and client needs are determined including intended usage, design and style preferences, potential energy and sustainable construction techniques, desired number of rooms, and approximate sizes of rooms. Materials, equipment, finishes, and fixtures are also discussed. The approximate price range of the house is determined, zoning requirements are discussed, and building codes are reviewed.

Compliance with various building codes and legislative requirements is necessary to obtain a building permit. For example, the intended building occupancy and usage could require compliance with the Americans with Disabilities Act (ADA). Variations in door opening sizes and countertop heights may be required in certain circumstances. Other access and egress accommodations may also be required. In another example, the owner or municipality may have an interest in sustainable or green construction methods that include specific materials and construction process requirements. With this information, the architect prepares a series of rough sketches for client review. The client makes final decisions and the architect proceeds to complete the working drawings.

1

Figure 1-1. Construction professionals, such as architects and contractors, utilize working drawings and specifications to coordinate their efforts in building a structure.

For speculative houses, the architect and contractor perform the design process. A *speculative (spec) house* is a house built by a contractor on the assumption that a buyer will be found during or after completion of construction. Architects are licensed by various approving agencies and affix their seal to the completed drawings. Care is taken to ensure that the completed drawings are in compliance with all building code and zoning requirements prior to beginning the construction process.

A variety of engineering reviews and approvals of the working drawings and specifications are performed. Structural engineers ensure that the various support systems including the foundation system, wall structure, and roof design meet or exceed all loading requirements. Electrical engineers review the design documents for compliance with electrical and fire code performance and safety. Other engineering work is performed as necessary to construct a structure that will be structurally and functionally sound.

Building Officials

After the drawings, prints, and specifications have been reviewed and approved by the owner, architect, and engineers, they are submitted to the appropriate governmental agencies for a particular location. These building officials review the construction documents to ensure that they are in compliance with all local building codes and zoning regulations.

Local governmental agencies adopt and approve a building code for a particular location. The International Residential Code® (IRC®) is a common model code that is adopted by governmental agencies that may adopt the code in total or approve local variations and additions. For example, local building codes may require that all structures be placed away from existing property lines by a minimum footage amount. Drawings indicating the placement of the building on the building lot are reviewed to ensure this requirement is met. Additionally, local codes may contain sustainability requirements related to green construction that require certain types of construction materials and methods to be utilized in a particular area. The National Green Building Standard, developed by the Home Innovation Research Labs, a wholly owned independent subsidiary of the National Association of Home Builders (NAHB®), has been approved by the American National Standards Institute (ANSI) as a model for sustainability certification of various types of residential structures.

For zoning, the location of the structure and the type of structure to be built must be in compliance with zoning regulations. Zoning regulations outline the allowable usages for various pieces of property as determined by a local governmental agency. Examples of zoning categories are single-family residential, multi-family residential, and light commercial. Prior to issuance of a building permit, zoning officials review the plans and specifications to ensure that the proper type of structure will be built on the designated property.

After all requirements are met on the construction documents, they are approved for construction to begin and a building permit is issued. Throughout the building process, a number of inspections are performed at various stages to be certain that the structure is being constructed in accordance with the working drawings and specifications as submitted and approved. Examples of inspections include foundation, rough framing, electrical, and plumbing inspections. Upon completion of construction, a final inspection is performed, again ensuring that the entire building is consistent with the construction documents. An occupancy permit is then issued to the owner.

Contractors, Subcontractors, and Suppliers

Contractors utilize working drawings, prints, and specifications to schedule the work that they will perform and to determine the types of work they will subcontract to others. Contractors use the appropriate construction documents to estimate material quantities and labor requirements in order to perform a cost estimate for the structure. Construction schedules are also determined based on the prints and specifications.

Subcontractors utilize the working drawings and specifications much in the same manner as a contractor pertaining to estimates of materials, labor, and scheduling. For example, an electrical subcontractor will determine quantities such as the number of various types of switches, receptacles, junction boxes, panel boards, and feet of various types of cable from the prints. The number of hours of labor required to install the electrical system will also be determined from this information.

Suppliers take the working drawings, prints, and specifications to determine various material quantities such as concrete, lumber, drywall, insulation, roofing, electrical materials, plumbing materials, masonry, heating and cooling systems, flooring, and any other materials included in the residence. Suppliers utilize information on both the prints and specifications to determine specific types of materials to be installed in the structure and work with the contractor and subcontractors to ascertain the materials specified are appropriate for current usage and available for construction.

TECH FACTS

A temporary certificate of occupancy (TCO) may be issued to allow owner occupation before the completion of the entire work covered by the permits, as long as the incomplete building is safe for occupancy.

Tradesworkers

The construction process in the field is governed by the working drawings, prints, and specifications. Each tradesworker on the job site performs and installs work using the construction documents as a guide. Close adherence to all measurements, materials, and methods shown on the prints creates a successful project where all components perform as designed and specified.

WORKING DRAWINGS AND SPECIFICATIONS

A *working drawing* is a drawing that contains the graphic information necessary to complete a construction job. Working drawings include plot plans, floor plans, elevations, sections, and details. A title block identifies each sheet. *Specifications* are written supplements to working drawings that provide additional building information. Specifications are organized by various standardized formats.

Plot Plans

A *plot plan* is a scaled drawing that shows the shape and size of the building lot; location, shape, and overall size of a house on the lot; and the finish floor elevation. Plot plans are drawn to smaller scales than floor plans. The use of a smaller drawing scale allows for drawings of larger areas such as building lots to be shown on a single print page. Solid contour lines on a plot plan show the finish grade of the building lot. Dashed contour lines, when included on a plot plan, show the existing grade. Other information shown on a plot plan includes a symbol designating true north and the point of beginning (POB) from which building corners and heights, location of streets, easements, and utilities are established. **See Figure 1-2.**

Plot Plans
Figure 1-2

Figure 1-2. Plot plans show the shape and size of the building lot and location and shape of the house. Floor plans show the shapes, sizes, and relationships of rooms.

Floor Plans

A *floor plan* is a scaled view of the various floors in a house looking directly down from a horizontal cutting plane taken 5'-0" above each finished floor. Floor plans show the layout of rooms and give information about windows, doors, cabinets, fixtures, and other features. The shapes, sizes, and relationships of rooms are also shown on floor plans. Dimensions show sizes of rooms, hallways, wall thicknesses, opening locations, and other measurements. Symbols and abbreviations provide additional information about the various building components. **See Figure 1-3.** A separate floor plan is required for each story of the house. Floor plans are generally the first drawings to be drawn for a set of plans.

Floor Plans

Figure 1-3

Figure 1-3. Floor plans show the shapes, sizes, and relationships of rooms.

Elevations

An *elevation* is a scaled view looking directly at an object such as a wall. Elevations show the true shape of the exterior and interior walls without any allowances for perspective in the drawings. Dimensions include floor-to-floor heights and heights of windows above finished floors. The two types of elevations are exterior and interior elevations. **See Figure 1-4.**

Exterior Elevations. An *exterior elevation* is a scaled view that shows the shape and size of the outside walls of the house and the roof. At a minimum, four exterior elevations are required to show exterior walls. Exterior elevations are generally drawn to the same scale as the floor plan. Building materials such as brick, stone, fiber-cement siding, vinyl siding, exterior insulation and finish systems (EIFS), and various wood finish materials are specified for the exterior walls through the use of symbols and notations. Door and window openings and their types and sizes are shown in their proper locations. Roof styles, slopes, and types of roof coverings are also shown.

Elevations

Figure 1-4

Figure 1-4. Elevations show the sizes and shapes of exterior walls, interior walls, and partitions.

Interior Elevations. An *interior elevation* is a scaled view that shows the shapes, sizes, and finishes of interior walls and partitions of the house. Interior elevations may be drawn to the same scale as the floor plan or to a larger scale when the architect is showing more detail. Interior elevations commonly show details of kitchen base and wall cabinets, sinks, dishwashers, ranges, and other built-in appliances. In addition, interior elevations show details of bathroom fixtures such as water closets, bathtubs, showers, and vanities.

Interior elevations also show special wall treatments in rooms. For example, details of interior elevations may show fireplaces, bookcases, and other built-in features. Symbols and notations are used to specify materials and special installation instructions.

Sections

A *section* is a scaled view created by passing a cutting plane through a portion of a building. **See Figure 1-5.** Common sections are taken through exterior walls to show information about foundation footings and walls, wall and floor framing, height of windows above floors, and eaves and roof construction.

Sections

Figure 1-5

Figure 1-5. Sections show features revealed by a cutting plane.

Cutting planes for sections are shown on floor plans. Direction arrows on the cutting plane line show the line of sight. Coded references shown with the cutting plane line give the sheet number of the section.

TECHFACTS

Insulation is rated according to its R-value. R-value is a measure of insulation's resistance to heat flow, and is dependent on the material type, thickness, and density. The higher the R-value, the greater the thermal performance.

Details

A *detail* is a scaled plan, elevation, or section drawn to a larger scale to show special features. Whenever a part of a building cannot be shown clearly at the small scale of the plan, elevation, or section, it is redrawn at a larger scale so that necessary information can be shown more clearly. For example, a fireplace, framing for a stairwell, special interior or exterior trim, an entrance doorway, or a section of a foundation may be drawn as a detail. Section details show the cross-sectional shape of features such as foundation footings and windows. The scale for the detail is determined by the complexity of the detail. **See Figure 1-6.**

Title Blocks

A *title block* is an area on a working drawing or print that is used to provide written information about the drawing or print. **See Figure 1-7.** The title block is located along the right side or bottom of the sheet. Title blocks give the number of the sheet and total number of sheets in the set of plans. For example, 1 OF 7 denotes the first sheet of a set of plans containing seven sheets. In a larger set of plans, initials may precede the sheet number to indicate a particular trade area. For example, E1 OF 3 denotes the first electrical sheet of three electrical sheets. Other letters commonly used to denote specific trade area prints are P for plumbing and M for mechanical, which includes heating, ventilating, and air conditioning (HVAC).

Details

Figure 1-6

Figure 1-6. Details show special features of plans as elevation or section views.

Title Blocks

Figure 1-7

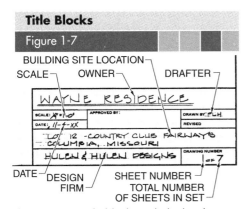

Figure 1-7. Title blocks include the sheet number, architect or design firm name, owner, and other pertinent information.

In addition to the sheet number, the title block may include the following information:

- design firm name
- architect seal
- project or building number
- date
- revisions
- drafter initials
- checker initials
- owner or client name
- building site address
- scale of drawings

Specifications

Written information related to the residential project is included in the specifications. **See Figure 1-8.** This will include information such as the specific lumber grades to be used for various structural components, the loading requirements for concrete slabs and foundations, and any other information required for construction professionals or building code review officials. General notes may also be included directly on a print sheet that may take the form of specifications for a small residential project.

PRINTS

A *print* is a reproduction of a working drawing. Originally, these reproductions were referred to as blueprints because the process used to make them produced a white line on a blue background. Any number of copies or blueprints could be made from working drawings by using a process similar to the process used for making photographic prints. Diazo prints were another type of print in the evolution of

print reproduction. Neither blueprints or diazo prints are used today, having been replaced by computer-controlled wide-format printers.

Digital printing services produce prints directly from digital files onto bond paper, vellum, or mylar. Original plans and blueprints can be scanned to create an electronic file for future document reproduction. CAD plotting can be done in both black and white and color. Electronic print files can also be archived onto an array of media types, such as CD, DVD, hard drives or document management systems.

Blueprints

The use of blueprints began in 1842 when a method of producing paper sensitized with iron salts was developed. The paper undergoes a chemical change when exposed to light. The part protected by pencil or ink lines on the original drawing shows as white lines on a blue background. Blueprints are not produced today since other methods have been developed to replace them.

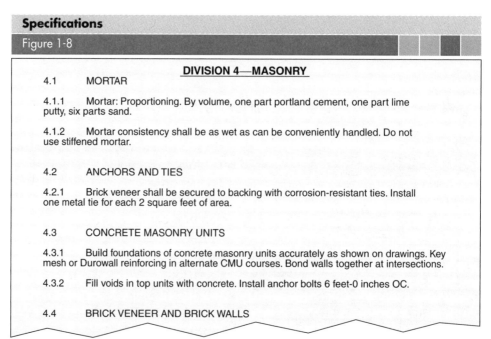

Specifications

Figure 1-8

DIVISION 4—MASONRY

4.1   MORTAR

4.1.1   Mortar: Proportioning. By volume, one part portland cement, one part lime putty, six parts sand.

4.1.2   Mortar consistency shall be as wet as can be conveniently handled. Do not use stiffened mortar.

4.2   ANCHORS AND TIES

4.2.1   Brick veneer shall be secured to backing with corrosion-resistant ties. Install one metal tie for each 2 square feet of area.

4.3   CONCRETE MASONRY UNITS

4.3.1   Build foundations of concrete masonry units accurately as shown on drawings. Key mesh or Durowall reinforcing in alternate CMU courses. Bond walls together at intersections.

4.3.2   Fill voids in top units with concrete. Install anchor bolts 6 feet-0 inches OC.

4.4   BRICK VENEER AND BRICK WALLS

Figure 1-8. Specifications include information such as the materials used in the construction and the responsibilities of those involved.

TECHFACTS

The blueprint process was developed in 1842 by Sir John Herschel, an English scientist and astronomer. The process, known as cyanotype, is also used for photography.

Diazo Prints

The diazo process made prints with blue or black lines on a white background. The diazo process provided accurate reproductions because the paper was not soaked with water and then dried as blueprints were, and the reproductions were easier to read than blueprints.

Two types of sensitized paper were used in the diazo process, one for each development method. In the wet development method, sensitized paper passed under a roller that moistened the exposed top surface, completing the chemical reaction to bring out the image. Prints made by this method had black or blue lines on a white background.

In the dry development method, sensitized paper was passed through a heated chamber where its surface was exposed to ammonia vapor. The dry diazo method created reproductions on plastic film or brown line copies.

Wide-Format Printers

With the use of computer-aided design (CAD), building information modeling (BIM), and the on-line transmission of architectural drawings, computer-controlled printers, sometimes referred to as plotters, are now used to create working drawings. **See Figure 1-9.** LED (light-emitting diode), inkjet, laser, and electrostatic wide-format printers have replaced blueprints and diazo print processes because the prints are quickly and easily produced and their white backgrounds and dark lines make them more legible. LED inkjet, laser, and electrostatic prints are also easily enlarged or reduced. Some wide-format printers have integrated scanners to enable the scanning and printing of existing paper prints.

LED Printers. LED, electrostatic, and laser prints are produced using a process similar to the process that office copiers and printers use. **See Figure 1-10.** LED printers take electronic print information received from a data source (typically an external electronic file or scan) and route the information through an integrated image processor. The processed information is then sent to a stationary LED array that writes an entire page width of the image information onto an electrically charged photoreceptive drum. Some LED printers use a positively charged drum with positively charged toner, while other LED printers use a negatively charged drum with a negatively charged toner. The LED array spans the width of the page, projecting the image onto the drum as it rotates.

In an LED printer with a positively charged drum, the projected light from the LED array discharges areas of the drum, making the exposed areas negative but retaining a positive charge in the unexposed areas. The drum then turns past a roller where positively charged toner particles are attracted to the negatively charged image areas on the drum surface. The drum continues to turn in synchronization with negatively charged copy paper that has a negative charge greater than the negatively charged areas on the drum. The toner particles are pulled from the drum to the paper and are fused to the paper by a pair of fuser rollers that apply heat and pressure. One advantage of LED printers is that they have fewer moving parts compared to other printers. This makes for a more reliable machine that requires less maintenance.

Print Production

Figure 1-9

HANDRAWN

ELECTRONIC

ORIGINAL DRAWINGS
CREATED

TRADITIONAL
DRAFTING

COMPUTER-AIDED
DESIGN

DRAWING FILE
SENT ELECTRONICALLY
TO PRINTER

PRINT MASTER
SCANNED
INTO PRINTER

PRINT MASTER
MANUALLY PLACED
ONTO PRINTER/COPIER

ELECTROSTATIC
PRINTER/COPIER

LED, or LASER
PRINTER/SCANNER

WORKING DRAWINGS
PRODUCED

Figure 1-9. Original drawings are produced using either traditional drafting or CAD. Working drawings are printed using a wide-format printer.

ELECTRONIC PRINT
INFORMATION

INTEGRATED IMAGE
PROCESSOR

NEGATIVELY CHARGED
IMAGE AREAS (WEAK)

POSITIVELY CHARGED
TONER PARTICLES

TONER ROLLER WITH
POSITIVELY CHARGED TONER

NEGATIVELY CHARGED PAPER
(STRONG)

POSITIVELY CHARGED
PHOTORECEPTIVE DRUM

LED ARRAY

FINISHED
PRINT

FUSED
IMAGE

FUSED ROLLERS APPLY
HEAT AND PRESSURE

Figure 1-10. LED printers use light-emitting diodes to project light onto a photoreceptive drum enabling fast production of detailed working drawings.

Laser Printers. Laser printers use the same technology as LED printers with the exception of the projection method. A laser printer uses a laser and mirrors as opposed to an LED array to write directly to the drum. Laser printers produce highly accurate drawings directly from an electronic design.

Electrostatic Printers. The process of producing electrostatic prints is the same as producing photocopies using an analog office copier, and very similar to LED and laser printers. To produce electrostatic prints, full-size working drawings are exposed to light and projected directly

through a lens onto a charged drum. The rest of the process is the same as LED and laser printers.

Prints made using the electrostatic method have black lines on a white background. These prints can be enlarged and reduced easily. One disadvantage of electrostatic prints is the potential for distortion by projection through a lens.

TECHFACTS

A wide-format LED printer can produce up to 22 D-size (24″ × 36″) prints per minute.

DRAFTING METHODS

Working drawings for prints may be made using traditional drafting practices or computer-aided design (CAD) software. A language of standard lines, symbols, and abbreviations is used in conjunction with drafting principles so that drawings are consistent and easy to read. The American National Standards Institute (ANSI) in conjunction with ASME International (formerly the American Society of Mechanical Engineers) publishes standards related to drafting conventions in their Y series standards. These standards are reviewed by various architectural and engineering societies on a recurring basis to ensure they remain current with new systems and practices.

Traditional Drafting

Basic tools such as T-squares, triangles, scales, and pencils are used to produce working drawings by the traditional method. Other drafting instruments such as dividers and compasses are also used to produce working drawings. **See Figure 1-11.**

Drafting Tools

Figure 1-11

DIVIDERS
SCALE
TRIANGLE
T-SQUARE

Figure 1-11. Drafting tools include T-squares, triangles, scales, and pencils. Drafting instruments, such as dividers, may also be used to create drawings.

TECHFACTS

Linetypes on working drawings are established in ANSI/ASME Y14.2-2008, *Line Conventions and Lettering.*

Drafting machines (combination T-square, scale, and triangles) and parallel straightedges (combination drafting board and modified T-square) are used for traditionally drafting as well. Drawings are started after properly taping the drafting paper to the drafting board. Initial linework is done using light construction lines, which are later darkened to produce the final drawing.

T-Squares. A *T-square* is a drafting tool used to draw horizontal lines and as a reference base for positioning triangles. The head of a T-square is held firmly against one edge of the board to ensure accuracy. T-squares are made of wood, plastic, or aluminum and are available in various lengths. Common T-squares are 24″ to 36″ in length.

Triangles. A *triangle* is a drafting tool used to draw vertical and inclined lines. The base of a triangle is held firmly against the blade of the T-square for accuracy. Two standard triangles —30°-60° and 45°— are available in a variety of sizes. A 30°-60° triangle is used to produce vertical lines and inclined lines of 30° or 60° sloping to the left or right. A 45° triangle is used to produce vertical lines and inclined lines of 45° sloping to the left or right. The triangles may be used together to produce inclined lines every 15°. Triangles are typically made of clear plastic. **See Figure 1-12.**

Drafting Instruments. Although a wide variety of precision drafting instruments is available, the compass and dividers are the most commonly used instruments. Compasses and dividers are available in varying sizes. **See Figure 1-13.**

A *compass* is a drafting instrument used to draw arcs and circles. One leg of a compass contains a needlepoint that is positioned on the centerpoint of the arc or circle to be drawn. The other leg contains the pencil lead used to draw the line. Two types of compasses are center-wheel and friction compasses. On center-wheel compasses, the center wheel is adjusted to change the radius of the arc. On friction compasses, arcs of various radii are obtained by opening or closing the legs. Center-wheel compasses are the most popular and most accurate.

Triangles
Figure 1-12

Figure 1-12. The 30°-60° and 45° triangles are used to draw lines 15° apart.

Compasses and Dividers
Figure 1-13

COMPASS

DIVIDERS

Figure 1-13. A compass is used to draw arcs and circles. Dividers are used to transfer measurements.

TECHFACTS

Alternative uses of a compass include drawing hexagons or octagons, bisecting arcs or angles, and transferring dimensions in place of a divider.

Dividers are a drafting instrument used to transfer dimensions. Each leg of a set of dividers contains a needlepoint. Two types of dividers are center-wheel and friction dividers. Friction dividers are more useful for general work.

Other drafting instruments include irregular (French) curves and architectural templates. Irregular curves are used to draw curves that do not have consistent radii. Architectural templates are used to save time when drawing standard items such as doors, windows, and cabinets.

Scales. A *scale* is a drafting tool used to measure lines and reduce or enlarge them proportionally. Three types of scales are the architect's scale, civil engineer's scale, and mechanical engineer's scale. **See Figure 1-14.**

Scales

Figure 1-14

TRIANGULAR

FLAT

ARCHITECT'S

CIVIL
ENGINEER'S

MECHANICAL
ENGINEER'S

Figure 1-14. Three types of scales are used to produce scaled drawings. The architect's scale is typically used for building trades plans.

TECHFACTS

Architect's scales are based on 12 units to the foot while engineer's scales are based on 10 units to the foot.

A digital measuring device can be used in place of an architect's, civil engineer's, or mechanical engineer's scale to accurately measure distances on a print.

Calculated Industries, Inc.

An *architect's scale* is a scale used when producing drawings of buildings and structural parts. The most common type of architect's scale is triangular in shape. One edge of the scale is a standard ruler divided into inches and sixteenths of an inch. The other edges contain 10 scales that are labeled 3, 1½, 1, ¾, ½, ⅜, ¼, 3/16, 3/32, and ⅛. For example, the ¼ scale means that ¼″ = 1′-0″. For larger scale drawings, the 1½″ =1′-0″ or the 3″ = 1′-0″scales are used.

A *civil engineer's scale* is a scale used when creating maps and survey drawings. Plot plans may also be drawn using a civil engineer's scale. A civil engineer's scale is graduated in decimal units. One-inch units on the scale are divided into 10, 20, 30, 40, 50, or 60 parts. These units are used to represent the desired measuring unit such as inches, feet, or miles. For example, a property line that is 100′-0″ long drawn with the 20 scale (1″ = 20′-0″) measures 5″ on the drawing.

A *mechanical engineer's scale* is a scale used when drawing machines and machine parts. A mechanical engineer's scale is similar to an architect's scale except that the edges are limited to fractional scales of ⅛, ¼, ½, and 1. Decimal scales are also available.

Pencils. Wood or mechanical pencils are used to draw lines. Wood pencils have a stamp near one end indicating the lead hardness. When using a mechanical pencil, a lead of the desired hardness is inserted into the jaws of the pencil.

Grades of lead range from 6B (extremely soft) to 9H (exceptionally hard). Hard leads are used to draw fine, precise lines. Medium leads are used to draw object lines. Soft leads are used primarily for sketching. The architect's range is HB, F, H, and 2H. F and H are most commonly used for producing drawings. **See Figure 1-15.**

Figure 1-15. Pencil leads range from extremely soft to exceptionally hard.

Computer-Aided Design (CAD)

Computer-aided design (CAD) is also known as computer-aided drafting or computer-aided drafting and design (CADD). Advantages of CAD include speed, accuracy, consistency, change-ability, duplication, and storage. A major additional benefit of a CAD system is its information-management capabilities. As drawings are made or changed, information about the materials used in the drawings is stored and updated, allowing the operator to extract it for estimating or pricing purposes. Advantages of CAD include legibility and consistency of line weights, notes, and symbols. **See Figure 1-16.**

CAD systems use hardware (computer equipment) and software (computer programs) to input (generate), manage (duplicate, file, and retrieve), and output (print) drawings. A wide variety of hardware and software is available for producing CAD-generated drawings.

Input Systems. Input systems are composed of a software program such as AutoCAD® and hardware such as a keyboard, computer, and monitor. **See Figure 1-17.** Other input devices such as a mouse, or other pointing device are commonly used.

A *keyboard* is an input device containing standard alpha and numeric keys as well as function keys. A *function key* is a key that performs a special task. A keyboard may be used to initiate a command, enter drawing coordinates, or enter text that will appear on the drawings.

A *computer* is a device that receives information from an input device, processes it, and displays the results on a monitor. It is important that the computer used for the CAD process contains a sufficient amount of random access memory (RAM) to efficiently run CAD programs.

A *monitor* is a high-resolution color display screen that allows drawings, data, and text to be displayed. Components in a CAD drawing are organized by layers, which are often drawn using different colors. For example, a floor plan for a building may be drawn in blue, the electrical plan drawn in red, and the mechanical plan drawn in yellow. Color allows features on the individual layers to be easily distinguished from one another. Layers can be turned on or off to view only the desired information.

CAD—Generated Plans

Figure 1-16

CONSISTENT
LINE WEIGHTS

EASILY RECOGNIZED
SYMBOLS

LEGIBLE
LETTERING

Rodger A. Brooks, Architect

Figure 1-16. CAD-generated plans have consistent line weights, symbols, and lettering.

A mouse is an input device used to input drawing commands that create and modify drawings. A mouse is moved on a flat surface, affecting the movement and location of the cursor on the monitor.

CAD Systems
Figure 1-17

Figure 1-17. A CAD system includes a keyboard, central processing unit (CPU), monitor, and input devices.

CAD drawings can be easily modified. Three-dimensional CAD drawings can be rotated, revolved, or viewed from other angles. Drawing files are easily copied, stored, or transmitted. Compact discs (CDs) containing CAD drawing files may be produced and shared, or CAD drawing files may be shared via e-mail or the Internet.

Output Systems. Output systems can display drawings on a monitor or print drawings on a printer. **See Figure 1-18.**

Many types of monitors are available to display CAD drawings. A larger monitor is commonly recommended for displaying architectural drawings to enable viewing of smaller details.

Printers output drawings by transferring the image to paper after receiving electronic information about the drawings from the computer. A wide-format printer is typically used as an output-printing device for CAD drawings.

CAD Drawings. CAD drawings are more consistent and standardized than drawings completed using traditional drafting methods. Line weights, symbols, and lettering on CAD drawings are precise and easy to read. The same elements on traditional drawings reflect the individual technique of the architect.

CAD drawings are more common due to lower prices of computer systems equipped with sufficient memory and storage capacity for CAD software. Architects use CAD because of the variety of software programs available and their ability to perform complicated tasks quickly.

Wide-Format Printers
Figure 1-18

KIP America

Figure 1-18. Wide-format LED printers are used to print working drawings. The printers may have an integrated scanner, stacker, or folder.

Building Information Modeling (BIM). *Building information modeling (BIM) is an integrated, electronically managed system that aligns all working drawings, structural drawings, and shop drawings into a consistent system.* **See Figure 1-19.** Electronically generated documents from a variety of sources are translated into a common set of construction drawings. One of the advantages of BIM is that any inconsistencies or conflicts between various sets of drawings can be recognized and resolved prior to discovery of these conflicts at the construction site.

Building Information Modeling (BIM)

Figure 1-19

Vico Software, Inc.

Figure 1-19. A building information model contains the geometric information needed to build the structure and may include particular construction details, job costs, and scheduling data.

LEARNER RESOURCES

ATPeResources.com/QuickLinks
Access Code: 281467

Name _____ Date _____

Multiple Choice

_____ **1.** ___ utilize working drawings, prints, and specifications to determine specific types of materials to be installed in the structure.
   A. Suppliers
   B. Architects
   C. Tradesworkers
   D. Engineers

_____ **2.** Accurate ___ ensure that the final project is completed in direct accordance with the intentions of the owner and architect and in compliance with engineering and legal standards.
   A. prints
   B. building permits
   C. shop drawings
   D. contracts

_____ **3.** Shapes, sizes, and relationships of rooms are most clearly shown on ___.
   A. plot plans
   B. floor plans
   C. elevations
   D. details

_____ **4.** LED wide-format printers have replaced blueprints and ___ print processes because the prints are quickly and easily produced.
   A. electrostatic
   B. inkjet
   C. diazo
   D. laser

_____ **5.** T-squares are ___.
   A. a drafting tool used to draw vertical lines
   B. made of wood, plastic, or aluminum
   C. not accurate
   D. only available in 24″ and 36″ lengths

_____ **6.** ___ printers use print heads that contain small nozzles that spray ink onto the paper.
   A. Laser
   B. LED
   C. Inkjet
   D. Electrostatic

_____ **7.** The primary use of compasses on drawings is to draw ___.
    A. horizontal and inclined lines
    B. vertical and inclined lines
    C. arcs and circles
    D. angles

_____ **8.** The ___ scale is preferred when drawing buildings and other structural parts.
    A. architect's
    B. civil engineer's
    C. mechanical engineer's
    D. drafter's

_____ **9.** An F pencil lead is harder than a(n) ___ pencil lead.
    A. 2H
    B. 4H
    C. B
    D. H

_____ **10.** Coded references on a cutting plane line show the ___.
    A. scale of the details
    B. sheet number of the section view
    C. architect's initials
    D. floor plan

_____ **11.** Two basic types of elevations are ___.
    A. rough and finished
    B. top and bottom
    C. interior and exterior
    D. scaled and freehand

_____ **12.** Section drawings show the ___ shape of features.
    A. reduced
    B. perspective
    C. cross-sectional
    D. enlarged

_____ **13.** The first drawing(s) of a set of plans to be drawn is/are generally the ___.
    A. elevations
    B. floor plans
    C. details
    D. plot plan

_____ **14.** Cutting planes for floor plans are taken ___ above the finished floor.
    A. 3'-0"
    B. 4'-0"
    C. 5'-0"
    D. 6'-0"

_____ **15.** The name and seal of the ___ are commonly found in the title block.
   A. architect
   B. drafter
   C. contractor
   D. owner

_____ **16.** Regarding floor plans, ___.
   A. the shape of the building on the lot is shown
   B. symbols and abbreviations give no additional information
   C. windows, doors, cabinets, fixtures, and other features are shown
   D. the sizes and shapes of the outside walls and roof are shown

_____ **17.** Regarding title blocks, ___.
   A. one title block is completed for each set of plans
   B. initials representing trade areas may precede sheet numbers
   C. an inspection checklist is a part of title blocks
   D. the symbol designating true north is shown

_____ **18.** Regarding printers, ___.
   A. laser printers use the same technology as LED printers with the exception of the projection method
   B. a disadvantage of electrostatic prints is the potential for distortion by projection through a lens
   C. LED inkjet, laser, and electrostatic prints are easily enlarged or reduced
   D. some LED printers use a positively charged drum with negatively charged toner

_____ **19.** Regarding scales, ___.
   A. an architect's scale is graduated in decimal units
   B. an architect's scale contains a ruler and 10 scales
   C. a civil engineer's scale is graduated in fractional units
   D. a mechanical engineer's scale is similar to a civil engineer's scale

_____ **20.** BIM is a system that___.
   A. aligns all working drawings, structural drawings, and shop drawings into a consistent system
   B. is used to recognize and resolve inconsistencies in a set of drawings prior to discovery of these conflicts at the contruction site
   C. translates electronically generated documents from one source into a common set of construction drawings
   D. is used to print drawings

True-False

T   F   **1.** The Y series of ANSI standards includes drafting conventions.

T   F   **2.** Electrostatic prints are produced using the same process used by office copiers.

T   F   **3.** Tradesworkers prepare working drawings of the final building design for approval by the owner.

T   F   **4.** Working drawings contain all graphic information necessary to complete a job.

T	F	**5.** Section views can show information about foundation footings and walls.
T	F	**6.** Elevations are generally drawn to the same scale as floor plans.
T	F	**7.** Each sheet of a set of working drawings contains a title block.
T	F	**8.** True south is designated on the plot plan to show building orientation on a lot.
T	F	**9.** Plot plans are drawn to a smaller scale than floor plans.
T	F	**10.** A separate floor plan is required for each story of a house.
T	F	**11.** Floor plans are generally the first drawings of a set of plans to be drawn.

Completion 1-1

_____ **1.** ___ are reproductions of working drawings.

_____ **2.** The mechanical engineer's scale is used when drawing ___ parts.

_____ **3.** The location of streets, easements, and utilities is shown on the ___ plan.

_____ **4.** The ___ of the T-square should be held firmly against the edge of the drawing board when in use.

_____ **5.** ___ are used to transfer dimensions on drawings.

_____ **6.** ___ on plans give the size of an object.

_____ **7.** ___ are written documents giving additional information about the plans.

_____ **8.** The slope of the roof is shown on the ___ elevations.

_____ **9.** Solid contour lines on plot plans show the ___ grade of the building lot.

_____ **10.** Advantages of ___ include legibility and consistency of line weights, notes, and symbols.

Completion 1-2

_____ **1.** The angle at A contains ___°.

_____ **2.** The angle at B contains ___°.

_____ **3.** The angle at C contains ___°.

_____ **4.** The angle at D contains ___°.

_____ **5.** The angle at E contains ___°.

_____ **6.** The angle at F contains ___°.

Name _____   Date _____

Identification 1-1

_____   **1.** Architect name

_____   **2.** Architect seal

_____   **3.** Owner name

_____   **4.** Date

_____   **5.** Sheet number

_____   **6.** Owner address

_____   **7.** Drafter initials

_____   **8.** Revisions

_____   **9.** Checker initials

_____   **10.** Lot number

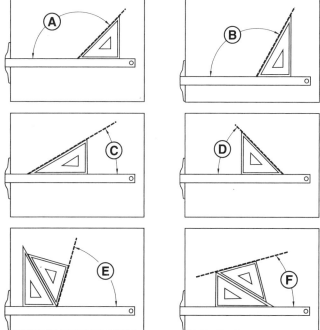

Identification 1-2

_____   **1.** 15°

_____   **2.** 30°

_____   **3.** 45°

_____   **4.** 75°

_____   **5.** 120°

_____   **6.** 135°

Identification 1-3

_____ **1.** Plot plan

_____ **2.** Property line

_____ **3.** Details

_____ **4.** Exterior elevation

_____ **5.** Point of beginning

_____ **6.** Dimension

_____ **7.** Title block

_____ **8.** Cutting plane

_____ **9.** Symbol

_____ **10.** Roof slope

_____ **11.** North

_____ **12.** Abbreviations

_____ **13.** Scale

_____ **14.** Floor plan

_____ **15.** Finish grade line

_____ **16.** Interior elevation

WORKING DRAWING CONCEPTS

Sketches provide a quick, concise method of communicating ideas. Pictorial sketches provide architects, clients, and builders with general information about the appearance of a finished dwelling. Three basic types of pictorial drawings are perspective, isometric, and oblique.

   Working drawings drawn as orthographic projections are often based on concepts developed from sketches. Plan, elevation, and section views are drawn to scale and dimensioned to show actual sizes.

OBJECTIVES

1. Define sketching and describe common sketching tools and materials.
2. Describe the proper sketching technique.
3. Define plane figure and explain how to draw various types of plane figures.
4. Define and describe the different types of pictorial drawings.
5. Define orthographic projection and describe its purpose.
6. Explain the purpose of dimensioning.
7. Describe the use of symbols and list common dimensioning conventions.

SKETCHING

Sketching is the process of drawing without instruments. Sketches are made by the freehand method. The only tools required are pencil, paper, and eraser. **See Figure 2-1.** The use of freehand sketching in a design industry that is increasingly using CAD systems has various implications for creativity. While CAD is the standard for the production of the final prints, freehand sketching is still done in the early stages of project development due to its more inexact nature compared to CAD systems.

Sketching pencils are either wood or mechanical. Softer leads, such as HB, F, and H, are commonly used for sketching.

Paper selected for sketching depends upon the end use of the sketch. Plain paper is commonly used. Papers are available in pads or sheets in standard sizes designated A, B, or C. Size A is 8½″ × 11″; size B is 11″ × 17″; size C is 17″ × 22″. The paper is either plain or preprinted with grids to facilitate sketching. Preprinted paper is available in a variety of grid sizes for orthographic and pictorial sketches. A grid size of ¼″ is common. Grids are commonly printed in light-blue, nonreproducing inks.

Erasers are designed for use with specific papers and leads. The eraser selected should be soft enough to remove pencil lines without smearing them or damaging the paper.

Sketching

Figure 2-1

PAPER

ERASER

PENCIL

Figure 2-1. Sketches convey ideas graphically and are drawn using basic tools such as pencils, paper, and erasers.

TECHFACTS

Erasing shields are used to protect a portion of a sketch while erasing. Erasing shields are small metal or plastic plates with various size cut-outs that allow for the erasing of small areas.

Sketching Techniques

When sketching, the pencil point should be pulled across the paper. Pushing the pencil point can tear the paper. While pulling the pencil, it should be slowly rotated to produce lines of consistent width.

Horizontal, vertical, inclined, and curved lines are used to produce three-view and pictorial drawings. Shading techniques are not used with three-view drawings; however, pictorial drawings may be shaded.

Horizontal Lines. A *horizontal line* is a line that is level or parallel to the horizon. When sketching a horizontal line, the end points are located with dots to indicate the position and length of the line. For short lines, the end dots are connected with a smooth wrist movement from left to right (for a right-handed person). Long lines may require intermediate dots. If grid paper is used, intermediate dots are not required. For long lines, a full arm movement may be required to avoid making an arc.

The top or bottom edges of the paper or pad may be used as a guide when sketching horizontal lines. Light construction lines are drawn first to establish the straightness of the line. The line is then darkened. Construction lines may be omitted when more sketching experience is gained.

Vertical and Slanted Lines. A *vertical line* is a line that is plumb or upright. When sketching a vertical line, the end dots are located and the line is drawn from the top to the bottom. The side edges of the paper or pad may be used as a guide when sketching vertical lines.

A *slanted line* is an inclined line that is neither horizontal nor vertical. When sketching a slanted line, the end dots are located and the line is drawn from left to right (for a right-handed person). To facilitate sketching, the paper is rotated so that the inclined lines are in either a horizontal or vertical position.

Plane Figures. A *plane figure* is a geometric shape with a flat surface. Common plane figures include circles, triangles, quadrilaterals, and polygons. **See Figure 2-2.**

A *circle* is a plane figure generated around a centerpoint. All circles contain 360°. The *circumference* is the perimeter (outside edge) of a circle. The *diameter* is the distance from circumference to circumference passing through the centerpoint. The *radius* is one-half the diameter. A *chord* is a line from circumference to circumference that does not pass through the centerpoint. An *arc* is a portion of the circumference. A *quadrant* is one-fourth of a circle. A quadrant has a 90° angle. A *sector* is a pie-shaped segment of a circle. A *semicircle* is one-half of a circle. Semicircles always contain 180°.

When sketching a circle, the centerpoint is located and several intersecting diameter lines are drawn. The radius is marked off on these lines and connected with a series of arcs. The lines are darkened to produce a smooth circle.

A *triangle* is a three-sided plane figure that contains 180°. A *right triangle* is a triangle that contains one 90° angle. An *obtuse triangle* is a triangle that includes one angle greater than 90°. An *acute triangle* is a triangle in which all angles are less than 90°. Equilateral triangles are acute triangles. An *isosceles triangle* is a triangle that contains two equal sides and two equal angles.

TECH TIPS

Long horizontal, vertical, or slanted lines can be sketched using a series of short lines, which are then connected to complete the long lines.

Plane Figures and Terminology

Figure 2-2

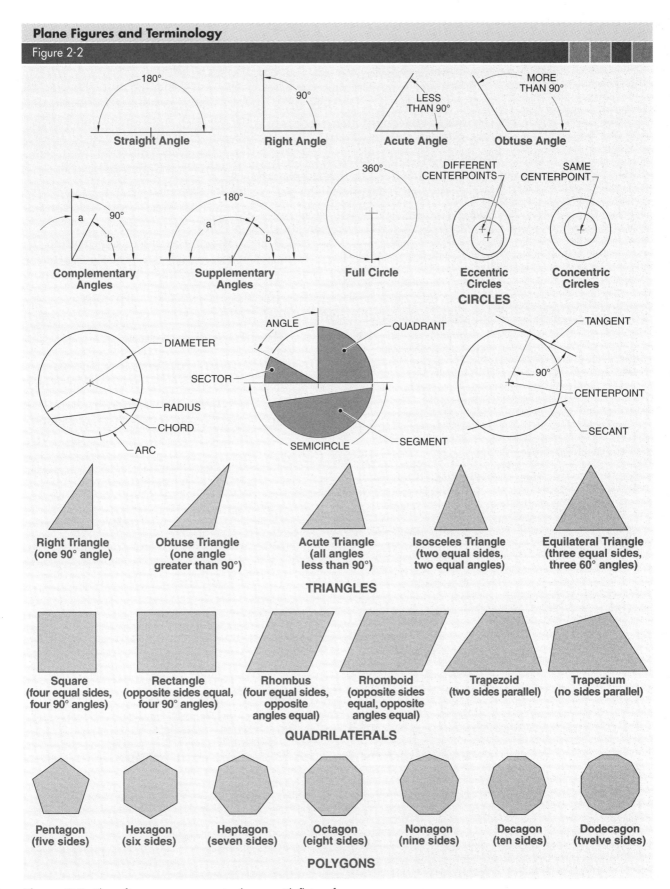

Figure 2-2. Plane figures are geometric shapes with flat surfaces.

An *equilateral triangle* is an acute triangle that contains three equal sides and three 60° angles.

When sketching a triangle, the base is drawn, the angles of the sides are determined, and straight lines are drawn. Generally, one or more of the sides is dimensioned and the angles noted.

A *quadrilateral* is a four-sided plane figure. All quadrilaterals contain 360°. A *square* is a quadrilateral that contains four equal sides and four 90° angles. A *rectangle* is a quadrilateral that contains four 90° angles with opposite sides equal. A *rhombus* is a quadrilateral that contains four equal sides with opposite angles equal and no 90° angles. A *rhomboid* is a quadrilateral that has opposite sides equal, opposite angles equal, but does not contain any 90° angles. A *trapezoid* is a quadrilateral that has two sides parallel. A *trapezium* is a quadrilateral that has no sides parallel. Squares, rectangles, rhombuses, and rhomboids are classified as parallelograms in mathematics.

When sketching a quadrilateral, the baseline is drawn and the locations of the corner points are determined. The corner points are connected with straight lines. Dimensions of two sides and angles are often included.

A *polygon* is a many-sided plane figure that is bounded by straight lines. A *regular polygon* is a polygon that has equal sides and equal angles. An *irregular polygon* is a polygon that has unequal sides and unequal angles. Regular polygons are named according to the number of their sides. For example, a triangle has three sides, a quadrilateral has four sides, a pentagon has five sides, and a hexagon has six sides.

When sketching a polygon, the length of each side is marked off at the appropriate angle. The lines are darkened to complete the polygon.

Pictorial Drawings

A *pictorial drawing* is a three-dimensional representation of an object. Pictorial drawings show the three principal measurements of height, length, and depth on one drawing. Three basic types of pictorial drawings used in the building trades are perspective, isometric, and oblique drawings. **See Figure 2-3.** Common uses of pictorial drawings for residential work include exterior perspective drawings, isometric drawings of plumbing systems, and oblique drawings of cabinets.

An exterior perspective drawing provides a realistic view of a building.

The Garlinghouse Company

Pictorial Drawings

Figure 2-3

ISOMETRIC

PERSPECTIVE

— THRU ROOF

KS

CO LT FD

CO

— BUILDING DRAIN

ISOMETRIC

OBLIQUE

Figure 2-3. Pictorial drawings show height (H), length (L), and depth (D) in one drawing.

Perspective Drawings. A *perspective drawing* is a pictorial drawing with all receding lines converging to vanishing points. Perspective drawings resemble photographs. Perspective drawings may be made with one, two, or three vanishing points. The object may be located above, on, or below the horizon to produce a worm's-eye, eye-level, or bird's-eye view, respectively. The number of vanishing points used and location of the object in relation to the horizon determine the type of perspective drawing. Two vanishing points and an eye-level view are commonly used for perspective drawings of houses. **See Figure 2-4.**

When sketching a perspective drawing, the type of drawing is determined and the appropriate number of vanishing points are located. The height of the object is established and receding lines that converge at the vanishing points are drawn. Object lines are darkened to complete the drawing. The proper location of the initial height line, its relationship to the horizon, and the distance between the vanishing points are critical in producing a realistic perspective drawing.

TECHFACTS

On isometric piping drawings, all horizontal pipes are drawn as 30° lines.

Figure 2-4. Receding lines of perspective drawings converge to one, two, or three vanishing points.

Perspective Drawings

Figure 2-4

Isometric Drawings. An *isometric drawing* is a pictorial drawing with horizontal lines drawn 30° above (or below) the horizon. Vertical lines remain vertical. All measurements are made on the 30° and vertical axes or lines parallel to them. Nonisometric lines are drawn by locating and connecting their end points on isometric lines.

Circles on isometric drawings appear as ellipses. An *ellipse* is a plane figure generated by the sum of the distances from two fixed points. These centerpoints are located to draw an ellipse.

When sketching an isometric drawing, the isometric axes are drawn and end points for the principal measurements of height, length, and depth are located. Vertical lines are projected from the length and depth end points, and receding lines are projected from the height end point to construct two isometric surfaces. The top surface of the cube is formed by projecting receding lines at the corners. The end points for other lines

on the isometric axes or lines parallel to them are located. These end points are connected and all nonisometric lines, circles, and arcs are completed. Object lines are darkened to complete the drawing. **See Figure 2-5.**

Oblique Drawings. An *oblique drawing* is a pictorial drawing with one surface drawn in true shape and receding lines projecting back from the face. Receding lines are commonly drawn at 30° or 45° angles. In oblique cavalier drawings, receding lines are drawn full-scale. In oblique cabinet drawings, receding lines are drawn at one-half scale. Oblique cabinet drawings are the most common type of oblique drawing. Circles appear in true shape on the front surface of oblique drawings and as ellipses on receding surfaces.

TECHFACTS

Pictorial drawings are also referred to as presentation drawings since they are commonly used to present design ideas to potential owners.

Isometric Drawings

Figure 2-5

120°

30° 30° — HORIZON

— ISOMETRIC AXES

NONISOMETRIC LINE

LOCATE END POINTS TO DRAW NONISOMETRIC LINES

X

½X

LOCATE CENTERPOINTS TO DRAW ELLIPSES

CIRCLES APPEAR AS ELLIPSES

Figure 2-5. The isometric axes are drawn 30° above horizontal.

When sketching an oblique cabinet drawing, the true shape of the front surface is drawn to scale showing the height and length of the object. Receding lines are drawn to one-half scale. All measurements along the oblique axis or lines parallel to them are made. Nonoblique lines are drawn by locating their end points on oblique lines. All nonoblique lines, circles, and arcs are completed. Object lines are darkened to complete the drawing. **See Figure 2-6.**

Orthographic Projections

An *orthographic projection* is a drawing in which each face of an object is projected onto flat planes, generally at 90° to one another. Each view is a two-dimensional drawing showing two principal measurements. The most common orthographic projection is a three-view, or multiview, drawing. The front view shows height and length; the side view shows height and depth; the top view shows depth and length. The three-view drawing is used in architecture, engineering, and construction to provide accurate graphic representations of the building project to be completed.

In an orthographic projection, lines are projected from every corner of the object to be drawn onto an imaginary transparent plane. Three planes are usually sufficient to show all details of most objects. These three planes produce the front, top, and side view of the object. In printreading, the front view is referred to as the front elevation, the side view as the side elevation, and the top view as the plan view. **See Figure 2-7.**

When describing a building to be built on a specific plot of ground, compass directions are used for each elevation. For example, the North Elevation is a view of the north side of the building and the South Elevation is a view of the south side of the building. A minimum of four elevations are required to show all exterior views of a building.

Figure 2-6. The oblique axis of an oblique drawing is drawn 30° or 45° above horizontal.

Oblique Drawings

Figure 2-6

TRUE SHAPE

30°   45°

OBLIQUE AXIS
(30° OR 45°)

2″
2″
2″
FULL SCALE

OBLIQUE CAVALIER

2″
2″
1″
ONE-HALF SCALE

OBLIQUE CABINET

ARCH SHOWN AS ELLIPSE

TRUE SHAPE

OBLIQUE SHAPE

ARCH SHOWN AS TRUE SHAPE

Orthographic Projections

Figure 2-7

VIEW	SHOWS
Front	Height & Length
Side	Height & Depth
Top	Depth & Length

Figure 2-7. The three-view drawing is the most common type of orthographic projection.

The top view of a three-view drawing shows the roof plan of a building. In order to see the floor plan, an imaginary horizontal cutting plane is passed through the building 5'-0" above the finished floor. Floor plans for basements and other floor levels of a multistory house are drawn by using additional imaginary cutting planes at 5'-0" above each finished floor level.

Projection lines that connect the parts of one view to another show the relationship of the elevations to the plan view. A transparent isometric box shows the house and indicates the various elevations and plan views. The box is then unfolded to show the relationship of views. Projection lines show that the principal measurements of height, length, and depth are consistent throughout the views. **See Figure 2-8.**

Southern Forest Products Association

A set of working drawings is used on a jobsite to accurately complete a construction project.

Visualizing the relationship of points from one elevation to another aids in understanding the concept of three-view drawings. **See Figure 2-9.** The simplified pictorial of the tri-level house contains wall surfaces designated A, B, C, and D. Points on these surfaces are designated with lowercase letters a through h. Surfaces A and B are seen on the front elevation in their true shape and size. Surfaces C and D are seen on the right side elevation in their true shape and size. Points on one view are lines on the other view. For example, the point representing the main roof ridge is designated ab on the front elevation. The order in which the letters are presented indicates that point a is closer to the observer than point b. The roof ridge is shown as horizontal line ab on the right side elevation.

When sketching a three-view drawing, the true shape of the front view showing height and length of the object is drawn to scale. Projection lines are drawn to define the height and depth of the side view and the depth and length of the top view. Additional projection lines are used to project other features of the object including offsets, slanted surfaces, and centerpoints for circles and arcs. Lines that cannot be seen on a particular view are drawn as hidden (dashed) lines. All object and hidden lines are darkened to complete the drawing.

Figure 2-8. Elevation views are related by projection of features from one view to another.

Projection Lines

Figure 2-8

Figure 2-9. A point on an elevation is shown as a line on the adjacent elevation and vice versa.

Three-View Drawings

Figure 2-9

DIMENSIONING

Prints used on a construction project are reproductions of architectural working drawings drawn to scale. A road map is a common example of a drawing made to scale. An area of several thousand square miles is shown on a small piece of paper by using a scale of a certain number of miles per inch.

Prints are drawn small enough so they can be handled easily, yet large enough to show necessary information clearly. Common drawing and print paper sizes in the United States are shown in the following table:

Letter Designation	Size
A	8½″ × 11″ (sheet)
B	11″ × 17″ (sheet)
C	17″ × 22″ (sheet)
D	22″ × 34″ (sheet)
E	34″ × 44″ (sheet)
E+	34″ × 44″ + (roll)

The length of each line on a print is reduced, or scaled, to a constant fraction of its true length so that all parts of the building are in exact relationship to each other. The scale most commonly used for floor plans and elevations is ¼″ = 1′-0″. For example, the floor plan of a 36′-0″ × 60′-0″ house drawn to the scale of ¼″ = 1′-0″ is drawn as a 9″ × 15″ rectangle (36′ × ¼ in./ft = 9″; 60′ × ¼ in./ft = 15″). For details of doors, windows, or other features, a larger scale, such as 1½″ = 1′-0″, may be used.

A complete set of plans is seldom drawn to the same scale because of the need to show details at a larger scale or the need to show the plot plan at a smaller scale. The scale for a sheet may be shown in the title block and/or below each plan, elevation, detail, or section view.

Architect's Scale

A triangular architect's scale has six ruled faces designed to measure in ten different scales. One of the edges is identical to a 12″ ruler divided into ¹⁄₁₆″ increments. The following are the ten scales on the triangular architect's scale:

- 3″ = 1′-0″
- 1½″ = 1′-0″
- 1″ = 1′-0″
- ¾″ = 1′-0″
- ½″ = 1′-0″
- ⅜″ = 1′-0″
- ¼″ = 1′-0″
- ³⁄₁₆″ = 1′-0″
- ⅛″ = 1′-0″
- ³⁄₃₂″ = 1′-0″

Architect's scales are read from left to right or right to left depending on the scale. **See Figure 2-10.** A ¼″ = 1′-0″ scale is read from right to left beginning at the 0 on the right end of the scale. The same set of markings is used for both the ¼″ = 1′-0″ scale and the ⅛″ = 1′-0″ scale. The correct line in relation to the scale used must be read. For example, 18′-0″ on the ¼″ = 1′-0″ scale is on the line representing 57′-0″ on the ⅛″ = 1′-0″ scale. Inches are read between the 0 and the end of the architect's scale.

TECH TIPS

Metric scales are available when creating drawings in the SI metric system. Common scales on a metric scale are 1:1, 1:2, 1:2.5, 1:5, 1:10, 2:1, 5:1, and 10:1.

Architect's Scales

Figure 2-10

READ FROM LEFT TO RIGHT

18′ ON ¼″ = 1′-0″ SCALE
57′ ON ⅛″ = 1′-0″ SCALE

READ FROM RIGHT TO LEFT

INCHES   FEET   INCHES

Figure 2-10. An architect's scale is used to produce scaled drawings.

Linear Measurement

Accurate readings of feet, inches, and fractions of an inch from a ruler or tape measure are essential in building construction. In addition, a tape measure can be used to scale measurements from a print.

When reading a tape measure or ruler, the number of feet is determined first. Many tape measures have highlighted areas indicating feet. **See Figure 2-11.** Next, the number of full inches is determined by reading the last number on the ruler prior to the measurement.

Figure 2-11. Most tape measures have highlighted portions indicating feet.

Feet Indicators

Figure 2-11

Next, the fractional part of the inch must be determined. Rulers divide an inch into equal fractional parts with longer lines denoting larger fractions and progressively shorter lines indicating smaller divisions.

Most tape measures and rulers used in the building trades are divided into ¹⁄₁₆″ increments. **See Figure 2-12.** There are 16 equal increments in each inch. Each inch on a tape measure or ruler is divided into ¹⁄₁₆″ increments that are indicated with marks of varying lengths. The ½″ mark is the longest mark between the two full inch marks. The ¼″ marks are slightly shorter than the ½″ marks and are placed one-half the distance between the ½″ mark and the full inch mark

on either side. The ⅛″ marks are slightly shorter than the ¼″ marks and are placed half the distance between the ¼″ marks and the full inch marks and the ¼″ marks and the ½″ mark. The ¹⁄₁₆″ marks are slightly shorter than the ⅛″ marks and placed half the distance between the adjoining ⅛″ marks.

Inch Increments

Figure 2-12

Figure 2-12. Tape measures and other rulers used in the building trades are often divided into ¹⁄₁₆″ increments.

Some rulers are divided into 32nds or 64ths of an inch using progressively shorter lines. With practice, reading the fractional marks based on their length and position within the adjoining inch and fractional marks can become quick and accurate.

Scaling Prints with a Tape Measure or Ruler. A tape measure or ruler divided into inches and ¹⁄₁₆″ increments may be used to make and read drawings at the ¼″ = 1′-0″ scale. The results, however, may not be as accurate because the small divisions on the architect's scale are not available. Prints should not be measured for scale at a construction site to obtain a dimension unless the dimension is verified by the architect or engineer.

Tradesworkers may use a tape measure on a job site to determine a specific detail or to transmit information back to the architect. Each ¼″ space on a tape measure is equal to 1′-0″ on a print with a ¼″ = 1′-0″ scale. Each ⅟16″ space on the tape measure is equal to 3″. Therefore, a distance of 1³⁄16″ on a print represents 4′-9″ at the scale of ¼″ = 1′-0″. The number of ¼″ spaces must be counted to find the number of feet. This number is added to the number of ⅟16″ spaces, which represent 3″ each to obtain the total of 4′-9″. **See Figure 2-13.**

Some dimensions on a print are found by simple mathematics. For example, if an overall dimension of 26′-0″ is shown for a wall having window openings 6′-6″ from each corner, the distance from the center of one window opening to the center of the other window opening is found by adding the given measurements for each window opening and subtracting them from the total wall length (6′-6″ + 6′-6″ = 13′-0″; 26′-0″ – 13′-0″ = 13′-0″).

Tape Measures
Figure 2-13

Figure 2-13. Tape measures are used by tradesworkers to measure components to be cut.

SYMBOLS AND CONVENTIONS

Symbols are drawn to scale to indicate their relative sizes. A *symbol* is a pictorial representation of a structural or material component used on prints. Walls, windows, doors, plumbing and fixtures, footings, partitions, chimneys, roofs, and other features are drawn in proportion to their size. **See Figure 2-14.**

Figure 2-14. Symbols are drawn in proportion to other construction materials.

Symbols
Figure 2-14

Dimensioning Conventions

The American National Standards Institute (ANSI) in conjunction with ASME International has developed specific standards for dimensioning drawings. ASME Y14.5M, *Geometric Dimensioning and Tolerancing,* establishes uniform practices for stating and interpreting dimensions on drawings. Through the use of this standard, architects can convey their ideas with the assurance that experienced printreaders can read them correctly.

Dimension lines may be terminated by arrowheads, slashes, or dots at the points on a drawing where they meet extension lines. The dimension is placed above the dimension line unless the space is too small. If the space is too small, the dimension is then placed in the nearest convenient space and related to the space by a leader line. **See Figure 2-15.**

Exterior Walls. Framed, masonry, and other types of exterior walls are dimensioned according to dimensioning standards. **See Figure 2-16.** The preferred method for framed walls is to dimension to the outside faces of stud corner posts. Most of the remaining structural members can be located in relation to these rough framing members. It is easier to locate openings for doors and windows if the dimensions start from the outside faces of stud corner posts than if the dimensions are given from the outside face of sheathing since sheathing is applied after the rough openings are located.

Figure 2-15. Arrowheads, slashes, or dots may be used to terminate dimension lines.

Concrete walls are dimensioned to their outside faces.

Figure 2-16. Walls are dimensioned to facilitate construction methods.

Solid masonry and concrete walls are dimensioned to their outside faces. Masonry veneer walls are dimensioned to the outside faces of the studs and to the outside faces of the masonry veneer wall. The outside dimensions of the foundation are usually the same as the outside dimensions of the masonry veneer wall. The faces of the studs must be located in relationship to the face of the masonry veneer wall because the frame structure is built before bricks for the veneer wall are laid.

Interior Partitions. Interior partitions vary in thickness depending on the structural framing materials and finishes. Dimensions are drawn to the center, the face of a stud partition, or the face of the finished wall. **See Figure 2-17.** Most common interior stud-framed stud partitions have an actual thickness of $3\frac{1}{2}''$, not including the drywall. Because of variations that may occur on the job site, the $3\frac{1}{2}''$ thickness aids in setting partitions accurately. Actual dimensions of a 2 × 4 stud are $1\frac{1}{2}'' \times 3\frac{1}{2}''$. Thus, a partition with $\frac{1}{2}''$ drywall on both sides is $4\frac{1}{2}''$ thick ($\frac{1}{2}'' + 3\frac{1}{2}'' + \frac{1}{2}'' = 4\frac{1}{2}''$). Partitions in bathrooms and kitchens may be thicker to accommodate plumbing soil stacks.

Concrete masonry units, tile, or other materials of standard width are generally dimensioned to the face of the finish material.

Windows and Doors. Locations of openings for windows and doors on the floor plans for frame construction are dimensioned to the center of openings. Locations of openings for windows and doors on floor plans for solid masonry construction are dimensioned to the center of the openings or to the finish masonry abutting the window or door. Dimensions to the centers of the openings are preferred. **See Figure 2-18.**

TECHFACTS

Interior partition thickness may be increased for rooms such as in-home theaters and game rooms to improve sound insulation.

Interior Partition Dimensioning

Figure 2-17

CENTERLINE — FACE

Stud Partition | Stud Partition | Concrete Masonry Unit Partition | Tile Partition

Figure 2-17. Partitions are dimensioned to their centerlines or faces.

Figure 2-18. Openings for windows and doors are dimensioned to their centerlines.

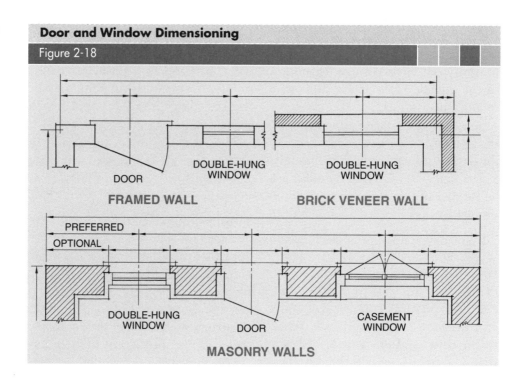

Door and Window Dimensioning

Figure 2-18

DOOR

DOUBLE-HUNG WINDOW

FRAMED WALL

DOUBLE-HUNG WINDOW

BRICK VENEER WALL

PREFERRED

OPTIONAL

DOUBLE-HUNG WINDOW

DOOR

CASEMENT WINDOW

MASONRY WALLS

LEARNER RESOURCES

ATPeResources.com/QuickLinks
Access Code: 281467

Name _____ Date _____

Sketching 2-1

Sketch the missing view of each three-view drawing.

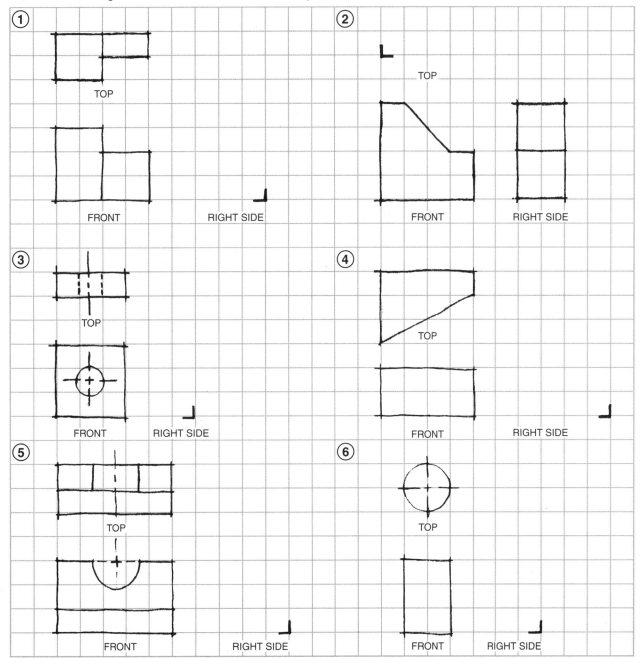

Sketching 2-2

Sketch oblique cabinet drawings of the multiview drawings on a separate sheet of paper.

① FRONT   RIGHT SIDE

② FRONT   RIGHT SIDE

③ LEFT SIDE   FRONT

④ FRONT   RIGHT SIDE

Sketching 2-3

Sketch front and right side views of the oblique drawings on a separate sheet of paper.

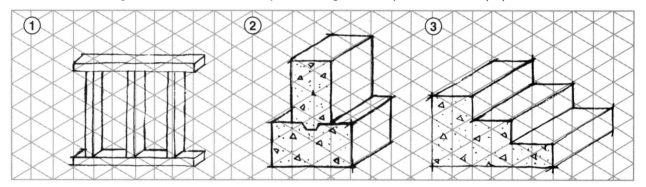

Sketching 2-4

Sketch front and right side views of the isometric drawings on a separate sheet of paper.

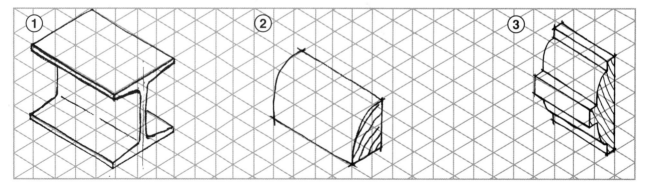

Sketching 2-5

Sketch oblique drawings of the section views of the moldings. Use 30° receding lines to the right.

① COVE

② RAKE

③ BRICK

④ DRIP CAP

⑤ SHOE

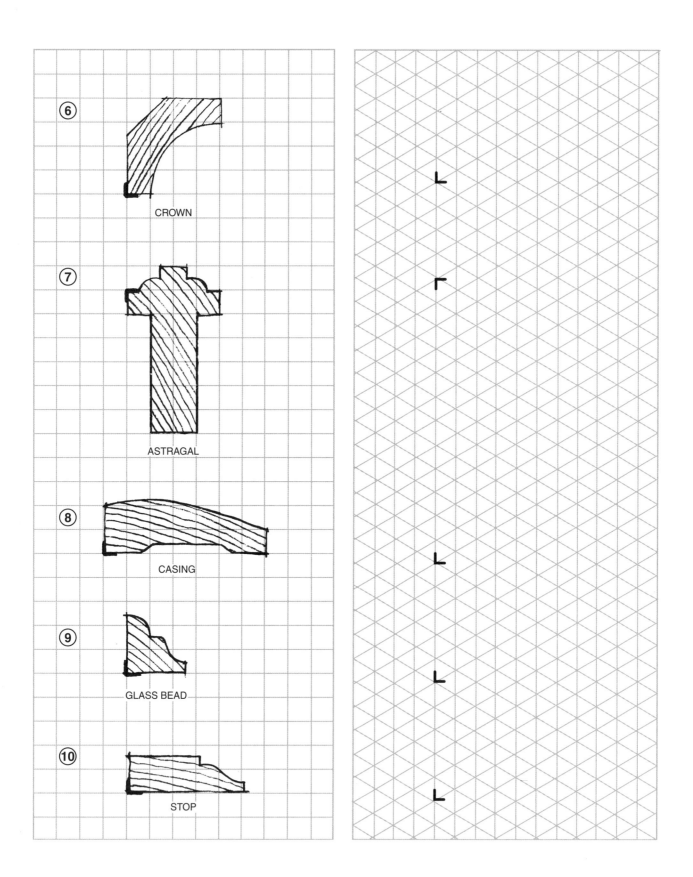

⑥ CROWN

⑦ ASTRAGAL

⑧ CASING

⑨ GLASS BEAD

⑩ STOP

46

Name _____ Date _____

Multiple Choice

_____ **1.** A basic type of pictorial drawing is ___.
- A. plan
- B. isometric
- C. elevation
- D. sketch

_____ **2.** C size paper is ___.
- A. 8½″ × 11″
- B. 11″ × 17″
- C. 17″ × 22″
- D. 18″ × 24″

_____ **3.** Isosceles and equilateral triangles are ___ triangles.
- A. acute
- B. obtuse
- C. right
- D. sector

_____ **4.** Quadrilaterals are ___ figures.
- A. three-sided plane
- B. three-sided solid
- C. four-sided plane
- D. four-sided solid

_____ **5.** In an oblique cabinet drawing, receding lines are drawn at ___ scale.
- A. one-fourth
- B. one-half
- C. three-fourths
- D. full

_____ **6.** The radius of a circle is ___ the diameter.
- A. the same length as
- B. one-half
- C. twice
- D. two and one-half times

_____ **7.** The top view of a three-view drawing of a house shows the ___.
- A. front
- B. site
- C. plan
- D. roof

47

8. The preferred method of dimensioning framed walls is to dimension to the ___.
    A. centerlines of stud corner posts
    B. inside face of stud corner posts
    C. outside face of stud corner posts
    D. most convenient location

9. A ___ movement is used when sketching long lines.
    A. smooth wrist
    B. full arm
    C. rigid
    D. steady

10. Dimension lines may be terminated by ___.
    A. extension lines
    B. dimensions
    C. outside faces of studs
    D. slashes

11. The diameter of a circle is a ___.
    A. straight line passing anywhere through the circle
    B. curved line passing anywhere through the circle
    C. straight line passing through the centerpoint
    D. curved line passing through the centerpoint

12. Each view of a three-view drawing gives ___ principal measurement(s).
    A. one
    B. two
    C. three
    D. four

13. A trapezoid has ___.
    A. opposite sides parallel
    B. opposite sides parallel and equal
    C. two sides parallel
    D. two sides parallel and two sides equal

14. A wood stud partition with ⅜″ drywall on each side of 2 × 4 studs is ___″ thick.
    A. 3½
    B. 4⅛
    C. 4¼
    D. 4½

15. A bird's-eye perspective is drawn ___ the horizon line.
    A. above
    B. on
    C. below
    D. from

True-False

T   F   **1.** Shading techniques are generally not used when producing three-view drawings.

T   F   **2.** A quadrant is one-half of a circle.

T	F	**3.** A right triangle contains one 90° angle.
T	F	**4.** Compass directions are commonly used to name exterior elevation drawings.
T	F	**5.** An arc is a portion of the circumference of a circle.
T	F	**6.** Oblique drawings may have one, two, or three vanishing points.
T	F	**7.** All circles contain 360°.
T	F	**8.** A complete set of plans is seldom drawn to the same scale.
T	F	**9.** A rhombus contains one 90° angle.
T	F	**10.** Circles on isometric drawings appear as ellipses.
T	F	**11.** Architect's scales are always read from left to right.
T	F	**12.** Solid masonry walls are dimensioned to their outside faces.
T	F	**13.** Rough openings for doors and windows are generally dimensioned to their centerlines.
T	F	**14.** The scale most commonly used for floor plans is ¼" = 1'-0".
T	F	**15.** Stud partitions vary in thickness depending on the finish.

Completion 2-1

_____ **1.** ___ is the process of drawing without instruments.

_____ **2.** ___ are plane figures with four 90° angles and four equal sides.

_____ **3.** Sketching pencils are either ___ or mechanical.

_____ **4.** Tracing ___ should be used when a sketch is to be duplicated on a diazo printer.

_____ **5.** Semicircles always contain ___°.

_____ **6.** ___ different scales are on the triangular architect's scale.

_____ **7.** ___ software programs can also be used for sketching.

_____ **8.** ___ lines are drawn level or parallel with the horizon.

_____ **9.** ___ polygons contain sides of equal length and equal angles.

_____ **10.** Pictorial drawings show the three principal measurements of ___, length, and depth.

_____ **11.** Perspective drawings may have one, two, or three ___ points.

_____ **12.** Concrete block partitions are generally dimensioned to the ___ of the finish material.

_____ **13.** The ___ view of a three-view drawing shows the height and depth of an object.

_____ **14.** The sum of two supplementary angles always equals ___°.

_____ **15.** ___ lines are plumb or upright.

_____ **16.** Plane figures have ___ surfaces.

_____ **17.** Circles on receding surfaces of oblique drawings appear as ___.

_____ **18.** Receding lines of oblique drawings may be 30° or ___°.

_____ **19.** An acute angle contains less than ___°.

_____ **20.** A(n) ___ of a circle is pie shaped.

_____ **21.** ___ are three-sided plane figures.

_____ **22.** A triangle always contains ___°.

_____ **23.** Right triangles always contain one ___° angle.

_____ **24.** ___ lines are straight lines that are neither horizontal nor vertical.

_____ **25.** Horizontal lines of isometric drawings are drawn ___° above the horizon.

Completion 2-2

_____ **1.** The ___ view shows height and length.

_____ **2.** The ___ view shows height and depth.

_____ **3.** The ___ view shows depth and length.

TOP VIEW

FRONT VIEW   SIDE VIEW

Name _____ Date _____

Identification 2-1

_____ **1.** Tangent

_____ **2.** Chord

_____ **3.** Radius

_____ **4.** Centerpoint

_____ **5.** Angle

_____ **6.** Segment

_____ **7.** Quadrant

_____ **8.** Diameter

_____ **9.** Sector

_____ **10.** Circumference

Identification 2-2

_____ **1.** Eccentric circles

_____ **2.** Square

_____ **3.** Hexagon

_____ **4.** Equilateral triangle

_____ **5.** Pentagon

_____ **6.** Right triangle

_____ **7.** Octagon

_____ **8.** Concentric circles

_____ **9.** Trapezium

_____ **10.** Rectangle

Identification 2-3

Refer to Randall Residence.

_____ **1.** West Elevation

_____ **2.** South Elevation

_____ **3.** East Elevation

_____ **4.** North Elevation

RANDALL RESIDENCE

Identification 2-4

_____ **1.** ⅜″

_____ **2.** ¾″

_____ **3.** 1¼″

_____ **4.** 1⅞″

_____ **5.** 2′-3⅛″

_____ **6.** 2′-3⅝″

_____ **7.** 1′-0⁹⁄₁₆″

_____ **8.** 1′-1⅛″

Identification 2-5

_____ **1.** 2′-6½″

_____ **2.** 1′-3″

_____ **3.** 3′-9″

_____ **4.** 6′-10″

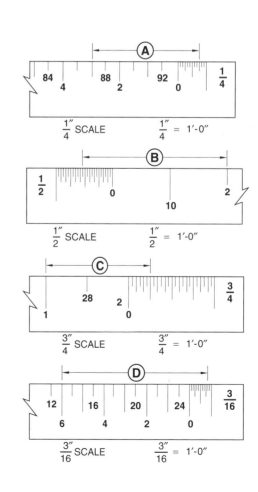

Completion 2-1

1. _____ ¼″ = 1′-0″

2. _____ ¼″ = 1′-0″

3. _____ ¼″ = 1′-0″

4. _____ ⅜″ = 1′-0″

5. _____ ¾″ = 1′-0″

6. _____ ½″ = 1′-0″

7. _____ 1″ = 1′-0″

8. _____ 1½″ = 1′-0″

9. _____ 1½″ = 1′-0″

10. _____ 3″ = 1′-0″

Completion 2-2

Determine the missing dimensions.

1. _____

2. _____

3. _____

4. _____

5. _____

6. _____

Multiple Choice

Refer to Joseph Residence on page 57.

_____ **1.** A(n) ___ drawing of the house is shown.
   A. perspective
   B. isometric
   C. oblique
   D. elevation

_____ **2.** A person standing at position X would see the ___ Elevation.
   A. North
   B. South
   C. East
   D. West

_____ **3.** A person standing at position Y would see the ___ Elevation.
   A. North
   B. South
   C. East
   D. West

_____ **4.** The kitchen entrance will be shown on the ___ Elevation.
   A. North
   B. South
   C. East
   D. West

_____ **5.** ___ door(s) will be shown on the South Elevation.
   A. No
   B. One
   C. Two
   D. Three

_____ **6.** ___ window(s) will be shown on the East Elevation.
   A. No
   B. One
   C. Two
   D. Three

_____ **7.** ___ window(s) will be shown on the West Elevation.
   A. No
   B. One
   C. Two
   D. Three

_____ **8.** The chimney will be shown head-on on the ___ Elevation.
   A. North
   B. South
   C. East
   D. West

_____ **9.** Wall surfaces ___ and ___ will be shown on the North Elevation.
    A. A; B
    B. C; D
    C. A; C
    D. B; D

_____ **10.** The front entrance will be shown on the ___ Elevation.
    A. North
    B. South
    C. East
    D. West

_____ **11.** A total of ___ door(s) and ___ windows will be shown on the South Elevation.
    A. 1; 2
    B. 2; 2
    C. 2; 3
    D. 2; 4

_____ **12.** A total of ___ door(s) and ___ window(s) will be shown on the North Elevation.
    A. 1; 1
    B. 1; 3
    C. 2; 2
    D. 3; 3

_____ **13.** Wall surfaces ___ will be shown on the East Elevation.
    A. A and C
    B. B and D
    C. F, E, and G
    D. A and B

_____ **14.** Wall surface F will be shown on the ___ Elevation.
    A. North
    B. South
    C. East
    D. West

_____ **15.** Wall surface A will be shown on the ___ Elevation.
    A. North
    B. South
    C. East
    D. West

Refer to Multiple Choice on page 55.

JOSEPH RESIDENCE

TRADE MATH

CHAPTER 3

Tradesworkers must be able to quickly and accurately translate dimensions from prints into actual construction components and a finished structure. Workers involved in the design, engineering, and construction of a building must be proficient in math to efficiently and successfully complete their portion of a construction project.

OBJECTIVES

1. Define whole number and place.
2. Explain how to add and subtract whole numbers.
3. Explain how to multiply and divide whole numbers.
4. Define fractions and decimals.
5. Explain how fractions are added and subtracted.
6. Explain how fractions are multiplied and divided.
7. Explain how decimals are added and subtracted.
8. Explain how decimals are multiplied and divided.
9. Describe the conversion process for fractions and decimals.
10. Explain metric measurement.
11. Define area and volume and explain how they are calculated.

WHOLE NUMBERS

A *whole number* is a number that does not have a fractional or decimal part. Whole numbers are commonly used for counting individual components and other items such as doors, windows, fixtures, bolts, or pipes. Numbers such as 1, 2, 3, 5, 12, 135, 1345, and 10,367 are whole numbers.

Whole numbers are either even or odd numbers. An *even number* is a number that can be divided by two without a remainder or decimal occurring. An *odd number* is a number that cannot be divided by two without a remainder or decimal occurring. **See Figure 3-1.** A *prime number* is an odd number that can only be divided by 1 or itself without a remainder or decimal occurring. Examples of prime numbers are 1, 3, 5, 7, 11, 17, and 23.

A *place* is the position that a digit occupies; it represents the value of the digit. **See Figure 3-2.** A digit has different values according to the place is occupies. For example, the digits 15 represent fifteen items, while the digits 51 represent fifty-one items.

Even and Odd Whole Numbers

Figure 3-1

ODD NUMBERS CANNOT BE DIVIDED BY 2 AN EXACT NUMBER OF TIMES

EVEN NUMBERS CAN BE DIVIDED BY 2 AN EXACT NUMBER OF TIMES

WHOLE NUMBERS HAVE NO FRACTIONAL OR DECIMAL PARTS

EIGHT FULL INCHES

SEVENTEEN FULL FEET

Figure 3-1. Whole numbers represent full units such as inches and feet.

Figure 3-2. The value of a digit varies depending on its place in a whole number.

Digit Values

Figure 3-2

COMMAS SEPARATE GROUPS OF THREE DIGITS WHEN NUMBERS CONTAIN FIVE DIGITS OR MORE

4 2 6
SIX ONES
TWO TENS
FOUR HUNDREDS

2 6 4
FOUR ONES
SIX TENS
TWO HUNDREDS

Adding Whole Numbers

Addition is the process of combining two or more whole numbers to obtain a total. A plus sign (+) indicates addition. A *sum* is the total that results from addition. For example, addition is used to determine the total length of a wall when the dimensions for several shorter lengths of wall segments are shown on a print.

Fundamentals. When whole numbers are added vertically, the numbers are placed above one another with the units places aligned. The units digit of each number is placed in the units place, the tens digit in the tens place, and so on. The columns are added from top to bottom, beginning with the units place. When the units sum is less than 10, the sum is recorded at the bottom of the column. When the units sum is greater than 10, the last digit of the sum is recorded and the remaining digit is carried to the next column to the left. This procedure is used in all columns to obtain a sum of the whole numbers. **See Figure 3-3.**

Applications. In printreading, whole numbers are added for a variety of applications. A common application of whole number addition is counting the number of items required for quantity takeoffs during estimating. For example, whole numbers are added to count the number of windows, doors, electrical switches, light fixtures, and other building components.

Dimensions on prints are commonly added to verify overall lengths. When adding feet and inches, inches are added first and then feet are added. Inches are added in base 12, with each 12″ equal to 1′-0″. Feet are added in base 10. For example, adding 6′-3″, 7′-6″, and 4′-6″ requires first adding the inches in base 12 (3″ + 6″ + 6″ = 15″ = 1′-3″), then adding the feet (6′ + 7′ + 4′ = 17′). The two subtotals are added to obtain the final sum (1′-3″ + 17′ = 18′-3″). **See Figure 3-4.**

Figure 3-3. Addition of whole numbers begins with properly aligning the digits vertically.

Addition of Whole Numbers

Figure 3-3

TENS PLACE
UNITS PLACE
2′-0″
+14′-0″
16′-0″
SUM

TENS PLACE
UNITS PLACE
¹2′-0″
4′-0″
3′-0″
3′-0″
+ 4′-0″
16′-0″
SUM

Addition of Feet and Inches

Figure 3-4

Figure 3-4. Addition of combined feet and inch measurements requires separate processes for each.

Subtracting Whole Numbers

Subtraction is the mathematical process of taking one number away from another number. Subtraction is the opposite, or inverse, mathematical operation of addition. The minus sign (–) indicates subtraction. The subtraction operation that begins with a quantity of three items and removes two to achieve a result of one is expressed as 3 – 2 = 1.

Fundamentals. The *minuend* is the total number of units prior to subtraction. The *subtrahend* is the number

of units to be removed from the minuend. The *result* is the difference between the minuend and subtrahend.

When whole numbers are subtracted vertically, the minuend is placed above the subtrahend with the units places aligned. Whole number subtraction starts with the units column on the right and moves from right to left through the columns. **See Figure 3-5.**

When the subtrahend digit in a column is larger than the unit in the minuend digit above, one unit is borrowed from the column immediately to the left. The borrowed unit may be

Subtraction of Whole Numbers

Figure 3-5

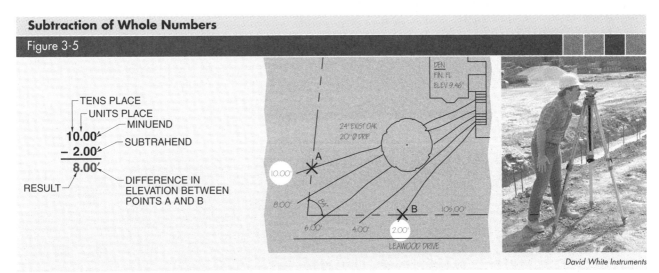

David White Instruments

Figure 3-5. Subtraction is used on a construction site to determine differences in elevations.

10, 100, 1000, or other multiples depending on the column. The following example illustrates borrowing ten units:

$$\begin{array}{r} 22 \\ -\ 9 \end{array} = \begin{array}{r} 1\overset{1}{2} \\ -\ \ 9 \\ \hline 13 \end{array}$$

TECHFACTS

Arabic numbers are expressed by ten digits—0 through 9. Roman numerals are expressed by the letters I, V, X, L, C, D, and M.

Applications. In printreading, whole numbers are subtracted to determine the remaining quantities or amounts of objects after another quantity has been removed. For example, when 15′ of the rear of a building lot is set aside as a utility easement and the total property depth is 87′, the usable distance is 72′:

$$\begin{array}{r} 87' \\ -15' \\ \hline 72' \end{array}$$

Similar to the addition of feet and inches, in subtraction the inches are subtracted first in base 12 and then feet are subtracted in base 10. **See Figure 3-6.** For example, to determine the missing dimension on the print, 4′-8″ is subtracted from 7′-0″ (7′-0″ – 4′-8″). Inches are subtracted first. Since 8″ cannot be subtracted from 0″, 1′-0″ is converted to 12″ to allow for subtraction to proceed

(12″ – 8″ = 4″). The remaining feet are then subtracted (6′ – 4′ = 2′). The two results are added (4″ + 2′ = 2′-4″).

Multiplying Whole Numbers

Multiplication is the mathematical process of adding a number to itself as many times as there are units indicated by the other number. The multiplication sign (×) is used to indicate multiplication. In effect, multiplication is an addition shortcut. For example, the notation of 10 × 8 is the same as adding ten to itself eight times (10 + 10 + 10 + 10 + 10 + 10 + 10 + 10 = 80). **Fundamentals.** The *multiplicand* is the number being multiplied. The *multiplier* is the number that indicates the number of times the addition should occur. The *product* is the result of multiplication. From the example 10 × 8 = 80, 10 is the multiplicand, 8 is the multiplier, and 80 is the product.

A multiplication table is a chart that can be studied and memorized to quickly recall various products of multiplication. **See Figure 3-7.** Memorizing that 7 × 12 results in a product of 84 is quicker than performing the function longhand.

Figure 3-6. When borrowing in the subtraction of feet and inches, care is taken to borrow 12″ for each 1′.

Subtraction of Feet and Inches

Figure 3-6

1′ BORROWED AND CONVERTED TO 12″

$$\begin{array}{r} 12 \\ 6\ 7'\text{-}0'' \\ -\ \ 4'\text{-}8'' \\ \hline 2'\text{-}4'' \end{array}$$

MISSING DIMENSION

Multiplication

Figure 3-7

MULTIPLICATION TABLE

1	2	3	4	5	6	7	8	9	10	11	12
2	4	6	8	10	12	14	16	18	20	22	24
3	6	9	12	15	18	21	24	27	30	33	36
4	8	12	16	20	24	28	32	36	40	44	48
5	10	15	20	25	30	35	40	45	50	55	60
6	12	18	24	30	36	42	48	54	60	66	72
7	14	21	28	35	42	49	56	63	70	77	84
8	16	24	32	40	48	56	64	72	80	88	96
9	18	27	36	45	54	63	72	81	90	99	108
10	20	30	40	50	60	70	80	90	100	110	120
11	22	33	44	55	66	77	88	99	110	121	132
12	24	36	48	60	72	84	96	108	120	132	144

7″ × 12″= 84″

Figure 3-7. Memorization of the multiplication table allows for quick and accurate calculations.

When multiple-digit whole numbers are multiplied vertically, the multiplicand is placed over the multiplier with the units places aligned. The first digit of the multiplier is multiplied across the entire multiplicand starting with the unit on the right, and the product is written in the first row below the horizontal line. The tens digit in the multiplier is then multiplied across the entire multiplicand, starting with the unit on the right, and the product is written in the second row below the horizontal line with the last digit of the product in the tens column. The two products are then added:

```
  365
× 42
  730
14 60
15,330
```

Any number multiplied by zero is zero. When there is a zero in the multiplier (for example, 407), only those numbers that have value are multiplied. The last digit of each separate product is placed under the digit used to calculate it. When all of the products have been calculated, the digits are added vertically. If the addition results in a sum of 10 or more in any given column, the ones digit is written in the proper place and the tens digit is carried to the next column:

```
  346
× 407
 2 422
138 4
140,822
```

One method to ensure the product accuracy is to reverse the multiplicand and multiplier and perform the multiplication again. For example, when properly calculated 45 × 236 results in the same product as 236 × 45.

Applications. In printreading, whole numbers are multiplied to determine areas and volumes and to determine material quantities for multistory structures. For example, an 8′ high by 17′ long wall has 136 sq ft of surface area:

```
  17
×  8
 136
```

A 12-story apartment project with each floor containing 19 lavatories requires 228 lavatories:

```
  12
× 19
 108
 12
 228
```

Dividing Whole Numbers

Division is the mathematical process of determining the number of times one number is contained in another number. The division sign (÷) is used to indicate division. An example of a division operation is 6 ÷ 2 = 3. Three is contained in six two times. Division is the inverse mathematical operation of multiplication.

TECHFACTS

Another method to ensure multiplication accuracy is to divide the product by the multiplier. The quotient should equal the multiplicand value.

Fundamentals. The *dividend* is the number to be divided. The *divisor* is the number that the dividend is divided by. The *quotient* is the result of the division operation. When a dividend is not divided evenly by a divisor, a remainder, fraction, or decimal will occur.

When long division is performed, the dividend is placed inside the division bar and the divisor outside the bar. The division operation is then carried out by dividing the divisor into the first number(s). **See Figure 3-8.** The number of times the divisor goes into the dividend is recorded on top of the division bar. The same operation is then carried out on the next number(s). If a remainder occurs, it is placed to the right of the quotient and noted as a remainder, placed over the divisor and expressed as a fraction, or expressed as a decimal.

An easy way to check the result of division is to multiply the quotient by the divisor. For example, $25 \times 4 = 100$ checks the division of the problem $100 \div 4 = 25$.

Applications. On prints, an architect might not provide specific dimensions to various features but will note them as being spaced equally or centered between two other features. Division is required to accurately locate the features. For example, two reinforced concrete pads and columns are equally spaced between two walls that are 36′ apart. Two pads equally spaced require that the distance between the walls be divided into three equal spaces. On-center (OC) spacing of the concrete pads is 12′-0″ ($36′ \div 3 = 12′\text{-}0″$ OC). **See Figure 3-9.**

Providing equal spacing between components with a given width requires a combination of multiplication, subtraction, and division. For example, four window units, each 5′ wide, are to be placed with exactly the same space between each of them and between adjoining walls that are 100′ apart. First, the overall width of the window units is determined by multiplying the width by the number of units ($5′ \times 4 = 20′$).

Figure 3-8. Proper alignment of units and accurate subtraction and multiplication are needed for accurate long division.

Division

Figure 3-8

```
DIVISION
BAR              32        DIVISOR (4) IS DIVIDED
                           INTO 12 THREE TIMES
            4)128
DIVISOR      12            QUOTIENT
             08
              8            DIVISOR (4) IS
DIVIDEND      0            DIVIDED INTO 8
                           TWO TIMES
```

Figure 3-9. Division is used to locate various building components where equal spacing is required.

Division Application

Figure 3-9

```
     12′
  3)36
     3
     06
      6
      0
```

COLUMNS SHOULD BE SPACED 12′-0″ OC

Next, the remaining space is determined by subtracting the overall width from the distance between the adjoining walls (100′ – 20′ = 80′). Finally, the exact spacing between the window units is determined by dividing the remaining space by the number of spaces between the four units (80′ ÷ 5 = 16′).

FRACTIONS AND DECIMALS

Fractions and decimals are a portion of a whole number. When expressing fractions, numbers are placed on each side of a horizontal or diagonal fraction bar, for example, ½. The number 2 indicates the total number of parts, and the number 1 indicates the number of parts included in the fraction. Decimals are represented by digits to the right of a decimal point that is placed to the right of a whole number. A decimal is expressed in base 10. The decimal of 0.5 indicates five-tenths of a whole number. **See Figure 3-10.**

Fractions are comprised of a denominator, numerator, and fraction bar. The *denominator* is the part of a fraction that indicates the total number of parts or divisions of a whole number. Denominators are placed below or to the right of the fraction bar. In ⅜, the denominator (8) indicates that a whole unit is divided into eight equal parts. The *numerator* is the part of a fraction that indicates the number of parts included in the fraction. Numerators are placed above or to the left of a fraction bar. In the ⅜ example, a numerator of 3 indicates that three of the eight equal parts are used to make up the total fraction. Fractions are common in linear measurement.

Decimal numbers are represented by digits to the right of a whole number, separated by a decimal point. A *decimal fraction* is a fraction with a denominator of 10, 100, 1000, 10,000, and so on. More digits in a decimal indicate greater accuracy. For example, 2.5 indicates two and five-tenths. A decimal of 2.568 indicates two and five hundred sixty-eight thousandths. Decimals are common in measuring elevations and heights.

TECHFACTS

The addition of zeros to a number with a decimal point in front of it does not change its value.

TECHFACTS

Elevations, such as those shown on plot plans, are typically expressed in decimal numbers.

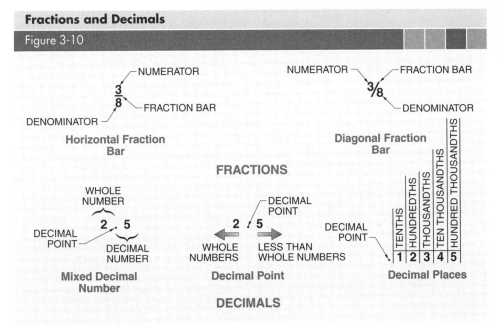

Fractions and Decimals

Figure 3-10

NUMERATOR

³⁄₈

FRACTION BAR

DENOMINATOR

Horizontal Fraction Bar

NUMERATOR — FRACTION BAR

³⁄₈

DENOMINATOR

Diagonal Fraction Bar

FRACTIONS

WHOLE NUMBER

2.5

DECIMAL POINT

DECIMAL NUMBER

Mixed Decimal Number

DECIMAL POINT

2 5

WHOLE NUMBERS — LESS THAN WHOLE NUMBERS

Decimal Point

DECIMAL POINT

TENTHS | HUNDREDTHS | THOUSANDTHS | TEN THOUSANDTHS | HUNDRED THOUSANDTHS

1 | 2 | 3 | 4 | 5

Decimal Places

DECIMALS

Figure 3-10. Smaller segments of whole numbers are described with fractions and decimals.

Adding Fractions

When adding fractions, the denominators of the fractions must be the same (common denominators). For example, $\frac{1}{16}$ and $\frac{3}{16}$ have common denominators and can be easily added, while $\frac{1}{8}$ and $\frac{1}{2}$ do not have common denominators. Fractions that do not have common denominators must be converted before adding.

Fundamentals. When adding a group of fractions with a common denominator, the fractions are arranged horizontally, the numerators are added, and the sum is placed over the denominator:

$$\frac{1}{8} + \frac{4}{8} + \frac{2}{8} = \frac{7}{8}$$

When adding groups of fractions, the sum of the numerators may be larger than the denominator:

$$\frac{1}{8} + \frac{3}{8} + \frac{5}{8} = \frac{9}{8}$$

An *improper fraction* is a fraction with the numerator larger than the denominator. An improper fraction must be converted to a mixed number. A *mixed number* is a fraction containing a whole number and a fraction. When converting an improper fraction to a mixed number, the denominator is divided into the numerator and the remainder is placed over the original denominator:

$$\frac{9}{8} = 9 \div 8 = 1\frac{1}{8}$$

When adding fractions with different denominators, the fractions must be converted so that their equivalents contain common denominators. The numerators are then added to obtain a sum:

$$\frac{1}{2} \times \frac{2}{2} = \frac{2}{4}$$
$$+\frac{1}{4} = \frac{1}{4}$$
$$\frac{3}{4}$$

TECHFACTS

A fraction should be reduced to its lowest terms after making a calculation. An improper fraction should be converted to a mixed number.

In some trades, fractions with very dissimilar denominators may be encountered. The denominators must be multiplied together to determine a common denominator. The numerators are then multiplied by the denominator of the other fraction:

$$\frac{3}{12} \times \frac{100}{100} = \frac{300}{1200}$$
$$+\frac{4}{100} \times \frac{12}{12} = \frac{48}{1200}$$
$$\frac{348}{1200}$$

Large fractions (such as $\frac{348}{1200}$) are reduced by dividing both the numerator and denominator by a common number. For $\frac{348}{1200}$, both 348 and 1200 can be divided by 12 to obtain $\frac{29}{100}$.

Applications. On most construction prints, portions of an inch are expressed as sixteenths ($\frac{1}{16}$), eighths ($\frac{1}{8}$), quarters ($\frac{1}{4}$), and halves ($\frac{1}{2}$). Dimensions with different denominators are frequently added to obtain an overall dimension. **See Figure 3-11.** When necessary, fractions are converted to their equivalents containing common denominators and the numerators of the fractions are added. Inches are then added in base 12. Feet are added in base 10 and the three sums are added to determine overall length.

Subtracting Fractions

When subtracting fractions, a common denominator for the fractions must first be determined. Where mixed numbers (fractions combined with whole numbers) are subtracted, the fractions are subtracted first and then the whole numbers are subtracted.

TECHFACTS

To ensure subtraction accuracy, add the result and subtrahend. The sum should be equal to the original minuend.

Fundamentals. After a common denominator has been determined and the fractions have been converted to their equivalents, the numerators are subtracted and the difference is placed over the denominator. For example, ⁵⁄₁₆ is subtracted from ¹¹⁄₁₆:

$$\frac{11}{16} - \frac{5}{16} = \frac{6}{16} \div \frac{2}{2} = \frac{3}{8}$$

In this case, the fraction is reduced by dividing both the numerator and denominator by 2 (6 ÷ 2 = 3 and 16 ÷ 2 = 8).

Applications. Fractions are frequently subtracted when determining required clearance or calculating omitted dimensions on a print. For example, it may be necessary to determine the distance between the base cabinet countertops and ceiling. **See Figure 3-12.** In some situations, it may be easier to perform calculations in inches (rather than feet and inches). In the example, the overall ceiling height is first converted to inches (8′ × 12″ = 96″ + ½″ = 96½″). Next, the floor-to-countertop height is subtracted from the overall ceiling

height (96½″ – 35¾″). Then, the fraction(s) are converted to equivalent fraction(s) with a common denominator; in this case, ½″ = ²⁄₄″. Since ¾″ cannot be subtracted from ²⁄₄″, one full inch is borrowed, converted to a fraction (⁴⁄₄), and added to the ²⁄₄ to allow subtraction to proceed (²⁄₄ + ⁴⁄₄ = ⁶⁄₄).

Wood Truss Council of America

Accurate measurement and math calculations are required in the construction of wood trusses.

Adding Dimensions

Figure 3-11

Figure 3-11. Accurate length calculations on prints require the addition of fractions of an inch, whole inches, and whole feet.

(1) SET UP OPERATION
3½″ + 12′-8½″ + 3½″ + 10′-0″ =

(2) ADD NUMERATORS OF FRACTIONS
½″ + ½″ + ½″ = ³⁄₂″ = 1½″

(3) ADD INCHES IN BASE 12
3″ + 8″ + 3″ = 14″ = 1′-2″

(4) ADD FEET IN BASE 10
12′ + 10′ = 22′

(5) ADD THREE SUBTOTALS
1½″ + 1′-2″ + 22′ = 23′-3½″

Figure 3-12. Subtraction of fractions, inches, and feet is utilized to calculate openings and remaining dimensions.

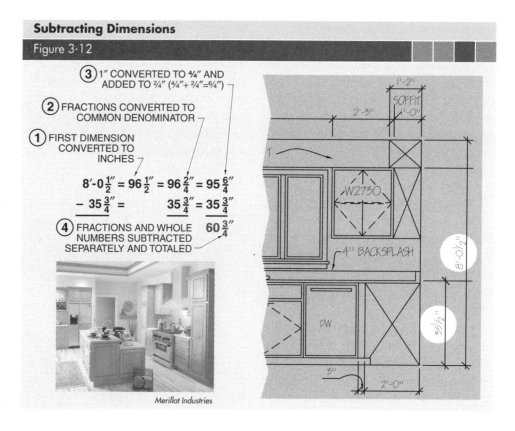

Subtracting Dimensions
Figure 3-12

The fractions are subtracted ($^6/_4$ – $^3/_4$ = $^3/_4$) and then the remaining whole inches (95″ – 35″ = 60″) are subtracted. The subtotals are added ($^3/_4$″ + 60″ = 60$^3/_4$″).

TECHFACTS

Fractions are the most common method of expressing partial inch dimensions in the building trades.

Multiplying Fractions

Fraction combinations that can be multiplied include two fractions, a fraction by a whole number, a fraction by a mixed number, a mixed number by a whole number, and two mixed numbers. Each type of multiplication requires a different process. **See Figure 3-13.**

Fundamentals. When multiplying two fractions, the numerator and denominator of one fraction are multiplied by the numerator and denominator of the other fraction. The product is reduced to its lowest terms as required. The product is reduced to lowest terms by dividing the numerator and denominator by the same number. For example, the product of $^{12}/_{48}$ can be reduced to lowest terms ($^1/_4$) by dividing the numerator and denominator by 12 (12 ÷ 12 = 1; 48 ÷ 12 = 4).

When multiplying a fraction by a whole number, the fraction numerator is multiplied by the whole number and the denominator is left unchanged. The fraction is reduced to its lowest terms as required.

When multiplying a fraction by a mixed number, the mixed number is first converted to its improper fraction equivalent. The numerator and denominator of the two fractions are multiplied and reduced to lowest terms as required.

When multiplying a mixed number by a whole number, the mixed number is first converted to its improper fraction equivalent. The improper fraction numerator is then multiplied by the whole number and reduced to lowest terms as required.

Multiplying Fractions
Figure 3-13

(1) SET UP OPERATION

$$\frac{1}{2} \times \frac{3}{4} =$$

(2) MULTIPLY NUMERATORS AND DENOMINATORS. REDUCE AS REQUIRED

$$\frac{1 \times 3}{2 \times 4} = \frac{3}{8}$$

MULTIPLYING TWO FRACTIONS

(1) SET UP OPERATION

$$\frac{3}{16} \times 2 =$$

(2) MULTIPLY NUMERATOR BY WHOLE NUMBER. REDUCE AS REQUIRED

$$\frac{3 \times 2}{16} = \frac{6}{16} = \frac{3}{8}$$

MULTIPLYING FRACTIONS BY WHOLE NUMBERS

(1) SET UP OPERATION

$$1\frac{3}{8} \times \frac{1}{2} =$$

(2) CONVERT MIXED NUMBER TO IMPROPER FRACTION

$$1\frac{3}{8} = \frac{11}{8}$$

(3) MULTIPLY NUMERATORS AND DENOMINATORS. REDUCE AS REQUIRED

$$\frac{11 \times 1}{8 \times 2} = \frac{11}{16}$$

MULTIPLYING MIXED NUMBERS BY FRACTIONS

(1) SET UP OPERATION

$$2\frac{1}{2} \times 3 =$$

(2) CONVERT MIXED NUMBER TO IMPROPER FRACTION

$$2\frac{1}{2} = \frac{5}{2}$$

(3) MULTIPLY NUMERATOR BY WHOLE NUMBER. REDUCE AS REQUIRED

$$\frac{5 \times 3}{2} = \frac{15}{2} = 7\frac{1}{2}$$

MULTIPLYING MIXED NUMBERS BY WHOLE NUMBERS

(1) SET UP OPERATION

$$2\frac{3}{4} \times 5\frac{1}{2} =$$

(2) CONVERT MIXED NUMBERS TO IMPROPER FRACTIONS

$$2\frac{3}{4} = \frac{8}{4} + \frac{3}{4} = \frac{11}{4}$$

$$5\frac{1}{2} = \frac{10}{2} + \frac{1}{2} = \frac{11}{2}$$

(3) MULTIPLY NUMERATORS AND DENOMINATORS. REDUCE AS REQUIRED

$$\frac{11 \times 11}{4 \times 2} = \frac{121}{8} = 15\frac{1}{8}$$

MULTIPLYING MIXED NUMBERS

Figure 3-13. Different mathematical operations are required for multiplication of various combinations of fractions, whole numbers, and mixed numbers.

When multiplying two mixed numbers, the mixed numbers are first converted to their fraction equivalents. The numerators and denominators are multiplied and the fraction is reduced as required.

Applications. A common application of multiplying fractions and mixed numbers is the calculation of the total rise of stairs. **See Figure 3-14.** The architect may note that a stairway has 14 risers, each with a unit rise of 7⅜″. The total rise of the stairs is 8′-7¼″.

Dividing Fractions

Dividing fractions is the opposite, or inverse, of multiplying fractions. When dividing fractions, the divisor is inverted (denominator placed over the numerator) and the fractions are then multiplied as previously described.

Calculators are often used on a job site to perform mathematical functions.

Figure 3-14. Multiplication of fractions is used to determine a stair landing height where a unit rise is indicated.

Multiplying Dimensions

Figure 3-14

① SET UP OPERATION

$$7\frac{3}{8}'' \times 14 =$$

② CONVERT MIXED NUMBER TO IMPROPER FRACTION

$$7\frac{3}{8}'' = \frac{59''}{8}$$

③ MULTIPLY NUMERATOR BY WHOLE NUMBER

$$\frac{59 \times 14}{8} = \frac{826}{8}$$

④ CONVERT IMPROPER FRACTION TO MIXED NUMBER

$$\frac{826}{8} = 103\frac{1}{4}'' = 8'\text{-}7\frac{1}{4}''$$

TECHFACTS

The numerator and denominator of a fraction can be multiplied or divided by the same number (except zero) without changing the value of the fraction.

Fraction combinations that can be divided include two fractions, a fraction by a whole number, a whole number by a fraction, a mixed number by a whole number, and two mixed numbers. Each type of fractional division requires a different process. **See Figure 3-15.**

Fundamentals. The dividend is the number to be divided. The divisor is the number that the dividend is divided by. The quotient is the result of the division operation. To divide two fractions, the numerator and denominator in the divisor are first inverted. For example, when dividing ⅞ by ¼, the divisor (¼) is inverted to ⁴⁄₁. The numerator and denominator of the dividend and the inverted divisor are then multiplied.

When dividing a fraction by a whole number, the whole number is converted to a fraction by placing it over 1. The divisor is inverted and the numerators and denominators are multiplied. The fraction is reduced as required. A similar process is used to divide a whole number by a fraction.

When dividing a mixed number by a whole number, the mixed and whole numbers must be converted to improper fractions. The divisor is then inverted and the fractions are multiplied and reduced to lowest terms as required. The same process is used to divide two mixed numbers.

TECHFACTS

A fraction can easily be divided by 2 by doubling the denominator.

Applications. The most common application of division in printreading is the centering or equal spacing of features, fixtures, or other items. **See Figure 3-16.** For example, centering a door opening between two walls that are 3'-6½" apart requires dividing 42 ½" (3'-6½") by 2. The door is centered on a mark 21¼" from either wall.

Another common application of division of fractions and mixed numbers is the determination of riser heights when constructing stairways. For example, a stairway with a total rise of 36⅞" requires five equal-height risers of 7⅜":

$$36\frac{7}{8} = \frac{295}{8}$$

$$\frac{295}{8} \div 5 = \frac{295}{8} \div \frac{5}{1}$$

$$\frac{295}{8} \times \frac{1}{5} =$$

$$\frac{295 \times 1}{8 \times 5} =$$

$$\frac{295}{40} = 7\frac{15}{40} = 7\frac{3}{8}''$$

Adding and Subtracting Decimals

The two types of decimal numbers are proper decimal numbers and mixed decimal numbers. A *proper decimal number* is a decimal number that does

Dividing Fractions

Figure 3-15

① SET UP OPERATION

$$\frac{7}{8} \div \frac{1}{4} =$$

② INVERT DIVISOR

$$\frac{7}{8} \times \frac{4}{1} =$$

③ MULTIPLY NUMERATORS AND DENOMINATORS

$$\frac{7 \times 4}{8 \times 1} = \frac{28}{8}$$

④ REDUCE AS REQUIRED

$$\frac{28}{8} = 3\frac{4}{8} = 3\frac{1}{2}$$

DIVIDING TWO FRACTIONS

① SET UP OPERATION

$$\frac{3}{4} \div 3 =$$

② CONVERT WHOLE NUMBER TO FRACTION

$$3 = \frac{3}{1}$$

③ INVERT DIVISOR

$$\frac{3}{4} \times \frac{1}{3} =$$

④ MULTIPLY NUMERATORS AND DENOMINATORS

$$\frac{3 \times 1}{4 \times 3} = \frac{3}{12}$$

⑤ REDUCE AS REQUIRED

$$\frac{3}{12} = \frac{1}{4}$$

DIVIDING FRACTIONS BY WHOLE NUMBERS

① SET UP OPERATION

$$6 \div \frac{3}{4} =$$

② CONVERT WHOLE NUMBER TO FRACTION

$$6 = \frac{6}{1}$$

③ INVERT DIVISOR

$$\frac{6}{1} \times \frac{4}{3} =$$

④ MULTIPLY NUMERATORS AND DENOMINATORS

$$\frac{6 \times 4}{1 \times 3} = \frac{24}{3}$$

⑤ REDUCE AS REQUIRED

$$\frac{24}{3} = 8$$

DIVIDING WHOLE NUMBERS BY FRACTIONS

① SET UP OPERATION

$$8\frac{3}{4} \div 4 =$$

② CONVERT MIXED NUMBER TO IMPROPER FRACTION

$$\frac{35}{4} \div 4 =$$

③ CONVERT WHOLE NUMBER TO FRACTION AND INVERT

$$\frac{35}{4} \times \frac{1}{4} =$$

④ MULTIPLY NUMERATORS AND DENOMINATORS

$$\frac{35 \times 1}{4 \times 4} = \frac{35}{16}$$

⑤ REDUCE AS REQUIRED

$$\frac{35}{16} = 2\frac{3}{16}$$

DIVIDING MIXED NUMBERS BY WHOLE NUMBERS

① SET UP OPERATION

$$1\frac{1}{4} \div 2\frac{1}{2} =$$

② CONVERT MIXED NUMBERS TO IMPROPER FRACTIONS

$$\frac{5}{4} \div \frac{5}{2} =$$

③ INVERT DIVISOR

$$\frac{5}{4} \times \frac{2}{5} =$$

④ MULTIPLY NUMERATORS AND DENOMINATORS

$$\frac{5 \times 2}{4 \times 5} = \frac{10}{20}$$

⑤ REDUCE AS REQUIRED

$$\frac{10}{20} = \frac{1}{2}$$

DIVIDING MIXED NUMBERS

Figure 3-15. Different mathematical operations are required for division of various combinations of fractions, whole numbers, and mixed numbers.

not have a whole number, such as 0.9. A *mixed decimal number* is a decimal number consisting of a whole number and a decimal number separated by a decimal point. For example, 4.75 is a mixed decimal number.

Fundamentals. When decimal numbers are added or subtracted vertically, the decimal points of the numbers must be aligned. Aligning the decimal points will align whole numbers over whole numbers, tenths over tenths, hundredths over hundredths, and so on. After the numbers are aligned, addition or subtraction proceeds in the same manner as addition or subtraction of whole numbers.

Applications. Dimensions such as elevations and distances around a building lot are commonly expressed in feet and hundredths of a foot on elevation drawings and plot plans. Determining distances between various building points and differences in elevations requires the addition and subtraction of decimals. **See Figure 3-17.** For example, the difference in elevation of two floor levels of a house is calculated by subtracting the elevation at the lowest grade point from the elevation at the highest grade point. If the highest reading is 13.46′ and the lowest point is 9.46′, the difference in elevation is 4.00′ (13.46′ − 9.46′ = 4.00′).

Multiplying Decimals

When multiplying decimals, the number of decimal digits to the right of the decimal point in the multiplicand and multiplier must carefully be determined. When multiplication is complete, the same number of decimal digits must be counted off in the product. Otherwise, multiplication of decimals is the same as multiplication of whole numbers.

Fundamentals. When decimals are multiplied vertically, the multiplicand is placed above the multiplier. **See Figure 3-18.** The first digit of the multiplier is multiplied across the entire multiplicand and the product is written in the first row below the horizontal line. The tens digit in the multiplier is then multiplied across the entire multiplicand and the product is written in the second row below the horizontal line with the last digit of the product in the tens column. The last digit of each separate product is placed under the digit used to calculate it. When all of the subtotals have been calculated, the digits are added vertically. If the addition results in a sum of 10 or more in any given column, the ones digit is written in the proper position and the tens digit is carried to the next column. The number of digits following the decimal point in the multiplicand and multiplier are counted. In the answer, the

Figure 3-16. Centering a fixture may require the division of a mixed number of feet, inches, and fractions of an inch by 2.

Adding and Subtracting Decimals

Figure 3-17

DECIMAL POINTS ALIGNED

```
 0.125
 3.5
+2.25
 5.875
```

ADD COLUMN BY COLUMN STARTING AT RIGHT

ADDING DECIMALS

DECIMAL POINTS ALIGNED

```
 13.46
− 9.46
  4.00
```

SUBTRACT COLUMN BY COLUMN STARTING AT RIGHT

SWALE

DECK

MAIN LEVEL
FIN. FL ELEV 13.46'

DEN
FIN. FL
ELEV 9.46'

GARAGE
FIN. FL ELEV 2.00'

DRIVEWAY

152.00'

15'-0"

40'-0"

Figure 3-17. Elevation differences expressed as mixed decimal numbers are calculated using decimal addition and subtraction.

Multiplying Decimals

Figure 3-18

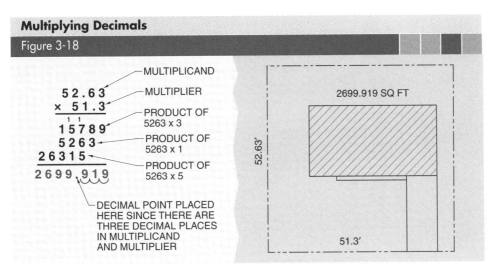

```
   52.63        MULTIPLICAND
 × 51.3         MULTIPLIER
  15789         PRODUCT OF 5263 x 3
  5263          PRODUCT OF 5263 x 1
 26315          PRODUCT OF 5263 x 5
2699.919
```

DECIMAL POINT PLACED HERE SINCE THERE ARE THREE DECIMAL PLACES IN MULTIPLICAND AND MULTIPLIER

2699.919 SQ FT

52.63'

51.3'

Figure 3-18. The decimal point must be properly located in the final product when multiplying decimal numbers.

same number of digits starting at the digit on the right is counted off and the decimal point is placed before the last counted digit.

Applications. Calculations such as area and volume are performed using decimal numbers. For example, the area of a building lot shown on a plot plan measuring 100.25' × 53.5' can be calculated by multiplying the decimal numbers (100.25' × 53.5' = 5363.375 sq ft).

Dividing Decimals

Dividing decimals is the same as dividing whole numbers. The decimal point must be properly placed for an accurate calculation. When performing long division, the decimal point of the quotient is positioned directly above the decimal point in the divisor.

Fundamentals. When performing long division of decimals, the dividend is placed inside the division bar and the divisor outside the bar. **See Figure 3-19.**

The decimal point in the dividend is moved to the right the same number of places as the decimal point in the divisor is moved to the right. A decimal point is placed on top of the division bar directly above the decimal point in the dividend. The division operation is then carried out by dividing the divisor into the first number(s). On top of the division bar, record the number of times the divisor goes into the dividend. The same operation is then carried out on the next number(s).

If the dividend has fewer decimal places than the divisor, add zeros to the dividend. There must be at least as many decimal places in the dividend as the divisor. As many zeros as desired can be added since adding zeros to the right of a decimal point does not change the value of the decimal (3.5 = 3.5000).

Figure 3-19. The decimal point must be properly located in the divisor, dividend, and quotient when performing long division.

Dividing Decimals

Figure 3-19

Applications. Decimal division is commonly used in operations such as calculating elevations or distances found on a plot plan. For example, determining one-half the height of an elevation of 32.87′ requires dividing 32.87 by 2 (32.87′ ÷ 2 = 16.435′).

TECHFACTS

Percentages are converted to decimals by moving the decimal point left two places.

Converting Fractions and Decimals

When performing mathematical calculations, it is often necessary to convert a dimension expressed in one format to another format. For example, it may be necessary to convert a measurement in decimal format to feet, inches, and fractions of an inch. It may also be necessary to perform calculations with feet and inches that are more easily carried out with the dimensions in a different format. For example, it may be necessary to convert a measurement in feet, inches, and fractions of an inch to decimal format before performing calculations. The ability to quickly and accurately convert dimensions from one format to another is valuable on a job site.

Decimals to Fractions. Decimals are calculated on a base 10 system. In a base 10 system, decimals are converted to fractions by placing the numbers to the right of the decimal point over 10, 100, 1000, or another base 10 unit. For example, 0.875 is converted to $^{875}/_{1000}$, which can be reduced in lowest terms to $^7/_8$. When decimal numbers include a whole number, the digits to the right of the decimal point are converted as previously shown and then the whole number is added. For example, 4.125 is converted to $4\frac{1}{8}$ (.125 = $^{125}/_{1000}$ = $^1/_8$; $^1/_8$ + 4 = $4\frac{1}{8}$). **See Figure 3-20.**

Fractions to Decimals. When performing mathematical operations with fractions, it may be preferable to convert the fractions to decimals for easier calculation. When converting a fraction to its decimal equivalent, the numerator is divided by the denominator. For example, $^5/_8$ is converted to 0.625 (5 ÷ 8 = 0.625). When adding a series of fractions with different denominators, such as $^5/_{16}$, $\frac{1}{2}$, and $^7/_8$, each is converted to a decimal and the addition operation is performed ($^5/_{16}$ = 0.3125; $\frac{1}{2}$ = 0.5; $^7/_8$ = 0.875; 0.3125 + 0.5 + 0.875 = 1.6875). The decimal can then be converted back to its fraction equivalent.

Converting Fractions and Decimals

Figure 3-20

CONVERTING DECIMALS TO FRACTIONS

CONVERTING FRACTIONS TO DECIMALS

Feet and Inches to Fractions and Decimals. Unlike decimals, which are in the base 10 system, inches are in the base 12 system. Inches are converted to their decimal foot equivalent by dividing the inch measurement by 12. For example, $4'' = 0.333'$ ($4 \div 12 = 0.333$). When fractions of an inch are involved, the fractional inch is converted to its decimal inch equivalent, the converted value is added to the whole inch(es) and divided by 12. For example, $4\frac{3}{8}'' = 0.36'$:

$$4\frac{3}{8} = 4 + \frac{3}{8}$$

$$\frac{3}{8} = 0.375$$

$$4 + 0.375 = 4.375$$

$$4.375 \div 12 = 0.36$$

$$4\frac{3}{8}'' = 0.36'$$

When feet, inches, and fractions of an inch are converted to decimal foot equivalents, three separate calculations are required. First, the fraction is converted to decimal feet, then the inch value is converted to decimal feet, and finally the foot value is added to the first two values. Each $\frac{1}{8}''$ equals $0.0096'$. For example, $5'-8\frac{3}{4}''$, when converted to its decimal foot equivalent, equals $5.7242'$.

Leica Geosystems

Total station instruments used for site layout provide very accurate dimensional data in decimal format.

First the fraction is converted to decimal feet:

$$\frac{3''}{4} = \frac{6''}{8}$$

$$6 \times 0.0096 = 0.0576'$$

Then the inches are converted to decimal feet:

$$8'' \div 12 = 0.6666'$$

Finally the whole feet and converted decimal feet values are added together:

$$5' + 0.0576' + 0.6666' = 5.7242'$$

TECHFACTS

A construction calculator is an efficient means of converting feet and inches to fractions and decimals.

The 0.0096 factor is used when maximum accuracy is required. For general construction applications, the 0.0096 factor is rounded to 0.01′ (⅛″ = 0.01′) for easier calculation. This is known as field conversion. When converting inches and fractions of an inch, three separate calculations are required. For example, when converting 6⅜″ to its decimal foot equivalent, the fraction is converted to decimal feet by multiplying by 0.01 ($3 \times 0.01 = 0.03'$). The inch value is then converted to decimal feet ($6 \div 12 = 0.5'$). Finally, the converted fraction value is added to the converted decimal foot value ($0.03' + 5' = 0.53'$).

Southern Forest Products Association

Metric lumber and panel sizes are based on actual standard lumber sizes and are expressed in millimeters (mm).

METRIC MEASUREMENT

In 1975, the United States Congress passed the Metric Conversion Act. In 1998, Congress took further action to encourage the use of the SI (Système International) metric system in the construction field. At the time, some building codes and manufacturers provided dimensions in both English and SI metric formats. When international materials or systems are used, dimensions may be stated in the metric system.

Metric Linear Measurement

The *meter* is the basic unit of measure-ment in the SI. One meter is equal to 39.37″ (1 m = 39.37″). A meter is divided into smaller units of centimeters and millimeters. One centimeter is equal to ¹⁄₁₀₀ meter (1 cm = 0.01 m) and one millimeter is equal to ¹⁄₁₀₀₀ meter (1 mm = 0.001 m). **See Figure 3-21.** Centimeters and millimeters are used to express small length dimensions, such as the diameter of a bolt. Meters are used to express longer dimensions, such as the length of a property line. The *kilogram* is the basic unit of weight in the SI. A kilogram is divided into smaller units including grams, centigrams, and milligrams. One gram is equal to 0.035 oz. One gram is equal to ¹⁄₁₀₀₀ kilogram (1 g = 0.001 kg). One centigram is equal to ¹⁄₁₀₀ gram (1 cg = 0.01 g) and one milligram is equal to ¹⁄₁₀₀₀ gram (1 mg = 0.001 g).

Metric Linear Measurement

Figure 3-21

Figure 3-21. The metric system uses base 10 for all calculations.

Metric Conversion. One of the main advantages of the SI is that it uses a base 10 system. One metric unit is converted to another metric unit by multiplying or dividing by multiples of 10, which moves the decimal point to the right or left. When a metric unit is converted to the next smaller unit, the value to be converted is multiplied by 10. For example, to determine the millimeter equivalent of 13.5 cm, the centimeter value is multiplied by 10 (13.5 cm × 10 = 135 mm), which moves the decimal point one place to the right. When a metric unit is converted to the next larger unit, the value to be converted is divided by 10. For example, to determine the meter equivalent of 320 cm, the centimeter value is divided by 100 (320 cm ÷ 100 = 3.2 m).

Conversion tables are used to convert common SI units to English units and English units to SI units. **See Figure 3-22.** Tables for other SI and English system conversions exist as well.

AREA AND VOLUME

Area is a two-dimensional surface measurement. Area is expressed in square units, such as square inches, square feet, and square yards. Area is commonly used to express measurements such as room size (400 sq ft [square feet]) or window area (432 sq in. [square inches]). *Volume* is the three-dimensional capacity of a space. Volume is expressed in cubic units, such as cubic feet or cubic yards. Volume is commonly used to ex-press measurements such as the amount of concrete (3 cu yd [cubic yards]) or amount of ventilation (1800 cfm [cubic feet per minute]).

Calculating Area

The formula used to calculate the area of a specific space depends on the shape of the space. One formula is used to calculate the areas of squares and rectangles, while other formulas are used to calculate the areas of triangles and circles. **See Figure 3-23.**

When calculating the area of a square or rectangular shape, the following formula is applied:

$A = w \times h \text{ (or } l)$

where

A = **area**

w = **width**

h **(or** *l***)** = **height (or length)**

For example, a floor measuring 12′ wide by 18′ long has an area of 216 sq ft:

$A = w \times l$

$A = 12 \times 18$

$A = 216 \text{ sq ft}$

When calculating the area of a triangular shape, ½ is multiplied by the base length by the height:

$A = ½ bh$

where

A = **area**

½ = **constant**

b = **base**

h = **height**

TECHFACTS

The SI metric system was the first standardized system of measurement. Gabriel Mouton is credited with origi-nating it in 1670.

ENGLISH/METRIC CONVERSION			
To Convert	**To**	**Multiply By**	**Example**
inches (in.)	millimeters (mm)	25.4	7″ × 25.4 = 177.8 mm×
inches (in.)	centimeters (cm)	2.54	2″ × 25.4 = 5.08 cm
feet (ft)	centimeters (cm)	30.48	10″ × 30.48 = 304.8 cm
feet (ft)	meters (m)	0.3048	6′ × .3048 = 1.8288 m
yards (yd)	meters (m)	0.9144	6 yd × .9144 = 5.4864 m
millimeters (mm)	inches (in.)	0.03937	320 mm × .03937 = 12.5984″
centimeters (cm)	inches (in.)	0.3937	22 cm × .3937 = 8.6614″
meters (m)	feet (ft)	3.281	6.5 m × 3.281 = 21.3265′
meters (m)	yards (yd)	1.0937	11 m × 1.0937 = 12.0307 yd

Figure 3-22. Conversion of English and metric values is accomplished using conversion tables.

For example, a triangular area with a base of 4′ and a height of 8′ has an area of 16 sq ft:

A = ½bh

A = ½ × 4 × 8

A = 16 sq ft

Two formulas may be used to calculate the area of a circular shape, one using the radius measurement and the other using the diameter measurement. When calculating the area using the radius, pi (π) is multiplied by the radius squared:

A = πr²

where

A = area

π = 3.1416 (constant)

r = radius

TECHFACTS

An ellipse has two diameters that define its shape—a major and a minor diameter. Area of an ellipse is calculated by multiplying .7854 by the major diameter by the minor diameter.

The symbol π is a conversion factor equal to 3.1416. For example, a circular area with a radius of 14′ has an area of 615.7536 sq ft:

A = πr²

A = 3.1416 × 14²

A = 3.1416 × 14 × 14

A = 3.1416 × 196

A = 615.7526 sq ft

When calculating the area using the diameter, .7854 is multiplied by the diameter squared:

A = 0.7854d²

where

A = area

0.7854 = constant

d = diameter

For example, a circular area with a diameter of 22″ has an area of 380.1336 sq in.:

A = 0.7854d²

A = 0.7854 × 22²

A = 0.7854 × 22 × 22

A = 380.1336 sq in.

Figure 3-23. Area formulas depend on the shape of the two-dimensional object.

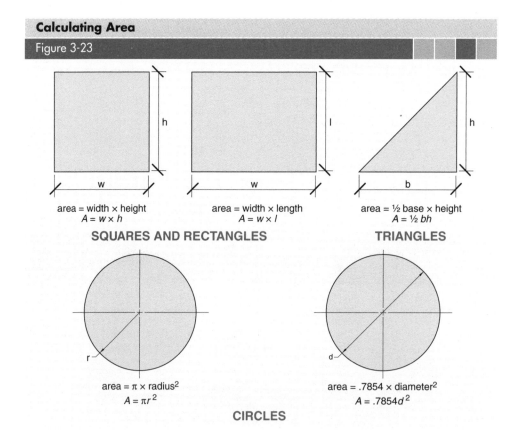

Calculating Area

Figure 3-23

area = width × height
$A = w × h$

area = width × length
$A = w × l$

area = ½ base × height
$A = ½ bh$

SQUARES AND RECTANGLES   **TRIANGLES**

area = π × radius²
$A = πr^2$

area = .7854 × diameter²
$A = .7854d^2$

CIRCLES

Applications. Area calculations are commonly used to determine material quantities for finish materials such as ceiling tile, paint, carpet, and roofing. Standard ceiling tiles are 2′ × 4′, each covering 8 sq ft (2′ × 4′ = 8 sq ft). After measuring the ceiling and determining the total ceiling area, the ceiling area (in sq ft) is divided by 8 to roughly calculate the number of ceiling tiles required.

The coverage area is commonly provided by the manufacturer for paint or other finishes. The coverage area per gallon of paint is compared to the area to be painted in order to calculate the number of gallons required. For example, a gallon of a particular quality of paint covers approximately 400 sq ft. A wall measuring 10′ × 20′ requires approximately ½ gal. of paint (10′ × 20′ = 200 sq ft; 200 sq ft ÷ 400 sq ft = 0.5 = ½ gal.).

Carpet coverage is commonly calculated in square yards (3′ × 3′ = 9 sq ft = 1 sq yd). After determining the total floor area, the area (in sq ft) is divided by 9 to determine the amount of carpet required to cover the floor (in sq yd).

For example, if the room measures 12′ × 15′, 20 sq yd of carpet is required to cover the floor (12′ × 15′ = 180 sq ft; 180 sq ft ÷ 9 = 20 sq yd).

Area calculations are also used to determine the amount of roofing materials required. Roofing materials, such as asphalt shingles, are commonly specified as squares. A roofing square is equal to the amount of roofing material to cover 100 sq ft. After determining the total roof area, the area (in sq ft) is divided by 100 to determine the number of roofing squares required for the job. For example, if one side of a gable roof measures 20′ × 45′, 18 roofing squares are required to cover the roof (20′ × 45′ × 2 = 1800 sq ft; 1800 sq ft ÷ 100 = 18 squares).

Calculating Volume

Volume is the three-dimensional capacity of a space. Therefore, three dimensions are used to define the space —width, height, and depth. When determining volume, the three dimensions—width, height, and depth—are multiplied together. **See Figure 3-24.**

Calculating Volume

Figure 3-24

volume = width × height × depth
$V = w \times h \times d$
SQUARES OR RECTANGULAR SHAPES

volume = 2 × π × radius² × length
$V = \pi r^2 \times l$
volume = 0.7854 × diameter² × length
$V = 0.7845d^2 \times l$
CYLINDERS

volume = $\dfrac{\pi \times \text{diameter}^3}{6}$

$V = \dfrac{\pi d^3}{6}$
SPHERES

Figure 3-24. Volume calculations provide cubic measurements. Concrete is typically ordered in cubic yards (cu yd).

When calculating the volume of a square or rectangular shape, the following formula is applied:

$$V = w \times h \times d$$

where

V = volume

w = width

h = height

d = depth

For example, a footing measuring $1' \times 2' \times 10'$ has a volume of 20 cu ft ($1' \times 2' \times 10' = 20$ cu ft).

$$V = w \times h \times d$$

$$V = 1 \times 2 \times 10$$

$$V = 20 \text{ cu ft}$$

TECHFACTS

One cubic yard is equal to 27 cubic feet (1 cu yd = 27 cu ft).

When determining the volume of a cylinder, the area of one end of the cylinder is calculated by multiplying pi by the radius squared ($A = \pi r^2$) or by multiplying 0.7854 by the diameter squared ($A = 0.7854d^2$). The area is multiplied by the length of the cylinder to calculate the volume:

$$V = \pi r^2 \times l$$

where

V = volume

π = 3.1416

r = radius

l = length

or

$$V = 0.7854d^2 \times l$$

where

V = volume

0.7854 = constant

d = diameter

l = length

For example, a cylinder with a radius of 14′ and a length of 26′ has a volume of 16,009.59 cu ft:

$$V = \pi r^2 \times l$$

$$V = 3.1416 \times 14^2 \times 26$$

$$V = 3.1416 \times 14 \times 14 \times 26$$

$$V = 16,009.59 \text{ cu ft}$$

or

$$V = 0.7854d^2 \times l$$

$$V = 0.7854 \times 28^2 \times 26$$

$$V = 0.7854 \times 28 \times 28 \times 26$$

$$V = 16,009.59 \text{ cu ft}$$

Concrete is specified for a job in cubic yards (cu yd).

When calculating the volume of a sphere, π is multiplied by the diameter cubed and the product is divided by 6:

$$V = \frac{\pi \, d^3}{6}$$

where
V = volume
π = 3.1416
d = distance
6 = constant

For example, a sphere with a diameter of 26′ has a volume of 9202.79 cu ft:

$$V = \frac{\pi \, d^3}{6}$$

$$V = \frac{3.1416 \times 26^3}{6}$$

$$V = \frac{3.1416 \times 26 \times 26 \times 26}{6}$$

$$V = \frac{55{,}215.761}{6}$$

$$V = 9202.79 \text{ cu ft}$$

TECHFACTS
The symbol π denotes the ratio of the circumference of a circle to its diameter. The circumference is determined by multiplying π by the diameter (C = πd).

Applications. Several examples of the use of volume calculations for construction are determining the amount of soil removed from excavations, specifying the amount of concrete for a slab, and determining the air-handling requirements for a heating, ventilating, and air conditioning (HVAC) system for a building. Volumes of soil and concrete are expressed in cubic yards.

A cubic yard, which is equal to 27 cu ft, is a volume measuring 3′ × 3′ × 3′. (3′ × 3′ × 3′ = 27 cu ft = 1 cu yd). To determine the number of cubic yards of soil or concrete, the cubic foot volume is divided by 27. For example, 6.389 cu yd of concrete is required for a 6″ thick concrete slab measuring 15′ × 23′:

6″ × 15′ × 23′ =
0.5′ × 15′ × 23′ = 172.5 cu ft
172.5 cu ft ÷ 27 = 6.389 cu yd

In HVAC applications, the volume of air to be moved is calculated and expressed in cubic feet per minute (cfm). Fans, air handlers, and other HVAC equipment are commonly rated in cfm capacity. When operating at 100% efficiency, a fan rated at 1700 cfm moves 1700 cu ft of air per minute.

TECHFACTS
Annual production of concrete in the United States is approximately 5,000,000,000 cu yd.

CertainTeed Corporation
Air flow, measured in cubic feet per minute (cfm), is calibrated with a flow hood.

LEARNER RESOURCES

ATPeResources.com/QuickLinks
Access Code: 281467

Name _____   Date _____

Computation 3-1

1. 18
   + 81

2. 125
   + 47

3. 5744
   + 588

4. 10,588
   − 95

5. 56,565
   + 875

6. 42
   − 17

7. 652
   − 89

8. 7505
   − 99

9. 4231
   − 877

10. 35,611
    − 577

11. 12
   × 12

12. 14
   × 85

13. 16
   × 36

14. 456
   × 19

15. 1567
   × 4329

16. $3\overline{)18}$

17. $6\overline{)45}$

18. $13\overline{)150}$

19. $18\overline{)5750}$

20. $73\overline{)6548}$

Multiple Choice

_____ 1. A ___ is a number that does not have a fractional or decimal part.
- A. multiplicand
- B. proper decimal number
- C. whole number
- D. minuend

_____ 2. ___ is the mathematical process of taking one number away from a larger number.
- A. Addition
- B. Subtraction
- C. Multiplication
- D. Division

_____ 3. The ___ is the result of multiplication.
- A. multiplicand
- B. quotient
- C. multiplier
- D. product

_____ 4. The ___ is the part of a fraction placed below or to the right of the fraction bar.
- A. divisor
- B. dividend
- C. numerator
- D. denominator

_____ 5. Decimals are converted to fractions by placing the number to the right of the decimal point over ___.
- A. 2
- B. 100
- C. inches
- D. feet

_____ 6. The sum of 42" and 16" is ___".
- A. 2.625
- B. 26
- C. 58
- D. 672

_____ 7. The SI metric system is a base ___ system.
- A. 6
- B. 8
- C. 10
- D. 12

_____ 8. The ___ is the basic unit of linear measurement in the SI metric system.
- A. kilogram
- B. meter
- C. gram
- D. kilometer

9. Area is a ___-dimensional surface measurement.
  A. one
  B. two
  C. three
  D. four

_____ **10.** A ___ is the position that a digit occupies; it represents the value of the digit.
  A. column
  B. location
  C. place
  D. row

_____ **11.** An 18" square by 14' concrete column contains ___ cu ft and requires ___ cu yd of concrete.
  A. 31.5; 1.17
  B. 35.84; 1.33
  C. 252; 9.33
  D. 4536; 168

_____ **12.** A built-up flat roof measuring 68' × 248' is ___ sq ft.
  A. 316
  B. 368
  C. 14,880
  D. 16,864

Computation 3-2

Reduce to lowest terms when necessary.

1. $\frac{1}{8} + \frac{3}{8} =$

2. $\frac{5}{16} + \frac{13}{16} =$

3. $\frac{1}{2} + \frac{3}{8} =$

4. $\frac{5}{8} + \frac{15}{16} =$

5. $\frac{13}{32} + 5\frac{3}{4} =$

6. $\frac{5}{8} - \frac{1}{8} =$

7. $\frac{7}{8} - \frac{1}{2} =$

8. $5\frac{1}{4} - \frac{3}{8} =$

9. $16\frac{5}{8} - 8\frac{7}{8} =$

85

10. $756\frac{5}{32} - 89\frac{1}{2} =$ **11.** $\frac{1}{8} \times 6 =$ **12.** $\frac{5}{16} \times 12 =$

13. $7\frac{7}{8} \times 14\frac{1}{2} =$ **14.** $18\frac{3}{4} \times 22\frac{5}{8} =$ **15.** $975\frac{5}{16} \times 5\frac{1}{2} =$

16. $625 \div 5\frac{1}{2} =$ **17.** $18\frac{3}{4} \div 2 =$ **18.** $56\frac{7}{8} \div 7 =$

19. $465\frac{1}{2} \div 4 =$ **20.** $15 \div 7\frac{1}{2} =$

True-False

T	F	**1.** A fraction with the numerator larger than the denominator is an improper fraction.
T	F	**2.** An odd number can be divided by two without a remainder or decimal occurring.
T	F	**3.** Multiplication is the mathematical process of determining the number of times one number is contained in another number.
T	F	**4.** In the fraction ⅜, 3 is the numerator.
T	F	**5.** A mixed number consists of a whole number and a fraction.
T	F	**6.** A quotient is the result of a division operation.
T	F	**7.** The dividend is the number to be divided.
T	F	**8.** A proper decimal number includes a whole number.
T	F	**9.** One millimeter is equal to 0.01 meter.
T	F	**10.** Volume is a three-dimensional capacity of space.

1. 12.5
   + 6

2. 13.85
   + 5.7

3. 125.65
   +7524.8

4. 432.66
   + 0.85

5. 1085.655
   + 145.39

6. 55.6
   − 0.9

7. 652.5
   − 18.75

8. 12.855
   − 6.9

9. 8321.15
   − 57.875

10. 9211.333
    − 55.67

11. 45.5
   × 8.5

12. 16.875
   × 12

13. 854.675
    × 13.5

14. 75.67
   ×87.333

15. 6584.75
    × 32.125

16. 5.5$)\overline{14.75}$

17. 12.875$)\overline{75.67}$

18. 6$)\overline{125.333}$

19. 186.3$)\overline{7489.675}$

20. 7.5$)\overline{53,244.8}$

87

Completion

_____ **1.** One meter is equal to ___".

_____ **2.** A room measuring 15′ × 25′ contains ___ sq ft.

_____ **3.** The ___ is the total that results from addition.

_____ **4.** The ___ is the total number of units prior to subtraction.

_____ **5.** Inches are added in base ___.

_____ **6.** The sign used to indicate multiplication is ___.

_____ **7.** A(n) ___ decimal number includes a whole number and decimal number separated by a decimal point.

_____ **8.** One gram is equal to ___ kilogram.

_____ **9.** Pi is abbreviated with the ___ symbol.

_____ **10.** When determining volume, ___ dimensions are multiplied together.

_____ **11.** An excavation measuring 15′-9″ × 73′ × 159′ contains ___ cu yd of soil.

Computation 3-4

Convert the following decimals to fractions.

_____ **1.** 0.50

_____ **2.** 0.125

_____ **3.** 0.625

_____ **4.** 0.875

_____ **5.** 0.25

Convert the following fractions to decimals.

_____ **6.** ³⁄₁₆

_____ **7.** ³⁄₈

_____ **8.** ⁵⁄₁₆

_____ **9.** ¹³⁄₃₂

_____ **10.** ¾

Name _____ Date _____

Identification 3-1

_____ **1.** 63

_____ **2.** 132

_____ **3.** 21

_____ **4.** 36

_____ **5.** 96

_____ **6.** 48

_____ **7.** 44

_____ **8.** 110

_____ **9.** 66

_____ **10.** 45

_____ **11.** 81

_____ **12.** 100

_____ **13.** 121

MULTIPLICATION TABLE

1	2	3	4	5	6	7	8	9	10	11	12
2	4	6	8	10	12	14	16	18	20	22	24
3	6	9	12	15	18	A	24	27	30	33	36
4	8	12	16	20	24	28	32	36	40	B	48
5	10	15	20	25	30	35	40	C	50	55	60
6	12	18	24	30	D	42	48	54	60	E	72
7	14	21	28	35	42	49	56	F	70	77	84
8	16	24	32	40	G	56	64	72	80	88	H
9	18	27	36	45	54	63	72	I	90	99	108
10	20	30	40	50	60	70	80	90	J	110	120
11	22	33	44	55	66	77	88	99	K	L	132
12	24	36	48	60	72	84	96	108	120	M	144

Computation

1. 255
  + 88

2. 7899
  + 722

3. 64
  − 45

4. 865
  − 76

5. 18
  × 90

6. 563
  × 75

7. $6\overline{)52}$

8. $18\overline{)235}$

9. $\frac{7}{16} + \frac{11}{16} =$

10. $\frac{1}{2} + \frac{7}{8} =$

11. $\frac{3}{8} - \frac{1}{16} =$

12. $12\frac{3}{4} - \frac{7}{32} =$

13. $\frac{3}{8} \times 12 =$

14. $17\frac{3}{8} - 11\frac{1}{4} =$

15. $21\frac{1}{4} \div 18 =$

16. $35\frac{7}{16} \div 4\frac{3}{8} =$

17. 12.355
  + 11.69

18. 514.85
  + 1543.4

19. 5.62
  − 0.39

20. 3662.432
  − 12.87

21. 5.65
  × 7.3

22. 459.667
  × 38.25

23. $3.33\overline{)55.125}$

24. $47\overline{)587.575}$

25. $3.3\overline{)696}$

90

Identification 3-2

_____ **1.** Divisor

_____ **2.** Multiplier

_____ **3.** Subtrahend

_____ **4.** Dividend

_____ **5.** Quotient

_____ **6.** Minuend

_____ **7.** Multiplicand

_____ **8.** Result

_____ **9.** Product

```
           16.00'  —Ⓐ
         −  6.25'  —Ⓑ
           ──────
            9.75'  —Ⓒ
```

```
              .40  —Ⓔ
     Ⓓ— 4)1.60  —
            1 6  —Ⓕ
           ────
            0 0
```

```
            6.2'  —Ⓖ
         ×    3'  —Ⓗ
           ─────
           18.6'  —Ⓘ
```

Completion

_____ **1.** A room measuring 24'-0" × 22'-6" requires ___ sq ft of ceiling tile and ___ sq yd of carpet.

_____ **2.** A rectangular building lot measures 75' × 167' and contains ___ sq ft.

_____ **3.** A porch measuring 8'-3" × 18'-6" has ___ sq ft of floor space.

_____ **4.** A 36" square column footing 18" deep requires ___ cu yd of concrete.

_____ **5.** A basement excavation measuring 68'-8" × 59'-6" × 11'-4" contains ___ cu yd of soil.

PRINTREADING

Refer to Stearns Residence—Main Level Floor Plan on page 93.

Completion

_____ **1.** The Master Bedroom has an area of ___ sq ft.

_____ **2.** The rear wall of the Living Room projects ___ beyond Bedroom #2.

_____ **3.** The window in the Office is ___ away from the Garage.

_____ **4.** The C window is centered along the 24'-7" dimension of the Garage wall, placing it ___ from outside of the wall.

_____ **5.** Bedroom #3 has an area of ___ sq ft and requires ___ sq yd of carpet.

Multiple Choice

_____ **1.** The #6 door is centered along the 5'-0" wall next to the overhead door. The center of the #6 door is ___ from the edge of the house.
    A. 1'-6"
    B. 2'-0"
    C. 2'-6"
    D. 3'-6"

_____ **2.** The Kitchen island is ___ sq ft.
    A. 1.75
    B. 8.75
    C. 9.25
    D. 9.36

_____ **3.** One section of the Kitchen cabinets measures 2'-0" × 10'-0" × 32". The volume of the cabinets is ___ cu ft.
    A. 20.6
    B. 53.3
    C. 65.3
    D. 640

_____ **4.** The A window in Bedroom #3 is centered along the wall. The total dimension of the wall is ___.
    A. 10'-8"
    B. 11'-7"
    C. 11'-11"
    D. 12'-3"

_____ **5.** The total distance from the edge of the Porch to the Garage wall is ___.
    A. 26'-0½"
    B. 27'-3½"
    C. 27'-6½"
    D. 28'-0½"

Refer to printreading questions on page 92.

STEARNS RESIDENCE

SYMBOLS AND ABBREVIATIONS

Symbols and abbreviations save time when producing working drawings and also conserve space on plans. Symbols and abbreviations are standardized to aid in the accurate interpretation of plans. In addition to standard architectural material and graphic symbols, specialized symbols are also available for electrical, plumbing, and heating, ventilating, and air conditioning systems.

OBJECTIVES

1. Define symbols and explain why they are used.
2. Define abbreviations and explain why they are used.

SYMBOLS

A *symbol* is a pictorial representation of a structural or material component required to complete a construction project. Prints use symbols to show materials, equipment, and building parts. **See Figure 4-1.** Symbols conserve space on prints, are easy to draw, and are easily recognized by experienced printreaders. The American National Standards Institute (ANSI), in conjunction with recognized trade associations, has standardized symbols for a vast majority of construction applications. CAD systems use symbol libraries from which the desired symbol is selected. Templates are commercially available for symbols drawn by the conventional method.

Symbols for the same material may appear differently from plan to elevation to section views. For example, the symbol for concrete masonry units has a different appearance for each view. **See Figure 4-2.** Other materials may have no standardized symbol for a particular view. For example, there is no standardized symbol for earth on a plan view.

Various symbols are used in combination to show the relationship of building materials. For example, a plan view of a fireplace in a brick veneer wall requires that the plan symbols for wood framing and brick be used when showing the wall. In addition, plan symbols showing the face brick, common brick, firebrick, and tile for the hearth are required. **See Figure 4-3.**

APA—The Engineered Wood Association

Building materials are represented on prints with symbols and abbreviations.

Symbols

Figure 4-1

Figure 4-1. Prints use standardized symbols to show building materials and fixtures.

Concrete Masonry Unit (CMU) Architectural Symbols

Figure 4-2

Elevation View   Plan View   Section View

CONCRETE MASONRY UNITS

Figure 4-2. Concrete masonry units have a different appearance in plan view, elevation view, and section view.

Openings for exterior walls and interior partitions are shown on elevation and plan views. The symbols used to show the doors and windows are drawn differently on each of these views. For example, the symbol for a double-hung window on an elevation view is drawn as if looking directly at the surface of the window. The symbol for the same window on a plan view is drawn as if looking directly down at the top of the window. **See Figure 4-4.**

TECHFACTS

Standard plumbing, piping, and valve symbols are designated per ASME Y32.3.3, *Graphical Symbols for Pipe Fittings, Valves, and Piping.*

Symbols in Combination

Figure 4-3

Figure 4-3. A symbol may be used in combination with other symbols.

Exterior Walls and Interior Partitions

Figure 4-4

Figure 4-4. Different symbols are used on elevations and floor plans to show the same window or door.

Electrical symbols are composed of graphic elements to which letters or numbers can be added. **See Figure 4-5.** For example, a lighting outlet is shown as a circle. If the outlet is designed for a specific task, the appropriate letter is added to designate that task. For example, a lighting outlet with a lampholder is shown with an L. Electrical switches are shown with letters and numbers. The letter S denotes the switch and the numbers indicate single-pole, double-pole, and so on. Various low-voltage systems and their components, such as alarms and computer or cable systems, are shown on floor plans with specialized symbols or on separate shop drawings. In many instances, a generic symbol is shown and notes identify the device or component.

Standardized symbols for plumbing include graphic elements with letters, as required, to show fixtures. Symbols for piping and valves include stylized and simplified line drawings. **See Figure 4-6.**

Heating, ventilation, and air conditioning (HVAC) symbols are comprised of graphic elements with text to show equipment and ductwork sizes and output. HVAC piping symbols use simplified line drawings with letters identifying the piping's use. For example, the HVAC symbol LPS indicates a low-pressure steam line.

ABBREVIATIONS

An *abbreviation* is a letter or series of letters or words denoting a complete word. Like symbols, abbreviations save time and conserve space on plans. Standardized abbreviations are developed by standards organizations such as ANSI. Abbreviations are used to denote materials, fixtures, and areas and to provide simplified instructions to tradesworkers. **See Appendix.**

Common Electrical Symbols

Figure 4-5

OUTLET BOX AND INCANDESCENT LIGHTING FIXTURE	CEILING WALL	SINGLE-POLE SWITCH	S
JUNCTION BOX	J J	THREE-WAY SWITCH	S₃
LAMPHOLDER WITH PULL SWITCH	L_PS L_PS	DIMMER	S_DM

LIGHTING OUTLETS   **SWITCH OUTLETS**

DUPLEX RECEPTACLE OUTLET–120 V		WALL MOUNTED DATA OUTLET	
SPLIT-WIRED DUPLEX RECEPTACLE OUTLET		TELEPHONE	
RANGE OUTLET	R	WALL-MOUNTED TELEPHONE/DATA OUTLET	

CONVENIENCE OUTLETS   **VOICE/DATA/VIDEO**

Figure 4-5. Electrical symbols are composed of graphic elements to which letters and numbers can be added.

Common Plumbing and HVAC Symbols

Figure 4-6

METER

GATE VALVE

CHECK VALVE

WATER HEATER

SOIL, WASTE, OR LEADER —
ABOVE GRADE

VENT

COLD WATER

HOT WATER

PLUMBING SYMBOLS

12 X 20

DUCT (1ST FIGURE,
WIDTH; 2ND FIGURE,
DEPTH)

20 X 12

EXHAUST, RETURN, OR
OUTSIDE AIR DUCT —
SECTION

20 X 12

SUPPLY DUCT —
SECTION

DIRECTION OF FLOW

HVAC SYMBOLS

Figure 4-6. Plumbing and HVAC symbols consist of graphic elements, stylized and simple line drawings, and letters and numbers.

Certain materials, fixtures, and other features may be referred to by their acronym. An *acronym* is an abbreviated word formed from the first letter of each word that describes the article. For example, the acronym GFCI refers to a ground-fault circuit interrupter, a type of electrical receptacle. **See Figure 4-7.**

Ground-Fault Circuit Interrupter

Figure 4-7

GFCI

OR

GFI

Figure 4-7. A ground-fault circuit interrupter receptacle is identified on a print as a receptacle outlet with the letters GFCI, or in some cases GFI.

The same abbreviation may be used to denote different items. For example,

R is the abbreviation for range, riser, and room. Generally, the location of the abbreviation will indicate its intent. Abbreviations that form a word are followed by a period to avoid confusion with the word. For example, SEW. is the abbreviation for sewer and KIT. is an abbreviation for kitchen.

Some words have more than one abbreviation. Both FIN. and FNSH are abbreviations for finish. When two abbreviations are given for the same word, the first abbreviation is preferred. In addition, some architects may use abbreviations that are not standardized, but their meanings are obvious to construction professionals-based on their location and use.

Symbols and abbreviations are used together to provide comprehensive information in a relatively small space. For example, the shape of a closet is shown on a plan view by parallel lines, which symbolize the framed partitions. The door symbol shows the swing of the door or a sliding door, and an abbreviation, either C, CL, or CLOS, designates the closet. **See Figure 4-8.**

Symbols and Abbreviations

Figure 4-8

Figure 4-8. Symbols and abbreviations are used together to provide comprehensive information.

LEARNER RESOURCES

ATPeResources.com/QuickLinks
Access Code: 281467

Name _____ Date _____

SKETCHING 4-1

Complete the chart by sketching the missing symbols. Refer to Appendix.

	ELEVATION	PLAN	SECTION
CONCRETE		LIGHTWEIGHT ①	SAME AS PLAN VIEW
CONCRETE MASONRY UNITS	②		③
WOOD	SIDING PANEL ④	STUD ⑤	OR ROUGH MEMBER ⑥ TRIM MEMBER ⑦
STRUCTURAL CLAY TILE	⑧		SAME AS PLAN VIEW
GLASS		⑨	SMALL SCALE LARGE SCALE ⑩

103

SKETCHING 4-2

Sketch the symbol indicated. Refer to Appendix.

For example: Three-way switch

S_3

1. Finish grade

2. Bush

3. Fence

4. Natural grade

5. Point of beginning

6. Property line

7. Water heater

8. Hose bibb

9. Ceiling lighting outlet

10. Junction box

11. Range outlet

12. Single-pole switch

13. Duplex receptacle outlet

14. Lighting outlet (wall)

15. Motor

16. Exposed radiator

17. Supply duct

18. Return duct

19. Thermostat

20. Water closet

Name _____   Date _____

Identification 4-1

Refer to Appendix.

_____ **1.** Brick wall

_____ **2.** Cut stone

_____ **3.** Common brick

_____ **4.** Brick veneer wall

_____ **5.** Concrete masonry units

_____ **6.** Insulation

_____ **7.** Gypsum board

_____ **8.** Firebrick

_____ **9.** Concrete

_____ **10.** Wood stud partition

_____ **11.** Rubble stone

_____ **12.** Face brick

_____ **13.** Stucco on frame wall

_____ **14.** Common brick on concrete masonry unit wall

_____ **15.** Wood stud wall

_____ **16.** Tile

_____ **17.** Glass block

_____ **18.** Cut stone on common brick wall

_____ **19.** Solid plaster partition

_____ **20.** Tile partition

Abbreviations 4-1

Write the word(s) for the abbreviation(s) in each notation.

_____	**1.** AL SASH
_____	**2.** 16" C TO C
_____	**3.** OAK FIN. FLR
_____	**4.** WALL-HUNG WC
_____	**5.** 4" CI
_____	**6.** 2400 SQ FT
_____	**7.** BR 1
_____	**8.** ½" GYP BD
_____	**9.** COMMON BRK
_____	**10.** 14 R UP
_____	**11.** ⅝" SC
_____	**12.** REFR CAB.
_____	**13.** PRCST CONC
_____	**14.** T&G SIDING
_____	**15.** 4 × 10 BM

Identification 4-2

Refer to Appendix.

_____	**1.** Duplex receptacle outlet
_____	**2.** Range outlet
_____	**3.** Lighting panel
_____	**4.** Motor
_____	**5.** Home run
_____	**6.** Natural grade
_____	**7.** Earth
_____	**8.** Point of beginning
_____	**9.** Three-way switch
_____	**10.** Pushbutton

PRINTREADING

Refer to Smith Residence—Floor Plan on page 111.

Completion 4-1

Complete the chart to list the number of outlets, fixtures, and switches shown in each room.

	$\bigcirc$	$\bigcirc_{FL}$	$\bigcirc_{PS}$	⊖	⊖	⊖$_R$	⊖$_{GFCI}$	⊖$_{GFCI}^{WP}$	S	S$_3$	S$_4$	(F)	(C)	(T)
EXAMPLE: LIVING ROOM-DINING AREA	2			6	1				2	2				1
1. BATHROOM 2														
2. BEDROOM 1														
3. BEDROOM 1 CLOSET														
4. BEDROOM 2														
5. BEDROOM 2 CLOSET														
6. HALL														
7. BATHROOM 1														
8. DEN														
9. DEN CLOSET														
10. KITCHEN														
11. UTILITY ROOM														
12. GARAGE														
13. EXTERIOR														
14. TOTAL														

NOTE: INCLUDE EXAMPLE IN TOTAL.

True-False

T   F   **1.** The hot water tank is located in the Kitchen.

T   F   **2.** Soil stacks are located in partitions behind toilets.

T   F   **3.** Four hose bibbs are shown.

T   F   **4.** LT indicates a light table in the Utility Room.

T   F   **5.** Medicine cabinets are located over lavatories in the bathrooms.

T   F   **6.** The house is heated by a forced warm air system.

T   F   **7.** Nine warm air registers are shown on the floor plan.

T   F   **8.** Nine cold air registers are shown on the floor plan.

T   F   **9.** The Kitchen range is gas operated.

T   F   **10.** A cabinet is shown over the refrigerator.

T   F   **11.** Seven stainless steel thresholds are shown on the floor plan.

T   F   **12.** Vinyl flooring is used in the Kitchen and Utility Room.

T   F   **13.** Ceramic tile flooring is used in the bathrooms.

T   F   **14.** Ceiling joists are spaced 16″ OC.

T   F   **15.** A planter box is shown on the east wall.

Multiple Choice

1. The ___, ___, and ___ have windows facing east.
A. UTIL RM; BR 1; LR
B. LR; KIT.; UTIL RM
C. BR 1; BR 2; DEN
D. LR; BR 2; B 2

2. Not counting the UTIL RM, HALL, B 1, B 2, and GAR., the house has ___ rooms.
A. three
B. four
C. five
D. six

3. The shortest route from BR 1 to the front door is ___.
A. HALL, DEN, LR
B. HALL, LR
C. HALL, BR 2, LR
D. HALL, DEN, KIT.

4. Exterior walls, excluding the garage, are ___.
A. concrete block
B. brick on concrete block
C. brick veneer
D. siding

5. ___ exterior walls are shown for the garage.
A. Framed
B. Brick veneer
C. Concrete block
D. Brick on concrete block

6. Windows in the LR are ___ windows.
A. double-hung
B. awning
C. fixed
D. jalousie

7. Lintels over windows are ___.
A. angle iron, and angle iron and plate
B. angle iron only
C. plate only
D. brick

_____ **8.** Ceiling joists over the LR run ___.

    A. north and south

    B. east and west

    C. north and south and east and west

    D. randomly

_____ **9.** Ceiling joists over the GAR. ___.

    A. run east and west

    B. are spaced 16" OC

    C. are not indicated on the floor plan

    D. require a beam

_____ **10.** Not including the GAR. door, ___ exterior doors are shown on the floor plan.

    A. two

    B. three

    C. four

    D. five

_____ **11.** Glass block is located in the GAR. and the ___.

    A. DEN

    B. KIT.

    C. UTIL RM

    D. DINING AREA

_____ **12.** Windows with fixed sashes are located on ___.

    A. both sides of the DEN door

    B. both sides of the front door

    C. one side of the front door

    D. one side of the rear door

_____ **13.** B 1 has a(n) ___ window near the CL.

    A. hopper

    B. casement

    C. awning

    D. double-hung

_____ **14.** A pocket door is shown ___.

    A. between the HALL and BR 1

    B. between the HALL and B 2

    C. for each L CL in the HALL

    D. between the DEN and KIT.

_____ **15.** Hose bibbs are shown on the ___ Elevation(s).

    A. East

    B. East and West

    C. North

    D. North and South

_____ **16.** Regarding the GAR., ___.

    A. a casement window is shown on the north wall

    B. three risers lead to the UTIL RM door

    C. the 6" concrete floor is brush finished

    D. there are 3 electrical outlets

_____ 17. Regarding the windows, ___.
        A. corner windows have only angle iron
        B. three corner windows are shown
        C. glass block sills are to be limestone
        D. all windows are casement windows

_____ 18. Regarding the plumbing, ___.
        A. each bathroom contains a tub-shower combination
        B. B 2 is adjacent to the DEN
        C. access panels are located in closets
        D. there are 2 hose bibbs

_____ 19. Regarding the scale, ___.
        A. the Smith Residence is drawn to the scale of ⅛″ = 1′-0″
        B. the Smith Residence is drawn to the scale of ¼″ = 1′-0″
        C. no scale is shown
        D. any scale applies

_____ 20. Regarding the masonry, ___.
        A. a limestone sill is shown beneath the LR windows
        B. all exterior walls are face brick
        C. face brick on edge finishes the inside of the garage
        D. face brick is installed to a height of 8′-0″

Completion 4-2

_____ 1. The water heater is located in the ___ room.

_____ 2. The front of the Smith Residence faces ___.

_____ 3. Tub and shower walls are finished with ceramic tile to a height of ___.

_____ 4. A(n) ___ sill is shown at the front door.

_____ 5. The L CL near the DEN has two shelves and one ___.

_____ 6. ___ floors are shown in the living room.

_____ 7. Glass block sills are ___ brick.

_____ 8. Three ornamental ___ posts are noted on the front porch.

_____ 9. A(n) ___ door separates the KIT. from the UTIL RM.

_____ 10. The Smith Residence is a(n) ___-story dwelling.

Refer to printreading questions on page 107.

**SMITH RESIDENCE
FLOOR PLAN**

NOTE: ALL WINDOWSILLS WILL BE FACE BRICK LAID ON EDGE. ALL DOOR SILLS TO BE LIMESTONE. GL BL SILLS TO BE FACE BRICK. CORNER WINDOWS TO HAVE ANGLE IRON & PLATE LINTELS. ALL OTHER EXT DOORS & WINDOWS TO HAVE ANGLE IRON LINTELS. BOTH BATH AND SHOWER ROOMS TO HAVE CERAMIC TILE ON WALLS TO HEIGHT OF 5'-0".

Name _____ Date _____

PRINTREADING

Refer to Hughes Residence—First Floor Plan on page 116.

True-False

T   F   **1.** Rafters in the GAR. are spaced 24″ OC.

T   F   **2.** Three WP receptacles are shown on the floor plan.

T   F   **3.** Six duplex convenience outlets, of which five are split-wired, are shown in the LR.

T   F   **4.** The door leading from the house into the GAR. is metal covered.

T   F   **5.** All dimensions are to centers of studs.

T   F   **6.** Flush doors are shown in the LAV.

T   F   **7.** The ceiling outlet in the GAR. is controlled by a three-way switch.

T   F   **8.** Three hose bibbs are shown.

T   F   **9.** The scale of the floor plan is ¼″ = 1′-0″.

T   F   **10.** The Kitchen door leading to the outside is designated as an E door.

Multiple Choice

_____   **1.** The first floor plan shows a(n) ___.
   A. complete Bathroom
   B. enclosed Entry passage
   C. open Living Room-Dining Room combination
   D. separate Garage

_____   **2.** Access to the second floor is gained by a stairway ___.
   A. partially open to the Entry
   B. open to the Living Room
   C. with 13 risers
   D. that makes a 180° turn

3. Access to the basement is gained by ___.

    A. winding stairs from the Entry
    B. stairs with 14 risers
    C. an exterior stairway
    D. a stairway open to the Entry

4. Regarding floor levels, the ___.

    A. Living and Garage areas are the same level
    B. Garage floor is lower than the Living Area
    C. Garage and Entry passage floor levels are the same
    D. Garage floor is level

5. The windows in the Living Room-Dining Room area are all ___.

    A. casement windows
    B. casement windows with mullions
    C. insulating glass
    D. casement or fixed-sash windows

6. The Kitchen and Lavatory windows are ___.

    A. double hung
    B. casement
    C. casement with mullion or double hung
    D. casement without mullion or double hung

7. Doors designated B on the floor plan are ___.

    A. swinging or sliding (pocket) doors
    B. panel doors
    C. of different sizes
    D. metal clad

8. Doors designated C and D are ___.

    A. louvered doors
    B. identical
    C. all 1¾" thick
    D. flush doors

9. Metal thresholds are provided ___.

    A. only at outside doors
    B. only at doors where flooring changes from one material to another
    C. at the Lavatory doorway
    D. at Garage doors

10. Regarding flooring, the ___.

    A. house has either oak or ceramic tile
    B. Garage floor and the Entry passage floor have the same material and base
    C. fireplace hearth is tile
    D. Entry has a slate floor

11. Regarding the Living Room-Dining Room area, ___.

    A. a wood base and plaster cornice are shown
    B. there are no ceiling outlets
    C. all convenience outlets are controlled by wall switches
    D. a pass-through is provided to the Kitchen

_____ **12.** Closets have ___.
    A. sliding doors
    B. shelves and rods
    C. shelves
    D. lights with pull switches

_____ **13.** The Kitchen has ___.
    A. a countertop range
    B. a ceramic tile floor and base
    C. an electric oven
    D. wall cabinets on three walls

_____ **14.** The Lavatory has ___.
    A. one ceiling light
    B. a ceramic tile floor and base only
    C. a soil stack located in the partition behind the toilet
    D. one light at the medicine cabinet

_____ **15.** Regarding Kitchen cabinets, ___.
    A. ceramic tile countertops are shown
    B. a dishwasher is shown to the right of the sink
    C. a freestanding range is supplemented by a built-in wall oven
    D. there is a pass through from the Kitchen to the Dining Room

Completion

_____ **1.** The finished opening for the overhead door is ___ wide.

_____ **2.** The fireplace has a(n) ___ hearth.

_____ **3.** The KIT. measures ___ × ___.

_____ **4.** A kitchen exhaust fan is located on the ___ wall of the KIT.

_____ **5.** ___ and ___ closets are located in the LAV.

_____ **6.** The fireplace opening is ___ wide.

_____ **7.** Wood columns supporting the roof over the ENTRY PASSAGE are ___" square.

_____ **8.** A(n) ___ door is shown between the DR and KIT.

_____ **9.** The front door to the house is designated ___.

_____ **10.** ___ B doors are required.

_____ **11.** The garage floor is pitched ___" to the garage door.

_____ **12.** Trusses in the GAR. are 24" ___.

_____ **13.** The oven and range are ___ operated.

_____ **14.** ___ glass is shown on the fixed sash window in the DR.

_____ **15.** All exterior receptacles are WP and ___ protected.

Refer to printreading questions on page 113.

FIRST FLOOR PLAN

SCALE: ¼" = 1'-0"

NOTE: ALL DIMENSIONS ARE TO FACE OF STUDS

MARK	SIZE	AM'T REQ'D	REMARKS	MARK	SIZE	AM'T REQ'D	REMARKS
A	3'-0" × 6'-8" × 1¾"	1	EXTERIOR FLUSH DOOR	D	2'-4" × 6'-8" × 1⅜"	4	FLUSH DOORS
B	2'-8" × 6'-8" × 1¾"	2	FLUSH DOORS 1-SLIDING 1-METAL COVERED	D₁	2'-4" × 6'-8" × 1⅜"	1	LOUVERED
				E	1'-3" × 6'-8" × 1⅜"	1	BIFOLD LOUVERED
C	2'-6" × 6'-8" × 1⅜"	4	FLUSH DOORS	F	2'-10" × 6'-8" × 1¾"	2	EXTERIOR 2-LIGHTS
C₁	2'-6" × 6'-8" × 1⅜"	2	LOUVERED	G	2'-8" × 6'-8" × 1¾"	1	EXTERIOR 2-LIGHTS

DOOR SCHEDULE

HUGHES RESIDENCE

PLOT PLANS

Local municipalities develop and provide information required for survey plats. Public streets and utilities are shown on survey plats. Plot plans show the building and improvement locations on a property. The governmental authority having jurisdiction issues permits and conducts inspections to ensure that minimum standards consistent with local ordinances are met.

OBJECTIVES

1. Describe how building codes and building permits work.
2. Explain survey plats.
3. Define plot plan and describe the scale used for plot plans.
4. Explain elevations and contour lines.
5. Describe symbols and abbreviations as used on plot plans.

BUILDING CODES

Building codes are used to enforce minimum building and safety standards and to ensure the use of proper materials and sound construction methods. The authority having jurisdiction in the area enforces local building codes, which are commonly based on model codes. A *model code* is a national building code developed through conferences between building officials and industry representatives around the country. Model codes can be adopted in part or in entirety by states or local communities. For example, the *International Residential Code®* is a model code developed by the International Code Council® (ICC).

Local municipalities and building officials may also adopt additional requirements for construction in their jurisdiction. One example of this is the addition of requirements for sustainable construction. *Sustainable construction* incorporates environmentally sensitive practices and materials into the building process. This is also commonly referred to as green construction.

Some states, like California, have developed building codes that incorporate requirements for sustainable construction. The CalGreen Code was adopted in California in 2009. It is the first statewide green building code in the United States. This code applies to both commercial and residential building permits and requires that new buildings meet a level of efficiency and sustainability. The purpose of this building code is to make water efficiency, indoor air quality, and the use of sustainable building materials mandatory.

There are several organizations and entities that have produced and created best practices and rating systems for sustainable construction such as the U.S. Green Building Council (USGBC). This organization has developed the LEED® (Leadership in Energy and Environmental Design) system as a rating tool for various construction projects. Many of the building requirements in the CalGreen Code can be used for LEED certification.

LEED for Homes is a voluntary rating system introduced in 2008 that encourages the design and construction of green homes. This rating system applies to affordable housing, mass-produced homes, custom homes, stand-alone single-family homes, duplexes and townhomes, suburban and urban apartments and condominiums, and lofts in historic buildings. LEED contributes to higher home efficiency through better energy and water-use practices. LEED homes are built to provide a better indoor environment and better air quality and are of greater value in that they sell for more money and in less time than non-green built homes.

Building permits must be obtained after the plans and specifications are completed by the architect and before construction begins. Construction documents are submitted to local building officials for review and approval prior to issuance of a building permit. The building permit must be displayed on the job site throughout construction. Inspectors enforce the local building codes by checking materials and construction methods at various points during construction. The final inspection is made after the house is completed. The house may be occupied only after it passes the final inspection and an occupancy permit is issued. **See Figure 5-1.**

Figure 5-1. Local building codes are based on model codes. Building permits are issued before construction begins.

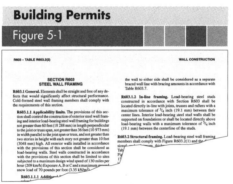

BUILDING CODE

BUILDING PERMIT

TECHFACTS

On survey plats, one section is equal to 640 acres.

SURVEY PLATS

A *survey plat* is a map showing a division of land, such as a portion of a quarter section of a township, subdivided into streets and lots. A survey plat is drawn by a licensed surveyor and contains legal descriptions of the land. It also shows the lot and the location of easements and public utilities. An *easement* is a strip of privately owned land set aside for the placement of public utilities.

A *township* is an area that is 6 miles long on each side, or 36 square miles. Townships are divided into sections and quarter sections. Townships are grouped based on a gridwork of North-South and East-West lines crisscrossing the United States. A *meridian* is the North-South line that defines a group of townships on the grid. A *baseline* is the East-West line that defines a group of townships on the grid. Individual townships are identified by their location in relation to meridians and baselines. For example, a township three rows North of a baseline and five rows East of a meridian is designated T3N, R5E.

Townships are divided into sections. A *section* is a division of a township and is one mile long on each side. Township sections are numbered 1 through 36 beginning at the northeast corner of the township. Sections are further subdivided into quarter sections. These are designated NE, SE, SW, and NW. **See Figure 5-2.**

PLOT PLANS

A *plot plan* is derived from information on a survey plot. A plot plan is a scaled view that shows the shape and size of the building lot; location, shape, and overall size of a house and other structures on the lot; and the finish floor elevation. In addition, locations of streets and utilities are shown. The plot plan is oriented from a point of beginning. A *point of beginning (POB)* is a location point from which horizontal dimensions and vertical elevations are made. This point is used to accurately locate all lot corners and to locate the building on the lot.

In LEED residential construction, efforts are made to orient the residence in a manner that takes advantage of any solar or wind energy. Architects access geospatial information that provides both solar and wind data for the property. Changing the orientation of the roof and walls by several degrees can improve energy performance.

Scale

A civil engineer's scale is used to draw plot plans. Plot plans are commonly drawn to the scale of 1″ = 10′-0″ or 1′ = 20′-0″ depending on the lot size and sheet size of the plan. Decimal dimensions are used on plot plans. For example, a property line that is 120′-6″ long is designated 120.50′, and a finish floor level of 5′-0″ is designated 5.00′. When locating a building on a lot, tradesworkers use tape measures showing feet, inches, and fractional inch increments. Therefore, decimal dimensions must be converted into fractions. **See Appendix.**

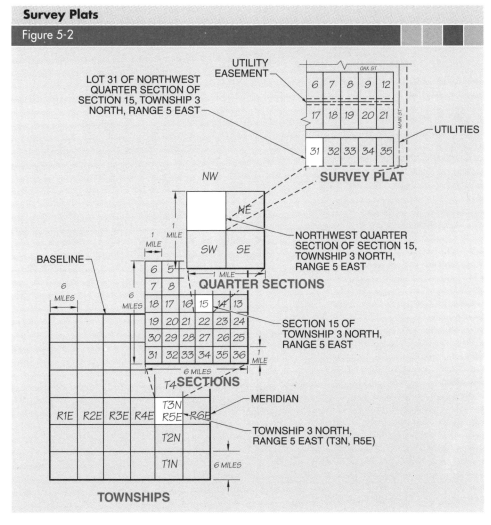

Survey Plats

Figure 5-2

Figure 5-2. Townships are subdivided into sections and quarter sections. The survey plat shows streets, utilities, and easements.

Elevations

An *elevation* is a vertical measurement above or below the point of beginning. (Note that the use of the word "elevation" here is different from an elevation view of a house.) The point of beginning is shown on the plot plan. A benchmark on the actual lot represents the point of beginning. A *benchmark* is a stake driven into the ground or a fixed point in the street or along the curb that is used as the point of beginning. For example, a benchmark with an elevation of 112′ indicates that the point is 112′ above the reference point used by the community. The reference point for a community may be in relation to mean sea level or to a specific point in the community.

Contour Lines. A *contour line* is a dashed or solid line on a plot plan that passes through points having the same elevation. Dashed lines represent the natural grade. *Natural grade* is the slope of the land before rough grading. Solid lines represent the finish grade. *Finish grade* is the slope of the land after final grading. **See Figure 5-3.**

Closely spaced contour lines denote steeply sloped lots. Contour lines spaced farther apart denote flatter lots. The spacing of contour lines is generally in 1′-0″ intervals for changes in elevation. For steeply sloped lots, the spacing may be in 2′-0″ or larger intervals for changes in elevation. Elevation notations are placed on the high side of contour lines.

Symbols and Abbreviations

Symbols and abbreviations conserve space on plot plans. **See Figure 5-4.** Symbols show roads, streets, sidewalks, the point of beginning, property lines, utilities, natural and/or finish grades, and other pertinent information. Trees and shrubbery to remain are shown with symbols. North is indicated with a symbol to orient the house on the lot.

Abbreviations on plot plans relate to roads and streets, the lot, location of the house on the lot, utilities, building materials, elevations, and similar items. For example, the abbreviation FIN. FL EL 10.25′ indicates a finish floor elevation of 10′-3″.

Figure 5-3. Contour lines show the slope of a lot.

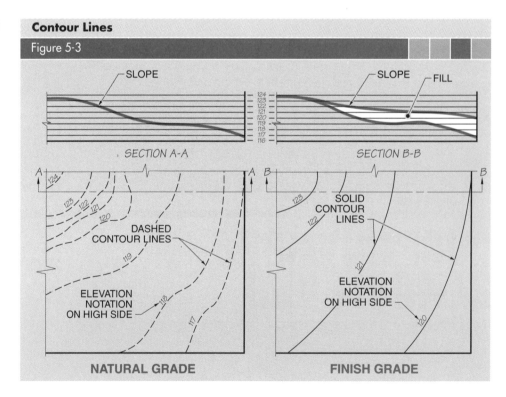

Symbols and Abbreviations on Plot Plans

Figure 5-4

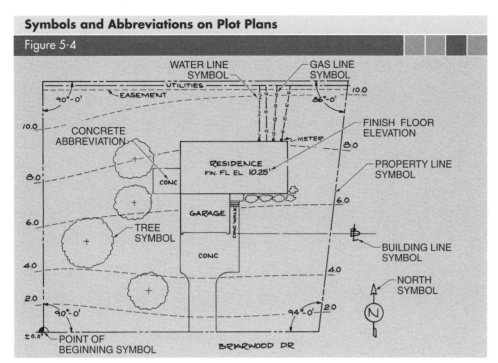

Figure 5-4. Symbols and abbreviations conserve space on plot plans.

READING PLOT PLANS

The plot plan for the Wayne Residence is drawn to the scale of 1″ = 20′-0″. **See Figure 5-5.** The lot, which is located on Country Club Fairways in Columbia, Missouri, is pentagonal. Dimensions for property lines and notations indicating the corner angles are given. For example, the angle of the southeast corner of the lot is 104°-23′-25″.

A 9′-0″ utility easement is shown between the curb and the property line along the street. An 8′ utility easement is shown along the northwest property line. The point of beginning is the southwest corner of the lot. The corner of the Garage is 25′-0″ north and 11′-0″ east of the property line. The finish floor elevation is 725′-0″. A concrete drive and 4′-0″ concrete walk are shown at the front of the house.

Contour lines show the finish grade of the lot. Numbers on the contour lines indicate elevations. The lot slopes down from west to east. The elevation near the southwest corner of the house is almost 726′ while the elevation at the southeast corner of the house is 718′. Retaining

walls are shown on the east and north sides of the house. The closely spaced contour lines from the retaining wall on the north side of the house represent a steep slope in the finish grade.

Symbols are used to show four trees that are to remain on the lot. In addition, symbols show foundation shrubbery along the front of the house between the front entrance and the Garage.

TECHFACTS

Load-bearing capacity, which is the ability of soil to support weight, affects the amount of settlement that occurs.

Trus Joist, A Weyerhaeuser Business

Exterior walls are erected after concrete for the foundation has set and hardened sufficiently.

Wayne Residence Plot Plan

Figure 5-5

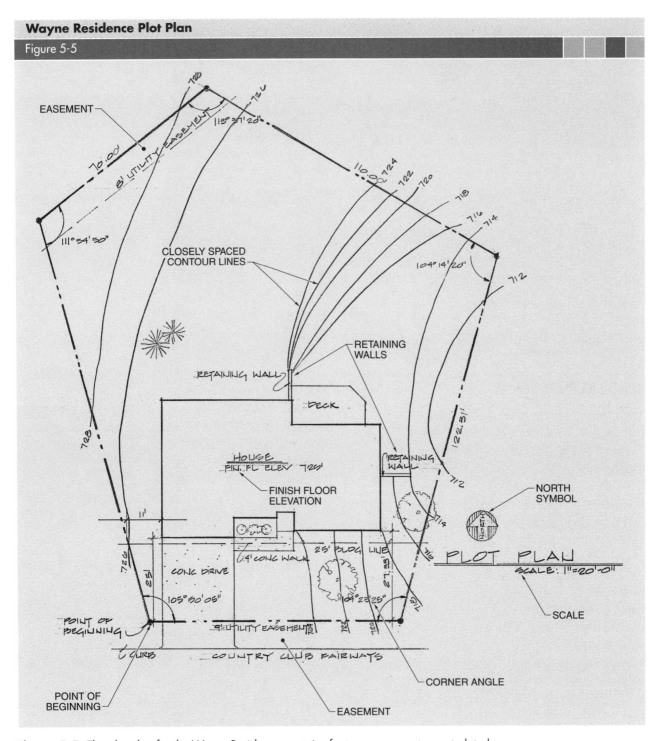

EASEMENT

CLOSELY SPACED
CONTOUR LINES

RETAINING
WALLS

RETAINING WALL

DECK

HOUSE
FIN. FL. ELEV 729'

FINISH FLOOR
ELEVATION

RETAINING
WALL

NORTH
SYMBOL

PLOT PLAN
SCALE: 1"=20'-0"

SCALE

CONC DRIVE

64' CONC WALK

25' BLDG LINE

POINT OF
BEGINNING

CURB

COUNTRY CLUB FAIRWAYS

CORNER ANGLE

POINT OF
BEGINNING

EASEMENT

Figure 5-5. The plot plan for the Wayne Residence contains features common to most plot plans.

LEARNER RESOURCES

Name _____ Date _____

SKETCHING 5-1

Sketch plot plan symbols as indicated. Refer to Appendix.

①
BUILDING LINE

②
POINT OF BEGINNING

③
PROPERTY LINE

④
TREE

⑤
UTILITY METER

⑥
IMPROVED ROAD

⑦
UNIMPROVED ROAD

⑧
FIRE HYDRANT

⑨
NORTH

⑩
POWER POLE
AND GUY

⑪
STREET SIGN

⑫
FENCE

Sketching 5-2

Sketch and/or letter the following to complete the plot plan.

1. 512' (elevation notation)
2. Existing trees (symbol)
3. 150.5' (dimension)
4. STORM DRAIN (symbol and notation)
5. WATER MAIN (symbol and notation)

6. GAS MAIN (symbol and notation)
7. POINT OF BEGINNING (notation)
8. 12.5' (dimension)
9. FIRST FL ELEV 513.5' (notation)

PLOT PLAN

Name _____ Date _____

True-False

T	F	**1.** Public streets and utilities are shown on plot plans.
T	F	**2.** The authority having jurisdiction in an area inspects the house during construction.
T	F	**3.** Building permits must be obtained before the plans are completed.
T	F	**4.** Townships are square areas one mile long on each side.
T	F	**5.** Baselines on maps showing townships run north and south.
T	F	**6.** A section contains one square mile.
T	F	**7.** Easements are private property containing public utilities.
T	F	**8.** Property dimensions on plot plans are generally given in feet and decimal parts of a foot.
T	F	**9.** The decimal 0.675 equals ⅝.
T	F	**10.** Solid contour lines show the natural grade of a lot.
T	F	**11.** Closely spaced contour lines on a plot plan represent a steep slope.
T	F	**12.** Trees and shrubbery should not be shown on plot plans.
T	F	**13.** The North symbol should always be included on a plot plan.
T	F	**14.** Utilities on plot plans may be shown with symbols and notations.
T	F	**15.** Spacing of contour lines on plot plans is generally in 1′-0″ intervals.

Multiple Choice

_____ **1.** A(n) ___ scale is used to draw plot plans.
   A. architect's
   B. civil engineer's
   C. mechanical engineer's
   D. tradesworker's

_____ **2.** A township contains ___ square miles.
   A. 1
   B. 6
   C. 16
   D. 36

_____ **3.** A township four rows North of the baseline and two rows East of the meridian is designated ___.
   A. T2N, R2E
   B. R3E, T3N
   C. T2N, R3N
   D. T4N, R2E

_____ **4.** Townships are divided into ___.
   A. sections
   B. communities
   C. towns and farms
   D. survey plats

_____ **5.** A plot plan shows the ___.
   A. size of the building lot
   B. legal description
   C. baseline
   D. adjacent lot

_____ **6.** A four-sided building lot with two 90° corners and one 83° corner also contains one ___° corner.
   A. 89
   B. 92
   C. 97
   D. 107

_____ **7.** A plot plan showing a finish floor elevation of 132'-10" is ___ above the point of beginning at an elevation of 128.5'.
   A. 3'-8"
   B. 4'-4"
   C. 4'-5"
   D. 4'-8"

_____ **8.** A rectangular building lot measuring 126'-0" × 212'-0" contains ___ sq ft.
   A. 252
   B. 338
   C. 22,424
   D. 26,712

_____ **9.** A(n) ___ is a vertical measurement above or below the point of beginning.
   A. height
   B. baseline
   C. elevation
   D. meridian

_____ **10.** A survey plat is a map showing a ___ of land.
   A. division
   B. building lot
   C. slope
   D. section

Name _____ Date _____

Refer to Wayne Residence—Plot Plan, Sheet 6.

Completion

_____ **1.** The concrete walk is ___' wide.

_____ **2.** The finish floor elevation is ___'.

_____ **3.** Solid ___ lines show the finish grade of the lot.

_____ **4.** The southwest property line of the lot meets the south property line at a(n) ___ angle.

_____ **5.** The utility easement along the street is ___' wide.

_____ **6.** The plot plan is drawn to the scale of ___.

_____ **7.** A deck is shown near the ___ corner of the house.

_____ **8.** The southwest corner of the house is ___ from the west property line.

_____ **9.** The concrete walk leads from the front entry to the ___.

_____ **10.** A(n) ___' utility easement runs along the northwest property line.

Multiple Choice

_____ **1.** Retaining walls are visible on the ___ Elevations of the house.
   A. North and East
   B. North and West
   C. South and East
   D. South and West

_____ **2.** Regarding the northwest property line, ___.
   A. it is 70.0' long
   B. a 104°-14'-20" angle is shown
   C. it is the longest property line
   D. it is 110.0' long

127

_____ **3.** Regarding the point of beginning, ___.
  A. it is 12.0' from the curb
  B. it is 716.0' above sea level
  C. a concrete drive is shown on that corner of the lot
  D. it is 11.0' from the house

_____ **4.** Regarding the utility easement, ___.
  A. two utility easements are shown
  B. utilities are located on the north side of the property only
  C. utilities are located on the south side of the property only
  D. utilities are located on the west side of the property only

_____ **5.** Regarding the driveway, ___.
  A. the Garage is located on the east side of the house
  B. a brick paver driveway is shown
  C. a concrete driveway is shown
  D. an asphalt driveway is shown

_____ **6.** Regarding the lot, ___.
  A. the front yard is the largest
  B. a steep slope runs north from the rear retaining wall
  C. trees are shown on four sides of the house
  D. the west side of the lot has a steep slope

_____ **7.** Regarding the building line, ___.
  A. it is set back 25'-0" from the curb
  B. the roof overhang cannot exceed 2'-0" to comply
  C. it is located on the north side of the house
  D. the garage can be built beyond it

_____ **8.** Regarding the lot, ___.
  A. the highest elevation shown is 111'-0"
  B. elevation does not vary over 2'-0"
  C. the natural grade is to remain
  D. the lowest elevation is on the east side of the house

_____ **9.** Regarding the lot, the ___.
  A. house is on a corner lot
  B. house faces Country Club Fairways
  C. basic shape is hexagonal
  D. front of the house faces north

_____ **10.** Regarding the title block for Sheet 6, the plans were ___.
  A. revised
  B. drawn by FGH
  C. developed by Hulen & Hulen Designs
  D. approved by the architect

FLOOR PLANS

Floor plans are a very commonly used portion of the prints in a set of plans. The overall shape and size of the house are shown on the floor plans. The sizes and relationships of rooms are given. Other prints relate to the floor plan to show construction details, locations, size, fixtures, and equipment. Dimensions, symbols, notations, and abbreviations are used to provide information for everyone involved in the construction process. Floor plans are generally drawn to the scale of ¼" = 1'-0" to allow adequate detail to be shown.

OBJECTIVES

1. Define floor plan and explain what a floor plan shows.
2. Explain how cutting planes relate to floor plans.
3. Describe orientation and relationship.
4. Describe simplified floor plans.
5. List the floor plans used for a one-story house and a two-story house.
6. Describe the floor plans for a one-and-one-half-story house.
7. Explain what the Foundation/Basement Plan of the Wayne Residence shows.
8. Explain what the Floor Plan of the Wayne Residence shows.

FLOOR PLANS

A *floor plan* is a scaled view of the various floors in a house looking directly down from a horizontal cutting plane taken 5'-0" above each finished floor. Floor plans show the broad aspects of shapes, sizes, and relationships of rooms and the layout of auxiliary space such as hallways, stairs, and closets. The layout of attached garages, carports, patios, and decks is also shown on a floor plan. Floor plans are generally the first set of plans to be created and are often the most used portion of the prints on the construction site.

Dimensions on floor plans give the overall size of the house and location of all wall offsets, partitions, doors, and windows. Wall and partition thicknesses are indicated and room sizes are shown. The location and sizes of closets, fireplaces, stairs, and other features are also dimensioned.

Symbols on floor plans represent materials, equipment, and fixtures. Ceramic floor tile, glass block, and common or face brick are examples of materials that are shown with symbols. Electrical equipment, such as receptacles

and outlets, and plumbing equipment, such as hose bibbs and floor drains, are shown with symbols. Fixtures such as kitchen sinks, bathroom lavatories, bathtubs, showers, and water closets are also shown with symbols.

Abbreviations on floor plans conserve space and help prevent clutter on the prints. Common abbreviations are used to designate various rooms such as LR (living room), BR (bedroom), DR (dining room), and B (bath). In addition, abbreviations are used to designate materials, equipment, and fixtures.

Notations (notes) on floor plans may be general, typical, or specific. A *general note* is a notation that refers to an entire set of prints. One example of a general note is ALL DIMENSIONS TO FACE OF STUDS, which refers to all dimensioned studs in the building. A *typical note* is a notation that refers to all similar items on the prints. For example, the notation PROVIDE FURRED SOFFIT OVER ALL KITCHEN WALL CABINETS refers to all kitchen wall cabinets shown on the floor plan. A *specific note* is a notation that refers to one certain item only. For example, the notation CER TILE FLR (ceramic tile floor) refers to that floor area only. Note that abbreviations may be used in notations to conserve space on the prints. **See Figure 6-1.**

Scale

Floor plans are drawn to scale. All rooms, hallways, stairs, and other areas are drawn to the same scale so that they are in a consistent size relationship to each other. The scale for the floor plan is generally given as a general note near the name of the plan. For example, the notation SCALE: ¼″ = 1′-0″ may be placed below the title FLOOR PLAN. The scale may also be given in the title block if the floor plan is the only drawing on the sheet or if all drawings on the sheet were drawn at the same scale.

Plan Views

Figure 6-1

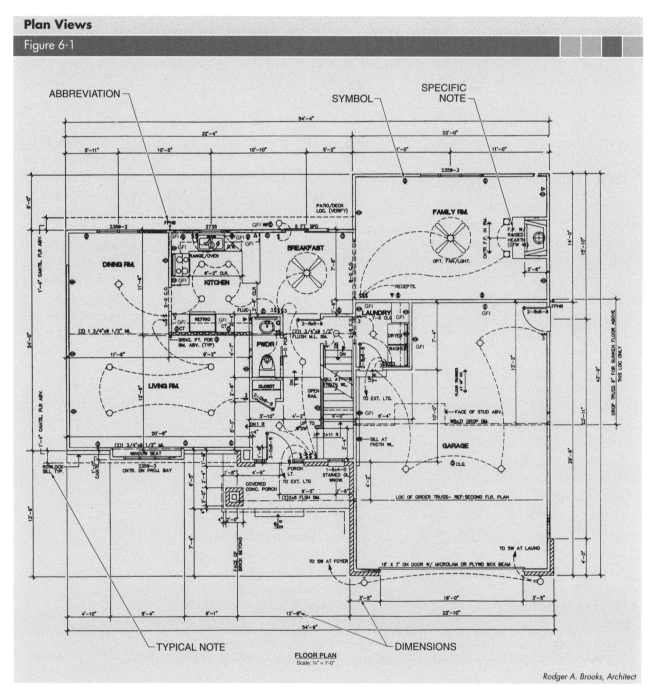

Rodger A. Brooks, Architect

Figure 6-1. Floor plans are scaled views of the various floors of a structure.

The most common scale for residential floor plans is ¼″ = 1′-0″ (¹⁄₄₈ scale). The ¼″ = 1′-0″ scale yields a floor plan large enough to convey sufficient information on standard size drawing sheets. Dimensions on scaled drawings give the actual size of the rooms, hallways, and other features. For larger houses and commercial buildings, a ⅛″ = 1′-0″ (¹⁄₉₆ scale) or ³⁄₁₆″ = 1′-0″ (¹⁄₆₄ scale) scale may be used.

Cutting Planes

Floor plans are horizontal sections made by an imaginary cutting plane taken through the house 5′-0″ above each finished floor. The cutting plane passes through walls, partitions, upper window sashes, kitchen wall cabinets, medicine cabinets, and other built-in-place or installed features. Solid lines show features below the cutting plane. Hidden (dashed) lines show features above the cutting plane. For example, kitchen base cabinets are shown with solid lines while kitchen wall cabinets are shown with hidden lines. **See Figure 6-2.**

Floor plans may also include information about structural members that support the roof or floor above. For example, the note 2 × 10 JOISTS OVER on a first floor plan indicates that the joists are overhead and support the second floor.

Orientation

Floor plans are generally drawn, based on orthographic projection concepts, with the front of the house toward the bottom of the sheet. However, floor plans may be oriented to fit the drawing sheet. For example, when a house is long and narrow, the front is usually placed facing the right edge of the drawing sheet. When floor plans for other floors are developed, they should be oriented in the same direction on each subsequent drawing sheet.

Floor Plan Cutting Plane
Figure 6-2

Figure 6-2. The cutting plane is positioned 5′-0″ above the finished floor. Solid lines represent features below the cutting plane. Dashed lines show features above the cutting plane.

Relationship

Floor plans for various floors are related to each other. Structural provisions are made so the load of roofs, floors and partitions is transferred to supporting members or partitions immediately below. Stairs are designed so they start on one floor and end in the proper place on the floor above or below. Heating and cooling ducts are designed to start at the furnace or fan blower, pass through first floor partitions, and end at registers in the desired locations in upper floor partitions or floors.

TECHTIPS
Roof rafters or trusses are positioned directly over exterior wall studs where possible so the roof weight is properly transferred to the foundation.

Floor plans and exterior elevations are drawn to the same scale, and the features on each of these types of drawings are directly related to each other. For example, windows that appear on the floor plan are the same size and the same distance from the building corners as they are on the elevations. The overall structure of the house is visualized by cross-referencing between the floor plans and elevation drawings.

The same information is generally only shown in one place on a set of prints to avoid redundancy and the potential for errors on the drawings. For example, a stairway that rises from the first to the second floor is not shown completely on the floor plans for either story. The first floor plan shows the exact location of the bottom riser and a few treads. A *riser* is the vertical portion of a stair step. A *tread* is the horizontal portion of a stair step. The print representation of the stairway is terminated on a break line. The second floor plan shows the top riser location and a few of the descending stair treads that also terminate on a break line. A notation, such as 16 R UP or 16 R DN indicates the total number of risers (R) for the stairway. A window that appears on a stairway landing can be shown on the first and second floor plan but is commonly only shown on one of these floor plans.

After the first floor plan has been created, it is used to locate walls, windows, stairways, and other features when creating the second floor plan. CAD and BIM systems allow an architect to quickly and easily maintain the proper relationship of floor plans for a multistory house. CAD and BIM systems also allow additional specific types of plans to be developed from basic floor plans for specific trade areas. **See Figure 6-3.** For example, a basic floor plan is drawn first, and notes and symbols are added. Plumbing information may then be added to create a floor plan for the plumbing work. Electrical information may be added to the basic floor plan for the electrical installations.

Layering of this type also minimizes clashes between structural components, electrical devices, and mechanical systems. For example, a properly executed CAD or BIM project will prevent a situation where a heating/cooling duct has to be rerouted at the job site due to interference with a horizontal beam.

Window and door placement in interior and exterior walls is commonly shown with a centerline to indicate the dimensions to the center of the opening. Where LEED principles are applied, locations of windows and doors as shown on floor plans will be designed in a manner that best utilizes natural light and ventilation.

SIMPLIFIED FLOOR PLANS

Simplified sketches of floor plans do not contain dimensions or detailed information. Symbols for materials of construction, windows, doors, and other basic building components are modified to permit visualization of room shapes and relationships without details. A set of prints should be studied in much the same order as a person might inspect a house. For houses with more than one floor plan, the first (main) floor plan is studied first. In a one-story house with a full basement, the floor plan (main floor plan) is studied first and the basement (foundation) plan is studied next.

Pictorial sketches can be useful in determining room shapes and relationships when studying floor plans. Such sketches show basic shapes and relationships but provide little detail. Overall construction concepts can be developed from the sketches.

Layering of CAD Drawings

Figure 6-3

Figure 6-3. Layering of CAD drawings allows plans with specific types of information to be developed.

One-Story House

A one-story house has one floor plan. Two floor plans are required if the house has a basement—one floor plan for the first floor and one plan for the basement. A floor plan is drawn as if a cutting plane had been passed through the house 5'-0" above the finished floor and the upper part had been removed so that the person reading the prints can look directly down on the floor. **See Figure 6-4.**

For the one-story house shown in Figure 6-4, entry to the house is through either the Living Room door or Kitchen door. The main entry is the Living Room door. A coat closet (CL) to the right of the Living Room

TECHTIPS

The attic of a house with a low roof pitch is usually too small for living purposes.

Figure 6-4. A one-story house on a concrete slab has one floor plan.

door serves as a windbreak and divides the entry area from the Dining Area. Picture windows are placed along the front of the house.

The Dining Area is between the Living Room and the Kitchen. It is not enclosed by partitions. One window is shown in the Dining Area wall. The Kitchen contains L-shaped base and wall cabinets. Base cabinets are shown with solid lines. Wall cabinets are shown with dashed lines since they are above the cutting plane. A window on the wall opposite the cabinets provides light and ventilation.

One-Story House

Figure 6-4

PICTORIAL

FLOOR PLAN

Three bedrooms and a bath are located off the hallway. The hallway is entered from the living room. The entry to the hallway is located so that it is not directly across from the Bathroom door or the door to Bedroom 1.

A linen closet is located at the end of the hallway near the Bathroom. This space could be devoted to a furnace if required. (Note that a chimney flue for the furnace is shown on the roof in the pictorial sketch.)

All bedrooms are well lighted with large windows. Bedrooms 2 and 3 have cross ventilation. Closets for Bedrooms 1 and 2 are located between the two bedrooms. The closet for Bedroom 3 is larger than the closets in the two other bedrooms. Bifold or sliding doors are required for this closet.

All Bathroom fixtures have been arranged along a common partition with the Kitchen. This fixture arrangement facilitates plumbing installation and reduces material and labor costs.

Two-Story House

A two-story house with a basement has three floor plans—one plan for the second floor, one plan for the first floor, and one plan for the basement. **See Figure 6-5.** The three cutting planes that produce the first floor, second floor, and basement floor plans are indicated by cutting plane lines designated A-A, B-B, and C-C, respectively. A-A is the projection for the first floor plan. Cutting plane line A-A passes through the house at the upper sash of the windows and the upper part of the doors on the main floor. B-B is the projection for the second floor plan. Cutting plane line B-B passes through the house at the upper sash of the windows on the upper floor. C-C is the projection for the basement plan. Cutting plane line C-C passes through the basement windows.

TECHFACTS

The Cape Cod Colonial is the earliest dwelling type built by the American colonists, and this design is still popular today.

Two-Story House

Figure 6-5

FINISHED
2ND FLR

FINISHED
1ST FLR

GRADE

**SECTION A-A—FIRST
FLOOR PLAN**

**SECTION B-B—SECOND
FLOOR PLAN**

**SECTION C-C—BASEMENT
(FOUNDATION)
FLOOR PLAN**

Figure 6-5. A two-story house with a basement has three floor plans.

First Floor Plan. The first floor plan shows that the Living and Dining Rooms are one large L-shaped room. The Kitchen, Bathroom, Breakfast Area, and rear exit occupy the remaining portion of the first floor. A stairway to the second floor starts at a landing one riser above the floor level. The stairway is open with a railing on the Living Room side. Stairs to the basement descend from the rear hallway and are built directly below the stairs to the second floor. A landing is provided as a safety measure inside the doorway before the basement stairs begin descending. Both stairways stop against break lines.

The second floor joists require additional structural members to be placed through the center of the house. A *joist* is a horizontal framing member that supports a floor. A load-bearing partition and a built-up beam provide the additional horizontal support for the floor joists. A *built-up beam* is a structural member made of laminated wood members and is designed to carry heavy loads.

In the Kitchen both base and wall cabinets are installed in a U-shaped configuration. Base cabinets are shown with solid lines. Wall cabinets are shown with dashed lines.

Note that the wall cabinet near the opening to the Dining Room extends beyond the base cabinet and provides additional storage space above the refrigerator. Additional information about cabinets is usually shown in detail views. Space is provided for a table along the wall opposite the sink. The appliances are arranged for efficient work flow from the storage area (refrigerator) through the preparation area (sink) to the cooking area (stove). The serving areas (either the Breakfast Area or Dining Room) are conveniently located. The window over the Kitchen sink provides light and ventilation.

The fireplace in the Living Room is drawn with the cutting plane passing 1'-0" above the floor to show details of its shape on the floor plan. The flue shown is for the basement furnace.

Floor plans provide dimensions for the proper placement of windows.

Second Floor Plan. The second floor plan shows the layout of rooms on the upper level. The top riser of the stairway is shown in its exact location. Treads descend until they stop against a break line. The stairway is open to the hallway and is protected by a railing. The window at the head of the stairs provides light.

Bathroom 2 is located above Bathroom 1 on the first floor. All plumbing fixtures in the house are arranged to be plumbed to a common partition. A small window is located in Bathroom 2.

Bedrooms 1, 2, and 3 all have windows in both exterior walls to provide cross ventilation. All bedroom closets have sliding doors to conserve space.

TECHFACTS

Door openings are located in walls to provide efficient access for building inhabitants.

A load-bearing partition, directly over the beam shown on the first floor plan, and other necessary structural members (not shown) continue to the wall over the stairs to support the overhead ceiling joists.

The chimney shown on the second floor plan shows two flues. One flue is for the fireplace on the first floor to exhaust smoke. The other flue is for the furnace in the basement to exhaust furnace gases.

Basement Floor Plan. The basement floor plan shows information about the foundation, windows, stairs, and building structure. The location of the bottom riser of the basement stairway is shown. Some of the treads are drawn and terminate against a break line.

The steel beam directly below the load-bearing partition on the first floor supports the joists that are placed 90° to the beam and are supported by the beam and the foundation walls. The beam terminates on a post at the edge of the stairway and does not continue to the wall, as it would pass through the stairway if it did. The notation 2 × 10 FLOOR JOISTS OVER and the directional symbol indicate the size and direction of the floor joists.

The fireplace foundation is carried down to the footing with only the furnace flue showing. A footing is a support base for a foundation wall or column. Basement windows are located in areaways to provide light and ventilation.

One-and-One-Half-Story House

A one-story house with a steeply sloped roof provides useful attic space that may be converted into living space. For example, the attic space in a traditional Cape Cod style house can be used as living space. Dormers can be added to provide additional floor area, ventilation, and architectural effect. A *dormer* is a projection from a sloping roof that provides additional interior area. Three common types of dormers are the gable, hip, and shed dormer. **See Figure 6-6.**

Two cutting planes are required for a Cape Cod style house—one for the first floor and one for the second floor. Each cutting plane is taken 5′-0″ above its finished floor. The cutting plane for the second floor plan reveals the irregular outline of walls with dormers. **See Figure 6-7.** An additional floor plan and cutting plane may be provided for a foundation plan if included.

READING FLOOR PLANS

The Wayne Residence is a contemporary one-story house with a full basement. (Refer to Wayne Residence, Sheets 1 and 2.) Sheet 1 shows the Foundation/Basement Plan. Sheet 2 shows the Floor Plan.

Foundation/Basement Plan

The title block shows that the Foundation/Basement Plan is drawing number 1 OF 7. This indicates that seven sheets comprise the complete set of plans for the Wayne Residence. The plan was drawn by Pam Hulen (initials PMH) of Hulen & Hulen Designs at the scale of ¼″ = 1′-0″. The Wayne Residence is to be built on Lot 12 of Country Club Fairways in Columbia, Missouri.

Cape-Cod-Style House
Figure 6-7

SECOND FLOOR PLAN

Figure 6-7. Cutting planes on the upper floor of a house with dormers reveal an irregular wall line.

Dormers
Figure 6-6

GABLE   HIP   SHED

Figure 6-6. Gable, hip, and shed dormers provide additional area and light for the upper floor.

The title of the drawing—FOUNDATION/BASEMENT PLAN—is shown below the plan and the scale (¼″ = 1′-0″) is repeated below the title. An arrow showing North indicates the orientation of the house and is used when referring to exterior elevation views of the house.

Foundation. The foundation walls are cast-in-place concrete, 8″ and 10″ wide, while the concrete footings are 16″ and 20″ wide. (Refer to Basement Wall and Walkout Details, Sheet 5.) Brick veneer is shown on the south and east sides of the foundation wall. A stepped 6″ brick ledge provides a base for the brick veneer. The west foundation wall is below grade level. Retaining walls are shown on the east and south walls to compensate for the drop in grade due to the slope of the lot. (Refer to Elevations, Sheets 3 and 4.)

Foundation walls can be formed using conventional wood or metal forms or by using insulating concrete forms (ICFs).

The north wall is the rear wall. (Refer to North Elevation, Sheet 4.) A lot that has an 8′-0″ drop in grade from front to rear gives builders an opportunity to provide a walkout basement. A *walkout basement* is a basement with standard-sized windows to provide light and standard-sized doors for entry and exit. A walkout basement can be finished to provide additional living space. The lot slope and use of retaining walls allows for a walkout basement in the Wayne Residence. A window well provides clearance for an awning window in the basement area designated for a Future Workshop. (Refer to Window Schedule, Sheet 5.)

TECHFACTS

Steel or plastic reinforcement is used in a building foundation to provide additional strength. Rebar, welded wire reinforcement, or plastic fibers are embedded in the concrete.

Steel columns 4″ in diameter are placed on foundation footings to carry the load of the beams that support the floor joists. The W (wide flange) beams are described by their nominal measurement over the flanges and their weight per running foot. A W8 × 10 beam is 8″ high and weighs 10 pounds per running foot.

Slab. The typical note 4″ CONC SLAB W/ 6 × 6—W1.4 × W1.4 WWR ON GRAVEL BASE is shown for the basement floor. The portion of the note 6 × 6—W1.4 × W1.4 WWR refers to a specific size of welded wire reinforcement. *Welded wire reinforcement* is heavy-gauge wire joined in a grid and is used to increase the tensile strength of concrete and help prevent cracks. This note is repeated for the unfinished portion of the basement and for the Garage slab.

Stairway. Entry to the basement from the main floor of the house is by the stairs. A 2′-6″ × 6′-8″ × 1⅜″ hollow-core, six panel wood door is at the foot of the stairs. Panels in these doors are formed from moldable fiberboard with wood components used in hollow-core construction. Natural or various wood finishes are available. The stairway contains 14 risers at 7.392″ each. Three-way electrical switches control a ceiling outlet above the landing.

Family Room. A 4'-9" × 4'-0½" vinyl-clad casement window and a 6'-0" × 6'-8" aluminum-clad sliding glass door provide natural light to this room. Electrical receptacles are located in all walls. The ceiling outlet is shown with its switch leg. A telephone outlet, represented by a triangle, is shown on the west wall.

Bathroom. A 2'-4" × 6'-8" × 1⅜" hollow-core, six panel wood door leads from the Family Room to the Bathroom. The Bathroom contains a water closet, vanity with lavatory, and bathtub. A ground-fault circuit interrupter (GFCI or GFI) receptacle is located near the lavatory, and wall switches control a combination ceiling outlet and fan.

Study. A 2'-6" × 6'-8" × 1⅜" hollow-core, six panel wood door leads to the Study. Casement windows provide light and ventilation. Electrical receptacles are located in framed walls. A switch located near the door controls the ceiling light. Future plans of the owner include enclosing the column and steel beam and adding a floor-to-ceiling combination storage and bookcase unit in the recessed area on the east wall. Alternate plans include using the Study as a fourth Bedroom.

Unfinished Basement. The Storage Area and Future Workshop are left unfinished during the initial construction of the house. The water heater, furnace, and fireplace foundation with flue are completed. A floor drain is located near the water heater. The power panel is located on the rear wall.

Registers for supply and return air are not shown on this set of plans. The mechanical subcontractor will design and install the heating and cooling system. The contractor will coordinate the mechanical subcontractor's work with that of other trades to assure that proper electrical and structural requirements are met.

Floor Plan

Title block information given on the Foundation/Basement Plan is repeated in the title block of the Floor Plan. The Floor Plan is drawn to the scale of ¼" = 1'-0". The arrow shows that the house faces south.

Overall exterior dimensions of the house are 44'-4" × 72'-8". Dimensions to the centers of the openings are given for locating doors and windows. A 24'-0" × 12'-0" Deck is located on the north side of the house. Doors from Bedroom 1 and the Living Room open to the Deck.

TECHTIPS

The drawing scale shown with a plan view, elevation, or section takes precedence over the scale shown in the title block.

Locations of interior load-bearing and non-load-bearing partitions are indicated on floor plans.

The main floor of the Wayne Residence contains the following rooms:

- Entry
- Hallway
- Bedroom 1
- Bedroom 2
- Bedroom 3
- Bathroom
- Master Bathroom
- Living Room
- Dining Room
- Kitchen
- Breakfast Area
- Laundry Room
- Screened Porch
- Garage

Entry and Hallway. The house is entered from a covered stoop through a 3'-0" × 6'-8" × 1¾" exterior door. The door is metal insulated and includes a deadbolt. Light is provided to the entry by a 15" sidelight. Wall switches control exterior and interior ceiling outlets and the ceiling outlet in the coat closet. A rod and shelf are shown in the coat closet.

The hallway provides access to the basement, bathroom, and bedrooms. Dashed lines show a 30" × 30" scuttle in the ceiling. A *scuttle* is an access opening in a ceiling or roof with a removable or movable cover. Dashed lines in the linen closet indicate shelf rods. Two ceiling lights controlled by three-way switches provide lighting for the hallway.

Bedrooms. Three 2'-6" × 6'-8" × 1⅜" hollow-core, six panel wood doors lead to the bedrooms. Bedroom 1 is the largest bedroom. It measures 11'-9½" × 17'-0". Bedrooms 2 and 3 are 11'-2" × 12'-3½". Electrical receptacles, ceiling lights with switch legs, and telephone outlets are shown in each bedroom. The closet in Bedroom 2 has bifold doors. Bedrooms 1 and 3 have walk-in closets. A small linen closet is also shown for Bedroom 1.

Bathrooms. The Master Bathroom contains a water closet, bathtub, and shower separated from the double-bowl lavatory. Wall cabinets, mirror, and soffit are shown in Elevations 2-5 and 3-5. Wall switches control ceiling lights in the Master Bathroom. A combination ceiling light and fan is also controlled by a wall switch. Ground-fault circuit interrupter receptacles are placed near the lavatories.

The hallway Bathroom contains a lavatory, water closet, and bathtub/shower combination. A wall switch controls the combination ceiling light and fan. A GFCI receptacle is placed near the lavatory.

TECHFACTS

A ground-fault circuit interrupter (abbreviated as GFI or GFCI) is a safety device that automatically de-energizes a circuit when the grounded circuit exceeds a predetermined value.

Living Room. The 19'-4½" × 21'-6" Living Room is located at the rear of the house. Four aluminum-framed fixed windows allow light to enter while providing a view of the backyard. The Deck, which is adjacent to the Living Room, is reached by a full glass door.

A masonry fireplace is built in the south portion of the Living Room. Cutting planes refer to Fireplace Details 1-6 and 2-6, which contain additional information.

Wood or steel framing members may be used to construct the framework of a building.

Recessed ceiling lights are controlled by three-way switches located on the east wall near the stair landing and near the patio door. Electrical receptacles are spaced around walls and electrical cables are installed in a manner so as not to interfere with the location of a future door to the Breakfast Area. A header is built into the wall to provide space for the future door. Dashed lines indicate structural support over a gypsum board wrap on the header over the opening leading to the Kitchen. A telephone outlet is shown on the west wall.

Southern Forest Products Association

Interior load-bearing partitions run perpendicular to ceiling joists, while non-load-bearing partitions run parallel to ceiling joists.

Dining Room. The panned ceiling with recessed lighting provides a formal look to the Dining Room. A *panned ceiling* is a ceiling consisting of two ceiling levels connected by sloped surfaces. (Refer to the Panned Ceiling Detail, Sheet 6.) This may also be called a tray ceiling. Vinyl-clad casement windows provide light and ventilation.

Kitchen and Breakfast Area. The Kitchen base cabinets are arranged in L-shaped, straight-run, and island installations. Wall cabinets are indicated by dashed lines. Sheet 6 includes several Kitchen elevations showing the cabinet

arrangement. The arrangement of storage, preparation, and cooking areas is designed to be compact and efficient. A desk on the east wall provides additional working space. The telephone outlet is located in the wall above the desktop.

Ground-fault circuit interrupter receptacles are located to safely provide electrical service at the countertop. A wall switch controls the disposal in the sink. A range receptacle serves the drop-in stove in the island cabinet. The stove has a downdraft vent system to remove cooking odors and smoke. Recessed ceiling fixtures over the bar cabinet are controlled by a single-pole switch. A three-way switch also controls the ceiling outlet in the Breakfast Area. A clock outlet is shown on the south wall. A vinyl-clad casement window is installed in the exterior wall above the Kitchen sink.

The Laundry, Screened Porch, and Garage are entered from the Kitchen. (Refer to Door Schedule, Sheet 5 for types and sizes of doors.)

Laundry. The Laundry contains space for the washer and dryer with wall cabinets above. A 240 V receptacle supplies electrical power for the dryer. The Laundry includes a pantry for additional storage. A pull chain lighting outlet is shown. A casement window is centered in the west wall of the Laundry.

Clothes washer outlet boxes provide water supply and waste connections for a clothes washer.

TECH TIPS

Dashed horizontal lines in base cabinets indicate shelves.

TECHTIPS

A weatherproof GFCI receptacle includes a cover to prevent moisture from entering the receptacle.

Screened Porch. The 10'-4" × 14'-0" Screened Porch has a 4" concrete slab that is sloped away from the house. (Refer to Foundation/Basement Plan, Sheet 1.) A screened door leads to the backyard, and a wood center-hinged patio door leads into the Breakfast Area. A weatherproof GFCI receptacle is shown on the east wall.

Garage. The 23'-4" × 21'-2½" Garage has a 4" concrete slab that slopes 2" from the north wall to the Garage door. (Refer to Foundation/Basement

Plan, Sheet 1.) A steel lintel provides a structural base for brick veneer above the overhead door.

A frostproof hose bibb (FP HB), or sillcock, is located on the north wall, and GFCI-protected electrical receptacles are located on the north, east, and west walls. Switches located at the two doors control lighting. The overhead Garage door will be operated by a garage door opener connected to the switched receptacle in the ceiling.

LEARNER RESOURCES

ATPeResources.com/QuickLinks
Access Code: 281467

Name _____ Date _____

Sketch the following on Warner Residence—Floor Plan. For example, the ceiling outlet (13) in the Dining Room is controlled by two three-way switches (15). *Note:* All exterior walls are brick.

1. Brick exterior wall
2. Double-hung window
3. Casement window
4. Exterior door
5. Interior door
6. Pocket door
7. French doors
8. Sliding door
9. Bifold doors

10. Cased opening
11. Water closet
12. Telephone
13. Ceiling outlet
14. Recessed ceiling outlet
15. Three-way switch
16. 120 V receptacle
17. 240 V receptacle

18. 120 V GFI receptacle
19. Pull chain
20. Weatherproof GFI receptacle
21. Ceiling exhaust
22. Kitchen sink
23. Bathtub
24. Hose bibb
25. Shelf and rod

**WARNER RESIDENCE—
FLOOR PLAN**

Name _____ Date _____

True-False

T   F   **1.** A portion of the stairway from the first to the second floor is shown on both floor plans.

T   F   **2.** Exterior elevations are generally drawn to a smaller scale than floor plans.

T   F   **3.** The broad aspects of shape, size, and relationship of rooms are shown on floor plans.

T   F   **4.** Layering on CAD drawings refers to the total area of the house.

T   F   **5.** Electrical fixtures and outlets on floor plans are shown with abbreviations only.

T   F   **6.** Cutting planes for floor plans are taken 3'-0" above the finished floor.

T   F   **7.** Floor plans may be oriented to fit the print sheet.

T   F   **8.** Stairways in plan views are terminated on a break line.

T   F   **9.** The note 2 × 10 JOISTS OVER on a first floor plan indicates that the joists are overhead and support the second floor.

T   F   **10.** Floor plans are generally drawn so that the front view of the house is toward the bottom of the sheet.

T   F   **11.** Abbreviations are not used on floor plans.

T   F   **12.** The cutting plane for second floor plans passes through the house at the upper sash of the windows on the main floor.

T   F   **13.** A two-story house with basement requires three floor plans.

T   F   **14.** A joist is a horizontal framing member that supports the floor.

T   F   **15.** The tread is the vertical portion of a stair step.

T   F   **16.** Floor plans are generally drawn to the scale of ¼" = 1'-0".

T   F   **17.** A typical note gives information pertaining to all similar items on the floor plan.

T   F   **18.** Dashed lines on floor plans show features above the cutting plane.

T   F   **19.** The scale for each room of a floor plan varies to fit the size of the room.

T   F   **20.** The first floor plan is generally studied before second floor or basement floor plan.

Printreading 6-1

Refer to Torrance Residence on page 147.

_____ **1.** A ___ house is shown.
      A. one-story
      B. one-story with basement
      C. one-and-one-half story
      D. two-story with basement

_____ **2.** The Living Room measures ___ × ___.

_____ **3.** The arch between the Entry and the Living Room is shown with ___ lines.

_____ **4.** The upstairs Bathroom contains a ___.
      A. shower, tub, and water closet
      B. vanity, tub, and water closet
      C. vanity, shower, and water closet
      D. vanity and water closet only

T   F **5.** Part of the ceiling in Bedrooms 1 and 2 is sloped.

T   F **6.** A dormer is shown on the rear of the house.

T   F **7.** A dormer is shown on the front of the house.

T   F **8.** The face of the rear dormer is directly above the face of the first floor wall line.

_____ **9.** The house is ___ wide across the front.

_____ **10.** The Patio is laid with ___.
      A. brick
      B. stone
      C. stone with brick details
      D. brick with stone details

_____ **11.** Bedroom ___ is the largest bedroom.

_____ **12.** Two built-in ___ are shown on the upper floor.

T   F **13.** Two risers are shown from the grade to the front door.

T   F **14.** Stairs to the upper floor begin in the Living Room.

T   F **15.** Four exterior doorways are shown on the first floor plan.

_____ **16.** The Dining Area is ___.
      A. part of the Living Room
      B. 11'-4" × 23'-0"
      C. adjacent to the Entry
      D. laid with carpet

_____ **17.** The Family Room has ___.
      A. two windows on the front wall
      B. two windows on the side wall
      C. one window on each wall
      D. no windows

_____ **18.** The house measures ___ from front to back.

T   F   **19.** The Kitchen sink is centered on the Kitchen windows.

T   F   **20.** The upstairs Bathroom measures 5′-6″ × 7′-0″.

TORRANCE RESIDENCE

Printreading 6-2

Refer to Chapman Residence on page 148.

_____ **1.** The house has ___.
- A. a full basement
- B. two fireplaces
- C. a two-car garage
- D. two levels

_____ **2.** The Living Room ___.
- A. is separated from the Dining Room by a room divider
- B. has direct access to Bedroom 1
- C. has a fireplace on the west wall
- D. is part of a Living-Dining Room area

_____ **3.** The Dining Area has ___.
- A. one awning window
- B. a swinging door to the Kitchen
- C. sliding glass doors to the Patio
- D. two casement windows

147

4. The Kitchen ___.

    A. has wall cabinets above the sink

    B. has two flush exterior doors

    C. is U-shaped

    D. also serves as a Laundry

5. The hallway ___.

    A. opens to all bedrooms

    B. has no door that swings out into it

    C. is L-shaped

    D. has two linen closets

6. Regarding closets, ___.

    A. Bedroom 1 has two closets

    B. linen closets have sliding doors

    C. Bedrooms 2 and 3 have closets of equal size

    D. Bathroom 2 has one linen closet

7. Regarding plumbing, ___.

    A. all fixtures in the bathrooms are located along the same wall

    B. two tubs are shown

    C. the Kitchen sink is located under the Kitchen window

    D. the washing machine is located on the east wall of the Kitchen

8. The South Elevation has ___ windows.

    A. double-hung

    B. hopper

    C. casement

    D. awning and horizontal sliding

FIRST FLOOR PLAN

CHAPMAN RESIDENCE

WINDOW & DOOR SCHEDULE	
A	AWNING
B	HOR SLIDING
C	DH
D	DH
E	DH
F	FL DOOR 1 LT
G	SL GL DOORS
H	FL DOOR 2 LT
J	PANEL DOOR
K	GARAGE DOOR
L	FL DOOR
M	FL DOOR
N	SL DOOR
P	BI-FOLD DOOR
Q	SL DOOR

ABBREVIATIONS	
WM	WASHING MACHINE
D	DRYER
REF	REFRIGERATOR
WH	WATER HEATER
R	RANGE
CL	CLOSET
LCL	LINEN CLOSET
LAV	LAVATORY
HOR	HORIZONTAL
DH	DOUBLE HUNG
FL	FLUSH
SL	SLIDING
GL	GLASS

9. The East Elevation has ___ windows.

    A. awning
    B. horizontal sliding
    C. double-hung and fixed sash
    D. double-hung and casement

10. The North Elevation has ___ and ___ windows.

    A. horizontal sliding; double-hung
    B. horizontal sliding; casement
    C. double-hung; casement
    D. awning; double-hung

Identification

Refer to Appendix.

1. Ceiling outlet

2. Bifold doors

3. Double-hung window

4. 240 V receptacle outlet

5. Three-way switch

6. Common brick

7. Telephone

8. Weatherproof receptacle

9. 120 V receptacle outlet

10. Double-acting door

Name _____ Date _____

PRINTREADING 6-1

Refer to Wayne Residence—Foundation/Basement Plan, Sheet 1.

True-False

T   F   **1.** The Porch slab is sloped away from the house.

T   F   **2.** The power panel is located directly beside the furnace.

T   F   **3.** Five 120 V receptacles are shown in the Study.

T   F   **4.** An areaway is shown on the east wall.

T   F   **5.** All exterior walls are brick veneer.

T   F   **6.** A frostproof hose bibb is located on the north wall.

T   F   **7.** Three retaining walls are shown on the exterior of the house.

T   F   **8.** The Garage slab is 4″ thick.

T   F   **9.** The basement contains a total of 4 doors.

T   F   **10.** The Foundation/Basement Plan is drawn to the scale ¼″ = 1′-0″.

T   F   **11.** All steel beams run east to west.

T   F   **12.** A three-way switch controls the ceiling outlet above the stair landing.

T   F   **13.** The overall length of the house is 72′-8″.

T   F   **14.** Casement windows are shown in the Study.

T   F   **15.** The water heater is located in the utility closet.

T   F   **16.** A #6 door is located at the foot of the stairway.

T   F   **17.** The foundation wall at the front of the Garage is notched 6″ for floor slope.

T   F   **18.** The Garage slab slopes 2″ to the door.

T   F   **19.** Steel posts in concrete footing pads in the Storage Area are 9′-2″ OC.

T   F   **20.** Three recessed ceiling fixtures in the family room are controlled by three-way wall switches.

Refer to Wayne Residence—Floor Plan, Sheet 2.

Multiple Choice

_____ **1.** Regarding the Dining Room, ___.
  A. six electrical receptacles are spaced on four walls
  B. awning windows are paired on the south wall
  C. a panned ceiling is shown
  D. wall openings are arched

_____ **2.** Regarding the stairway, ___.
  A. 16 R DN is shown
  B. the stairs are straight run
  C. an interior door is located at the top of the stairs
  D. riser height is 7.392"

_____ **3.** Regarding the Master Bathroom, ___.
  A. a combination tub-shower is shown
  B. the overall size is 7'-3½" × 8'-8"
  C. lighting is provided by a switch-chain outlet
  D. a 3'-0" interior door is shown

_____ **4.** Regarding the Kitchen, ___.
  A. a partition separates the Kitchen and Breakfast Area
  B. a double-bowl sink is shown in the island cabinet
  C. a clock outlet is shown on the west wall
  D. three-way switches control a light fixture above the island

_____ **5.** Regarding the Kitchen, ___.
  A. GFI receptacles serve the countertop
  B. a telephone outlet is located in the west wall
  C. there are three ceiling-mounted light fixtures
  D. a dishwasher is located in the island

_____ **6.** Regarding the Laundry, a ___.
  A. casement window is shown in the south wall
  B. casement window is shown in the west wall
  C. double-hung window is shown in the south wall
  D. double-hung window is shown in the west wall

_____ **7.** Regarding the Laundry, ___.
  A. lighting is provided by a recessed fixture
  B. a floor drain is centered in the room
  C. entry is from the Screened Porch
  D. the pantry has a pull chain light fixture

_____ **8.** Regarding the bedrooms, ___.
  A. all bedrooms are the same size
  B. Bedroom 2 and Bedroom 3 are the same size
  C. Bedroom 1 is smaller than Bedroom 2
  D. Bedroom 1 is the same size as Bedroom 2 and Bedroom 3

_____ **9.** Regarding the bedrooms, ___.

        A. Bedroom 1 is located in the northwest corner of the house

        B. telephone outlets are shown in each bedroom

        C. sliding windows are shown in each bedroom

        D. 28″ interior doors lead to the hallway

_____ **10.** Regarding the bedrooms, ___.

        A. Bedroom 2 has a walk-in closet

        B. Bedroom 3 has a walk-in closet

        C. Bedroom 1 has two linen closets

        D. all closets are the same size

_____ **11.** Regarding the bedrooms, the Deck may be entered directly from ___.

        A. Bedroom 1

        B. Bedroom 2

        C. Bedroom 3

        D. the Master Bath

_____ **12.** Regarding the Living Room, ___.

        A. a cased opening separates the Living Room from the Dining Room

        B. casement windows provide a view of the backyard

        C. the handrail for the stairway is on the west wall

        D. recessed ceiling fixtures are controlled by three-way switches

_____ **13.** Regarding the Garage, ___.

        A. a frostproof hose bibb is located on the south wall

        B. the interior light is controlled by three-way switches

        C. the Garage is accessible from the Laundry Room

        D. there are four GFI receptacles

_____ **14.** Regarding the Screened Porch, ___.

        A. two casement windows are shown in the west wall

        B. a screen door is shown on the east wall

        C. its overall size is 10′-4″ × 14′-0″

        D. entry to the house is through the Laundry

_____ **15.** Regarding the Entry, ___.

        A. a bank of wall switches controls the Porch light, ceiling light, and Entry closet light

        B. sidelights are shown to the left of the exterior door

        C. a telephone outlet is located near the Entry closet

        D. ceramic tile is shown on the floor

PRINTREADING 6-3

Refer to Wayne Residence—Foundation/Basement Plan and Floor Plan, Sheets 1 and 2.

Completion

_____ **1.** Floor plans for the Wayne Residence are drawn to the scale of ___.

_____ **2.** The front of the house faces ___.

_____ **3.** The Garage is 21'-2½" × ___.

_____ **4.** Access to the attic is through a(n) ___ scuttle.

_____ **5.** The concrete footing pad for the fireplace measures ___.

_____ **6.** Seven ___" columns support the steel beams.

_____ **7.** Two ___ outlets provide lighting in the Future Workshop.

_____ **8.** The front foundation wall is stepped down to provide a(n) ___ ledge.

_____ **9.** The Entry is ___ wide.

_____ **10.** The hall bath on the main floor has ___ GFI receptacle(s).

_____ **11.** ___ lavatories are shown in the vanity for the Master Bedroom.

_____ **12.** ___ linen closets are shown on the main floor.

_____ **13.** Bedroom windows on the south wall measure ___ C to C.

_____ **14.** The Dining Room measures 13'-4½" × ___.

_____ **15.** A(n) ___" concrete pier is shown below the front stoop.

_____ **16.** The linen closet at the head of the stairs is ___ deep.

_____ **17.** Lighting for the Deck is controlled by wall switches located in Bedroom 1 and the ___.

_____ **18.** The Garage contains ___ GFI receptacles.

_____ **19.** The east foundation wall is ___" thick.

_____ **20.** A microwave oven is located on the ___ wall of the Kitchen.

_____ **21.** The light fixture in the walk-in closet in Bedroom 3 is operated by a(n) ___.

_____ **22.** Bedroom 1 measures 11'-9½" × ___.

_____ **23.** The Wayne Residence measures ___ across the front.

_____ **24.** The fireplace opening faces ___.

_____ **25.** The ___ bath is the only bathroom with a separate shower.

ELEVATIONS

Elevations (or elevation views) show the exterior of a house or other structure. A minimum of four exterior elevations is required to show all sides of a house. The basic design of the house and the type of roof are shown. Elevations are directly related to floor plans and are generally drawn to the same scale. Symbols and notations are used to simplify elevations. In some cases, interior elevations may also be included in a set of plans to show interior wall details.

OBJECTIVES

1. Define elevations and explain their use in prints.
2. Describe the roof, window, and door information that is shown on elevations.
3. Describe the use of symbols and abbreviations on elevations.
4. Describe the building design process and the main architectural styles.
5. List styles of roofs and describe roof slope.
6. Describe the use of wall openings for windows and doors on elevations.
7. Describe exterior finish information shown on elevations.
8. Describe information shown on the South Elevation for the Wayne Residence.
9. Describe information shown on the East Elevation for the Wayne Residence.
10. Describe information shown on the North Elevation for the Wayne Residence.
11. Describe information shown on the West Elevation for the Wayne Residence.

ELEVATIONS

An *elevation* is a scaled orthographic projection showing the walls of a building. Elevations may be drawn as exterior or interior elevations and may also show additional features of the building. Four exterior elevations, each showing a different side of the building, are part of the working drawings typically prepared by the architect. Exterior elevations show the house design, the location of openings, and the materials to be used.

North, East, South, and West are the four major directions of the compass. Compass directions are most commonly used to designate exterior elevations. The North Elevation shows the side of the building facing north, not the direction a person faces to see that side of the house. The East Elevation shows the side of the house facing east, the South Elevation shows the side of the house facing south, and the West Elevation shows the side of the house facing west. **See Figure 7-1.**

The prints in a set of working drawings all relate to each other. It is often necessary to refer to several print sheets to find all the information on one subject. A complete and comprehensive set of prints is drawn so that the foundation plan, floor plans, and elevations exactly match regarding the location of windows and doors, materials, and other details. Exterior elevations provide a significant amount of information needed to complete the exterior work on a construction project.

Elevations provide a general sense of the building design by showing the exterior finish materials, location of offsets, patios, stairways, bays, dormers, chimneys, and other features. Elevations may also indicate the dimensions and materials to use for footings and foundations.

James Hardie Building Products

Elevations provide a general sense of the building design and show the relationship between building features.

Plan Views and Elevation Views

Figure 7-1

Figure 7-1. Exterior elevations show the exterior sides of a building without adjustments for perspective.

Roof information on elevations includes type of roof design (gable, hip, shed, gambrel, flat, or a combination of these styles), slopes, materials to be used, vents, gravel stops, projection of eaves, and soffits. Where solar panels are to be installed, they may be shown on the roof elevations.

Window and door openings are shown on elevations. For windows, various symbols show window types, sizes, swings, and locations. In a similar manner, standard symbols for doors indicate the types of doors, sizes, number of lights in each door, and locations. Where solar shades or other energy saving window and door treatments are to be installed, they are also shown on elevation drawings.

Typically, elevations contain very few dimensions. Dimensions shown on elevations are usually vertical dimensions that include established grade to finished basement floor, established grade to finished first floor, heights from floor to floor, heights of special windows above a floor, and heights from roof ridges to tops of chimneys. These dimensions are usually provided in feet and inches.

Exterior finish materials appear on exterior elevations and are noted with symbols and abbreviations. Finish materials include types of siding, concrete, concrete masonry units, insulating concrete forms (ICFs), brick, stone, stucco, exterior insulation and finish systems (EIFS), roof shingles, or other materials. Treatment of exterior trim around windows, entrance doorways, columns, posts, balustrades, cornices, and other features are also shown on exterior elevations. Other miscellaneous details shown on exterior elevations include electrical fixtures, utility outlets, hose bibbs, gutters and downspouts, flashing, and waterproofing.

Symbols

Symbols showing building materials and fixtures save space on elevations. Most elevations for residential construction are drawn to the scale of ¼″ = 1′-0″, which is ¹⁄₄₈ the size of the actual building. A scale such as ¼″ = 1′-0″ dictates the use of symbols to clearly show the materials to be used. **See Figure 7-2.**

Building Material Symbols on Elevations

Figure 7-2

FACE BRICK OR COMMON BRICK | HORIZONTAL LAP SIDING | STRUCTURAL CLAY TILE | GLASS

CUT STONE | SHINGLES | CONCRETE MASONRY UNITS | STUCCO

STONE RUBBLE | WOOD PANEL | CONCRETE | SHEET METAL FLASHING

Figure 7-2. Symbols are used on elevations to show building materials.

Abbreviations

Abbreviations are also used on elevations to conserve space. Abbreviations may be used alone, in notations, or with symbols to describe materials. Standard abbreviations are typically used to avoid misinterpretation. Only uppercase letters are used in abbreviations. Abbreviations that form a word are followed by a period. For example, IN. is the abbreviation for inch.

California Redwood Association

A contemporary design includes more complex rooflines, geometric windows, and curved or angled windows and walls.

BUILDING DESIGN

Houses are most commonly designed with room and living space arrangements taken into account as the primary design element. The floor plan is developed first, based upon the living space required. After the room arrangement has been determined, the exterior of the house is planned. Local ordinances and conditions regarding lot size, setback, allowed exterior finish materials, egress requirements, utility availability and location, sustainability or LEED design elements, and house size are considered. Client preferences, types of materials to be used, and overall costs are carefully reviewed.

The use of sustainable construction techniques can have an impact on building design. For example, the location of the structure on the building lot may be influenced by sun and wind patterns to take advantage of light patterns and maximize the insulating properties of natural airflow. The choice of window location and design may also be based on sustainable construction techniques. In addition, roofing materials and shape may incorporate sustainable design characteristics.

Styles

Houses are often designed in a particular style. This style may be traditional or contemporary. A *traditional design* is an architectural design that reflects long-standing design elements. For example, popular designs such as Cape Cod, Colonial, and Old English each have distinctive design elements that appeal to various customers. Traditional design elements commonly include horizontal and vertical window alignment and straight walls with few angular offsets. A *contemporary design* is an architectural design that reflects some more modern trends and may include more complex rooflines, geometric windows, and curved or angled walls.

Details such as the general proportions, roof type, windows, and trim must be consistent with the design. Elevations show the elements of style and design. Whenever a change is shown in a wall or roofline, a modification of the basic rectangular shape of the house is indicated on the elevation.

All visible lines on elevations are drawn as object (solid) lines. Any part of the building below grade level is shown with hidden (dashed) lines. For example, foundation footings, walls below grade, and areaways (window wells) for below-grade windows are shown with hidden lines.

Roofs

The roof of a house protects the structure from the elements. For an attractive and functional finished project, the roof style must be consistent with the style of the house. The six basic roof styles are flat, shed, gable, hip, gambrel, and mansard. **See Figure 7-3.** These roof styles may be modified or combined to produce various roofline designs. Roof styles are most easily seen on elevations.

A flat roof must slope at least ⅛″ per foot of run for proper water runoff. Shed roofs slope in one direction (indicated with arrow) with opposing walls constructed to different heights. Gable roofs slope in two directions and are the most common roof style. Hip roofs slope in four directions. All walls of buildings with hip roofs are the same height. Gambrel roofs have a double slope in two directions. Gambrel roofs are a popular roof style on barns and country-style houses. Mansard roofs have a double slope in four directions and are used for multistory dwellings.

Slope. Roofs must slope to provide proper water runoff. *Slope* is the relationship of unit rise to unit run of a roof. *Unit rise* is the vertical increase in height per foot of run. *Unit run* is a unit of the total run based on 12″. Roof slope is shown on elevations with the pitch symbol. **See Figure 7-4.**

Roof slope may also be expressed as pitch. *Pitch* is the angle a roof slopes from the roof ridge to the outside walls of the building. Pitch is expressed as a fraction.

TECHFACTS

Roof slope is typically shown on a drawing using a pitch symbol. However, fractional pitch may be used on drawings to indicate roof slope. Fractional pitch is calculated by dividing the total rise by the total span.

Roof Styles

Figure 7-3

Figure 7-3. Six basic roof styles are used in residential construction. Roof styles are shown on elevations.

Roof Slope

Figure 7-4

Figure 7-4. Roof slope is shown on elevations with a pitch symbol.

Wall Openings

Windows, doors, and other wall openings such as louvers and vents are shown on elevations in their exact locations. The floor plan, details, and door and window schedules must be referred to for additional window and door information. For example, the elevation shows the general exterior appearance of a window and its vertical location in the wall. The floor plan, however, provides dimensions for the location of the window, typically from the center of the window opening to the corner of the house. The window size may be given on an elevation or on a window schedule, often located on another sheet. **See Figure 7-5.** The architect may include additional window and door information within the written specifications

Windows. The most common window types used in residential construction are fixed sash, double-hung, horizontal sliding-sash, casement, awning, and hopper windows. Elevations show the window sash and hinge locations on a swinging-sash window. Dashed lines are used to show window swing. The apex of the triangle drawn on the window designates the side to be hinged. **See Figure 7-6.**

The size of the light may be shown on elevations. A *light* is a pane of glass. For example, the sash of a window designated 28/24 indicates that the light size is 28″ × 24″. Note that the width is given first when designating window size, followed by the height.

Doors. Flush and panel doors are commonly used in residential construction. A *flush door* is a door with flat surfaces with the stiles and rails within the door. A *panel door* is a door with individual panels between the stiles and rails.

Flush wood doors have either a solid core or a hollow core. A *solid-core door* is a flush door with wood surface veneer and an inner core made of solid wood blocks, engineered wood products, or high-density foam. Solid-core doors are commonly used for exterior openings.

Solid-core doors at least 1¾″ thick are required for exterior openings. At least three hinges are used to support the weight of solid-core doors. A *hollow-core door* is a flush door with wood surface veneers, a solid wood frame, and a mesh core. Hollow-core doors are commonly used for interior openings. A minimum of two hinges are required for interior doors.

TECHFACTS

High-performance windows commonly consist of a multipane unit that is coated with a low-emittance (low-E) coating with argon or krypton gas between the panes.

Figure 7-5. Drawings in a set of prints are related. A window shown on an elevation is also shown on the floor plan. The rough opening size is commonly included on the window schedule.

Window Types

Figure 7-6

Figure 7-6. Symbols on elevations show the window type specified.

Metal doors may be flush or panel style. Metal doors are insulated to minimize thermal transmission and to provide fire protection. Lights, arranged in a wide variety of patterns, make metal doors attractive for exterior openings.

Door hand is the direction a door swings. Door hand is determined from the outside of the door. Hinges and door hand are not shown on elevation views. The floor plan indicates the hinged side and door hand. **See Figure 7-7.**

Exterior Finish

Elevations show the exterior finish of a house or other building. Materials, trim, and miscellaneous details are shown with symbols and described by notations and dimensions. Wood, masonry, and siding of various shapes and materials are shown. Shingles and other roof coverings are drawn as symbols and described on elevations using notes.

Elevations also show decorative features designed to enhance the appearance of the house, including columns, posts, balustrades, and decorative trim around doors, windows, and eaves. Weatherproof electrical receptacles, exterior lighting, frostproof hose bibbs, gutters and downspouts, and flashing may also be shown on elevations.

TECHFACTS

When reading an elevation, first orient yourself with the direction of the North arrow on the floor plan.

READING ELEVATIONS

The plans for the Wayne Residence contain two sheets with exterior elevations. Sheet 3 includes the South and East Elevations while Sheet 4 includes the North and West Elevations.

The title blocks on Sheets 3 and 4 show the name of the plans, scale, drafter, lot number and address, design firm, and sheet numbers. The name of each elevation is provided with its scale. The scale for all exterior elevations of the Wayne Residence is $\frac{1}{4}'' = 1'\text{-}0''$.

South Elevation

The South Elevation shows the front of the house. (Refer to Sheets 1, 2, and 6 showing the symbol designating North. The symbol orients the house and identifies the elevations.)

The hidden (dashed) lines on the South Elevation show the concrete foundation footing and foundation wall. A 1'-0" diameter concrete pier provides additional support for the stoop. The foundation wall is stepped down along the Bedroom area of the house to provide a 6" ledge for the brick veneer. Vertical dimensions indicate distances between finished floors and ceilings. The grade level is shown sloping to the east end of the house.

The South Elevation is finished with brick veneer. Casement windows, marked A and B, are shown. The apex of the hidden lines indicates the hinged side of each window. The Window Schedule on Sheet 5 provides additional window information. Dimensions from the house corners to the centers of the rough openings for these windows are shown on the Floor Plan, Sheet 1. Shutters are indicated on each side of the windows on the South Elevation.

The entry door is a 3'-0" × 6'-8" × 1¾" exterior, metal panel door that is insulated. (Refer to the Door Schedule on Sheet 5.) One sidelight flanks the door. As shown on Sheet 2 of the plans, the center of the rough opening for the door and sidelight is 31'-3" from the framing for the southeast corner of the house (7'-8" + 13'-2" + 7'-8" + 2'-9" = 31'-3") or 31'-7" (31'-3" + 4" = 31'-7") from the finished southeast corner. A column on the stoop supports the roof overhang at the stoop.

The four-section overhead garage door is shown on the South Elevation. (Refer to Sheets 1 and 2 for additional information regarding the garage door and its rough opening size.)

The hip roof on the Wayne Residence has a 6 on 12 slope. The roof is covered with cedar shakes and has a 1'-6" overhang. A chimney is shown rising above the roof.

Notes specify brick bonds to be used on the chimney. (Refer to the Roof Plan on Sheet 5 for additional information regarding the roof and chimney.)

Doors

Figure 7-7

Figure 7-7. Door hand and symbols are shown on plan views.

East Elevation

Foundation footings and walls are stepped down at the retaining wall to compensate for the drop in the lot grade. The east wall is brick veneer with two casement windows, one in Bedroom 1 and the other in the Family Room. The east wall at the rear of the house is finished with 12″ wood lap siding. The East Elevation shows a full-glass wood frame door in the Living Room and a casement window for the Study on the lower level. (Refer to Sheets 1 and 2 and the Window and Door Schedules on Sheet 5 for additional information regarding these wall openings.)

Vertical dimensions provide measurements between finished floors and ceilings. The deck wraps around the north wall of the house. Horizontal dimensions for the deck are shown on Sheet 2. Roof and chimney information is similar to that shown for the South Elevation.

North Elevation

The North Elevation on Sheet 4 shows the rear of the house. Concrete piers, which provide a base for the 4 × 4 ACQ posts supporting the deck, are 1′-0″ diameter. The acronym ACQ stands for alkaline copper quaternary. *Alkaline copper quaternary* is a wood preservative used to prevent decay and make the wood suitable for exterior use. The concrete foundation footing and foundation wall are stepped down at the retaining wall to compensate for the changes in grade on the building lot.

The finish material on the rear wall is 12″ wood lap siding. A vinyl-clad awning window is shown in the areaway of the Future Workshop. (Refer to Sheet 1 and the Window Schedule on Sheet 5 for information on this window.) A break line is used on the areaway so the awning window may be shown with object (solid) lines. A sliding glass door is shown for the Family Room. (Refer to Sheet 1 and the Door Schedule on Sheet 5 for additional information on the sliding glass door.)

A wood-framed, center-hinged patio door leads to the Deck from Bedroom 1, and a wood-framed screen door is shown on the screened Porch. Vinyl-clad casement windows are shown for the Master Bath and Breakfast Area. Fixed aluminum-framed patio replacement windows are shown for the Living Room. (Refer to Sheet 1 and the Window Schedule on Sheet 5.)

Information given for the roof is similar to information given on the other elevations, with the addition of seven roof vents. Roof vents provide ventilation for the attic. The vents are placed on the rear of the house so they will not detract from the overall appearance when the house is viewed from the street.

West Elevation

The West Elevation shows the screened porch and garage end of the house. The concrete foundation footing and foundation wall are shown. The footings for the screened Porch and Garage are at the same level. The lower foundation footing relates to the Future Workshop. An end view of the portion of the Deck that extends from the north side of the house is shown on the West Elevation. The west wall is brick veneer with one vinyl-clad casement window for the Laundry and one six-panel, solid-core wood door for the Garage. (Refer to Sheets 1 and 2 and the Window and Door Schedules on Sheet 5.) Information given for the roof is similar to information given on the other elevations.

TECHFACTS

Inhalation of sawdust from treated wood and panel products should be avoided. An approved particulates mask, gloves, and goggles should be worn.

LEARNER RESOURCES

ATPeResources.com/QuickLinks
Access Code: 281467

Name _____ Date _____

SKETCHING 7-1

Sketch elevation symbols in the spaces provided. Refer to Appendix.

BRICK

CONCRETE

CONCRETE
MASONRY UNITS

CUT STONE

DOUBLE-HUNG
WINDOW

DOOR

Sketching 7-2

Complete the sketch to show the windows hinged on the sides indicated by checkmarks.

Sketching 7-3

Add symbols and notations as required to complete the sketch of the South Elevation.

1. Roof slope 5 on 12

2. Cedar shake roof

3. Full-length shutters on both sides of windows and doors

4. Brick veneer to 4'-0" above finish grade with wood lap siding above

5. Casement window with mullion between the door and window shown

SOUTH ELEVATION

Sketching 7-4

On separate sheets of paper, sketch North, East, South, and West Elevations of the Warner Residence. Add symbols and notations as required.

25 YR SEAL-DOWN ASPHALT SHINGLES ON 15# ROOFING FELT OVER ½" OSB ROOF SHEATHING

12
5

BR1

CL

CL

CL

RANGE

KIT.

DR

BREAKFAST NOOK

B

HALL

CL

CL

ENTRY

LR

CL

BR2

P

FLOOR PLAN
SCALE: 1/4" = 1'-0"

Name _____ Date _____

True-False

T   F   **1.** Elevations are pictorial drawings showing exterior views of a building.

T   F   **2.** Elevations show where exterior openings are located.

T   F   **3.** Major points of the compass may be used to designate elevations.

T   F   **4.** Various prints in a set of plans are related to each other.

T   F   **5.** Most elevations for residential construction are drawn to the scale of ⅛″ = 1′-0″.

T   F   **6.** Abbreviations in notations on elevations may be used with symbols to show building materials.

T   F   **7.** Abbreviations that form a word are followed by a period to distinguish them from the actual word.

T   F   **8.** A Cape Cod house has a traditional design.

T   F   **9.** A flat roof must slope at least ⅛″ per foot to provide for water runoff.

T   F   **10.** The slope of a roof is the relationship of unit rise to unit run.

T   F   **11.** Elevations show horizontal dimensions for door and window openings.

T   F   **12.** The apex of the triangle drawn on a window on an elevation points to the hinged side.

T   F   **13.** A window designated 32/48 indicates that the glass is 48″ wide.

T   F   **14.** Flush doors may be either solid core or hollow core.

T   F   **15.** Three hinges are required for exterior doors in residential construction.

Matching

_____ **1.** Gable roof   A. Double slope in two directions

_____ **2.** Hip roof   B. Double slope in four directions

_____ **3.** Flat roof   C. Minimum slope of ⅛″ per foot

_____ **4.** Gambrel roof   D. Single slope in two directions

_____ **5.** Mansard roof   E. Single slope in four directions

Multiple Choice

_____ **1.** The North Elevation is the ___.
    A. elevation facing north
    B. elevation facing south
    C. direction a person faces to see the north side of the house
    D. front of the house

_____ **2.** The scale of ¼″ = 1′-0″ indicates the drawing is ___ the size of the actual building.
    A. ¼
    B. ¹⁄₁₂
    C. ¹⁄₄₈
    D. ¹⁄₉₆

_____ **3.** ___ roofs are popular on barns and country-style houses.
    A. Flat
    B. Hip
    C. Gambrel
    D. Mansard

_____ **4.** In relation to roofs, unit run is the ___.
    A. vertical increase in roof height
    B. unit of total run
    C. overall distance between building corners
    D. overall distance, less space for brick veneer, between corners

_____ **5.** The hinged side of a door can be determined from the ___.
    A. plot plan
    B. floor plan
    C. elevation
    D. section

_____ **6.** Doors for exterior openings are required to be ___ and at least ___″ thick.
    A. hollow core; 1⅜
    B. hollow core; 1¾
    C. solid core; 1⅜
    D. solid core; 1¾

_____ **7.** The size of a window may be given ___.
    A. on the elevations
    B. on a window schedule
    C. with the height stated first followed by the width
    D. on the plot plan

_____ **8.** Information commonly found on elevations includes ___.
    A. dimensions for locating rough openings for doors and windows
    B. overall size and shape of the lot
    C. dimensions from established grade to finished first floor
    D. size and location of joist spacing

Name _____   Date _____

Refer to Wayne Residence—Elevations, Sheets 3 and 4.

Multiple Choice

_____   **1.** The Wayne Residence is a ___.
  A. one-story house with living space in the attic
  B. two-story house with attached garage
  C. one-story house with full basement
  D. one-story, L-shaped house

_____   **2.** The elevations show the ___.
  A. garage on the South and West Elevations
  B. deck on the North, East, and South Elevations
  C. porch on the South and West Elevations
  D. swing of the exterior doors

_____   **3.** ___ roof vents are shown on the North Elevation.
  A. Four
  B. Five
  C. Six
  D. Seven

_____   **4.** Brick veneer walls are shown on the ___, ___, and ___ Elevations.
  A. North; West; South
  B. East; West; North
  C. West; South; East
  D. South; East; North

_____   **5.** The main level ceiling is ___ above the main level floor.
  A. 8'-0⅛"
  B. 8'-1⅛"
  C. 9'-0⅛"
  D. 9'-1⅛"

_____   **6.** A total of ___ E windows is shown on all elevations.
  A. two
  B. four
  C. six
  D. eight

_____ **7.** The slope of the roof is ___ on 12.
      A. 4
      B. 5
      C. 6
      D. 7

_____ **8.** A total of ___ retaining wall(s) is shown for the Wayne Residence.
      A. one
      B. two
      C. three
      D. four

_____ **9.** A brick ledge is required in the foundation walls shown on the ___ and ___ Elevations.
      A. East; West
      B. North; South
      C. North; West
      D. South; East

_____ **10.** Lap siding is shown on the ___ and ___ Elevations.
      A. South; East
      B. North; West
      C. North; East
      D. North; South

_____ **11.** Elevations are drawn to the scale of ___″ = 1′-0″.
      A. ⅛
      B. ¼
      C. ⅜
      D. 1

_____ **12.** Floor-to-ceiling height in the basement is ___.
      A. 7′-9½″
      B. 8′-1⅛″
      C. 8′-7½″
      D. 7′-0″

_____ **13.** The screened porch is shown on the ___ and ___ Elevations.
      A. South; East
      B. South; West
      C. North; East
      D. North; West

_____ **14.** The front entry door is ___.
      A. a flush door
      B. shown on the North Elevation
      C. a panel door
      D. a wood door

_____ **15.** Shutters are shown ___.
      A. with all B windows
      B. with all A and B windows
      C. on the North Elevation
      D. on the South Elevation

True-False

T   F   **1.** The basement window for the Future Workshop is below finished grade level.

T   F   **2.** The South and East Elevations are shown on Sheet 3.

T   F   **3.** Brick quoins project 1″ and are 24″ wide.

T   F   **4.** A 1′-6″ diameter concrete pier is shown supporting the column on the front porch.

T   F   **5.** Cedar shakes are specified for the roof.

T   F   **6.** The garage floor is above finished grade level.

T   F   **7.** The plans were drawn by PLH.

T   F   **8.** All doors opening to the deck are the same type and size.

T   F   **9.** Paired windows are hinged toward the center.

T   F   **10.** East and West Elevations are drawn to a larger scale than North and South Elevations.

T   F   **11.** The foundation wall on the front of the house is stepped down to provide for the sloping lot.

T   F   **12.** The deck has grade-level access.

T   F   **13.** The retaining wall on the back of the house is sloped to follow the lot slope in the backyard.

T   F   **14.** The lower windows on the East Elevation are aligned vertically.

T   F   **15.** The top of the retaining wall on the East Elevation is flat.

Completion 7-1

_____ **1.** The Wayne Residence is located in ___, Missouri.

_____ **2.** One window and one door are shown on the ___ Elevation.

_____ **3.** A sidelight is shown to the right of the exterior door designated # ___.

_____ **4.** The ___ Elevation shows the front of the house.

_____ **5.** The front yard slopes to the ___ end of the house.

_____ **6.** Finish material on the rear wall is ___″ lap siding.

_____ **7.** ___ 1′-0″ diameter concrete piers support 4 × 4 deck posts.

_____ **8.** A handrail is shown on ___ sides of the deck.

_____ **9.** Masonry information related to the chimney is specified by dimensions and ___.

_____ **10.** ___ brick quoins are located on each front corner of the garage.

Completion 7-2

Place checkmarks in the appropriate boxes to show the windows and doors designated on each elevation view. For example, the checkmark shown indicates that a G window is shown on the North Elevation.

ELEVATION	WINDOWS						DOORS					
	A	B	C	E	F	G	1	2	3	4	5	10
SOUTH												
EAST												
NORTH						✓						
WEST												

Completion 7-3

_____ **1.** The 4 × 4 posts supporting the deck are treated with ___.

_____ **2.** The East Elevation has brick veneer and ___″ lap siding.

_____ **3.** A total of ___ shutters is required for the South Elevation.

_____ **4.** Brick quoins are set out ___″ from the face of the brick veneer.

_____ **5.** The basement ceiling is ___ above the basement floor.

_____ **6.** A(n) ___ door is shown on the West Elevation.

_____ **7.** The roof extends ___ beyond the face of the brick veneer.

_____ **8.** A total of ___ E windows is shown on the North Elevation.

_____ **9.** Roof vents are shown on the ___ Elevation.

_____ **10.** A total of ___ porch column(s) is/are required at the front entrance.

SECTIONS

CHAPTER 8

Sections are created by passing a cutting plane through a portion of a building to show construction details. Longitudinal and transverse sections show the relationships of rooms and floors. Details of platform, balloon, and post-and-beam framing, as well as brick veneer and masonry construction, are shown using sections.

OBJECTIVES

1. Describe how sections and details appear on prints.
2. Compare longitudinal and transverse sections.
3. List and describe the main types of residential construction.
4. Describe platform framing.
5. Describe balloon framing.
6. Describe post-and-beam framing.
7. Discuss brick veneer and masonry construction.
8. Describe the longitudinal and transverse sections of the Wayne Residence.

SECTIONS

Floor plans and elevations provide dimensions indicating overall building size and locations for various building components; show the materials to be used for walls, partitions, and floors; and indicate locations of rough openings for doors and windows. Sections provide additional detailed information about the building. A *section* is a scaled view created by passing a cutting plane vertically through a portion of a building. Sections drawn to a larger scale than the plan from which the cutting plane is taken are known as details. Details provide greater clarity of features due to their larger size.

Typical Details

A typical detail is an enlarged section that shows the materials and construction details common throughout the building. For example, a typical foundation footing and wall section shows, in detail, materials required and necessary dimensions for constructing foundation footings and walls wherever they appear on the set of plans.

A typical wall detail is created by passing a cutting plane vertically through the foundation, footing, and wall shown on the plan view. **See Figure 8-1.** Arrows indicate the direction of sight for the section. For example, the detail of the section is identified as Detail 1 of Sheet A10. The Typical Wall Detail indicates the size of the footing and foundation wall and the size and spacing of rebar. The footing is 10″ × 16″. The foundation wall is 8″ thick. Two #4 rebar are placed horizontally throughout the length of the footing. The foundation wall contains #4 rebar placed horizontally and vertically 4′-0″ OC (on center). The 4″ concrete slab contains 6 × 6—W1.4 × W1.4 welded wire reinforcement.

ITW Ramset/Redhead

Sections provide information about roof and wall sheathing, insulation, and underlayment.

Figure 8-1. Sections are created by passing a cutting plane through a building feature to show its interior details. Details are sections that are drawn to a larger scale.

Wall Detail

Figure 8-1

CUTTING PLANE

DETAIL NUMBER

SHEET NUMBER

SLOPE FLOOR
DOWN 6" TO FD

10" X 16" CONC. FOOTING W/ 2#4'S CONT.

8" CONCRETE FOUNDATION WALL

24'-7"

PLAN VIEW

FIBERGLASS SHINGLES

1 LAYER #15 FELT PAPER

5/8" OSB DECK

ALUM DRIP

ALUM GUTTER W/ DOWNSPOUT

1X6 WOOD FASCIA VINYL CLAD

PERF VINYL SOFFIT ON BOTTOM OF TRUSS (RUN MATERIAL PARALLEL TO HOUSE WALL) WITH 45 DEGREE JOINT AT CORNERS

DECORATIVE DRYVIT SILL SEE ELEVATIONS

1 1/2" DRYVIT STUCCO SYSTEM ON 1/2" OSB PLYWOOD SHEATHING

TJI WOOD BAND

FINISH GRADE

PROTECTIVE BOARD OVER WATERPROOFING

DRAINAGE GRAVEL

4" DIA PERF DRAIN PIPE. EXTEND TO DAYLIGHT

WOOD ROOF TRUSSES @ 2'-0" OC

12" FIB. GL BATT INSULATION

5/8" GYP BD

WOOD HEADER (SEE ROOF FRAMING PLAN)

WINDOW SEE SCHEDULE

2X4 WOOD STUDS AT 16" OC W/ FULL THICKNESS BATT INSULATION

1/2" GYP BD

4" WOOD BASE

3/4" PLYWOOD SUBFLOOR ON TJI COMPOSITE FLOOR JOISTS@16" OC

2X6 PT WOOD PLATE W/ 1/2" DIA ANCHOR BOLTS @ 4'-0" OC

8" CONCRETE FOUNDATION WALL W/ #4'S @ 4'-0" OC VERT AND HORIZ

4" CONC SLAB W/ 6X6-W1.4 X W1.4 WWR WWF ON 6 MIL VAPOR BARRIER OVER 4" WELL-COMPACTED TERMITE TREATED GRANULAR FILL

10" X 16" CONC FOOTING W/ 2#4'S CONT

1'-2"

8'-1"

10'-0"

1'-6"

10"

1'-4"

1
A10

TYPICAL WALL DETAIL

SCALE 3/4"=1'-0"

SECTION DRAWN AS DETAIL

Plan Ahead, Inc.

A 2 × 6 pressure-treated wood sill is secured to the foundation wall with ½″ diameter anchor bolts. Composite floor joists are placed 16″ OC and covered with ¾″ plywood subfloor. Interior wall surfaces are covered with ½″ gypsum board and the ceiling is covered with ⅝″ gypsum board. Exterior walls are sheathed with ½″ oriented strand board (OSB), which is then finished with 1½″ Dryvit® system. The Dryvit system is a type of exterior insulation and finish system (EIFS). An *exterior insulation and finish system (EIFS)* is a system used to provide exterior building protection through application of exterior insulation, insulation board, reinforcing mesh, a base coat of acrylic copolymers and portland cement, and a finish coat of acrylic resins. EIFSs provide an uninterrupted layer of rigid insulation that is attached directly to the building sheathing using adhesives and/or mechanical fasteners.

Longitudinal and Transverse Sections

Passing vertical cutting planes completely through a house to show the relationship of rooms and floors creates longitudinal and transverse sections. A *longitudinal section* is a section created by passing a cutting plane through the long dimension of a house. A *transverse section* is a section created by passing a cutting plane through the short dimension of a house. **See Figure 8-2.** The cutting planes for longitudinal and transverse sections are shown on the floor plan.

In the example, the longitudinal section—Section A-A—is created by passing a cutting plane through the Bathroom, down the Hall, and through the Living Room. The subfloor is ½″ plywood and 1 × 2 cross bridging reinforces the 2 × 10 floor joists placed 16″ OC. Beam pockets in the foundation walls and a 4″ diameter steel post support a W8 × 15

steel beam. The ceiling is covered with ⅝″ gypsum board.

The transverse section—Section B-B—is created by passing a cutting plane through the front door and Entry, across the Hall, and through the Kitchen. Interior walls are covered with ½″ gypsum board. Doors are referenced to a door schedule, shown on another sheet of the prints. Kitchen cabinets and appliances are shown on the west wall of the house. The countertop and 4″ backsplash are made from plastic laminate. A 12″ soffit is above the wall cabinets. Batt insulation is placed between the 2 × 8 ceiling joists that are placed 16″ OC. Rafters are also placed 16″ OC. The exterior of the house is face brick, and the roofing is 25 yr asphalt shingles on 15 lb roofing felt over ½″ OSB sheathing.

RESIDENTIAL CONSTRUCTION

Three common types of residential construction are frame construction, brick veneer construction, and solid masonry construction. Three styles of frame construction are platform (western), balloon, and post-and-beam framing. A brick veneer building may also be considered to be frame construction since the supporting structure is wood or steel framing faced with brick.

In solid masonry construction, the exterior walls are concrete, brick, concrete masonry units, insulating concrete forms (ICFs), stone, structural clay tile, or a combination of masonry products. The other parts of the building, including the floor structure, its supports, and the interior partitions, are conventional frame construction.

TECHTIPS
Steel beams and posts are usually coated with a paint primer to prevent corrosion.

TECHFACTS
Balloon framing has largely been replaced by platform framing due to decreased availability of longer lengths of lumber.

Longitudinal and Transverse Sections

Figure 8-2

Figure 8-2. Longitudinal and transverse sections are created by passing cutting planes through plan views.

Platform Framing

The most common type of residential frame construction is platform framing. *Platform framing* is a system of frame construction in which each story of a building is framed as a unit, with wall studs being one story in height. Exterior walls in a platform-framed building consist of bottom plates, studs, and double top plates. The floor unit consists of joists, subfloor, and solid or cross bridging. The main characteristic of platform framing is that a complete floor system is built as a platform at each level.

In platform framing, studs in exterior walls, load-bearing interior partitions, and beams through the center of a building support floor members. **See Figure 8-3.** Exterior wall studs are cut and arranged to provide rough-framed openings for the doors and windows. Horizontal members, such as joists or rafters, support floor or roof members. An OSB or plywood subfloor and exterior wall sheathing tie the building members together and provide the stiffness needed to resist strong winds and other lateral forces.

A sill plate is the lowest member of platform framing. Sill plates are pressure-treated lumber, typically 2 × 6s or 2 × 8s, that are bolted to the top of the foundation wall to act as a base for the floor joists. Floor joists or floor trusses rest on the sill plates and are tied together around the perimeter of the structure by a header joist, which maintains floor joist alignment. Floor joists or floor trusses are commonly spaced 16″ OC so that subfloor panel edges fall directly over the joists. Longer floor joists are supported by glued laminated (glulam) or steel beams on steel posts set on concrete footings. Solid or cross bridging may be installed between the floor joists to strengthen and stiffen the floor and prevent the joists from twisting.

OSB or plywood subfloor panels are fastened to the top of floor joists in a staggered pattern. The exterior walls and partitions are then laid out and built on the subfloor, squared, raised into position, plumbed, and properly braced. Each exterior wall panel is covered with exterior sheathing and housewrap to provide both lateral structural support and energy efficiency.

Second floor joists or trusses are placed on top of the double top plates of the first floor walls and bearing partitions and are fastened together. The second floor OSB or plywood subfloor panels are then fastened to the tops of the joists to cover the platform. Exterior walls and interior partitions are laid out and built on the subfloor, squared, raised into position, plumbed, and properly braced. Prefabricated trusses may be set in place on the top of the walls of the top floor of the structure to provide a nailing surface for roof sheathing as well as a surface for attaching ceiling finish materials. If trusses are not used, ceiling joists are laid on the uppermost double top wall plates, and rafters are cut and placed on the wall plates to transfer the load of the roof to the walls. The roof is then sheathed and covered with the roof finish materials.

TECHTIPS
Oriented strand board (OSB) is a panel product made of layers of wood strands bonded together with a phenolic resin.

Exterior walls in platform framing commonly have a double top plate and solid headers.

Platform Framing

Figure 8-3

RIDGE BOARD

RAFTER

GABLE-END STUDS

CEILING JOISTS

DOUBLE TOP PLATE

DOUBLE TOP PLATE

SUBFLOOR

STUD

BOTTOM PLATE

PARTITION PLATE

DOUBLE TOP PLATE

HEADER JOIST

BEARING PARTITION

CORNER POST

BOTTOM PLATE

CROSS BRIDGING

STUD

FIRST FLOOR JOISTS

BOTTOM PLATE

SILL PLATE

REBAR

WALL SHEATHING

STEEL BEAM

FOUNDATION WALL

HEADER JOIST

SUBFLOOR

WALL SHEATHING

Figure 8-3. Studs in platform-framed buildings are one story high.

Balloon Framing

Balloon framing is a system of frame construction in which one-piece exterior wall studs extend from the first floor line or sill plate to the double top plate. Balloon framing is not commonly used in new construction but may be encountered in remodeling work. Studs at bearing partitions are as long as conveniently possible to reduce shrinkage. Minimal shrinkage is especially valuable when brick veneer, EIFS, or stucco is used as an exterior finish material on a building over one floor in height.

TECHFACTS

Pressure-treated sill plates are required by most model building codes.

As in platform framing, the sill plate in a balloon-framed building is also the lowest member and is bolted to the top of the foundation wall. **See Figure 8-4.** Floor joists and studs are fastened together on the sill, and fire-stop blocks are fastened to the floor joists and studs. The floor joists may be stiffened with cross bridging, and the subfloor is fastened to the tops of the floor joists. Let-in braces, metal straps, or plywood panels are used to stiffen the structure.

A 1 × 4 ribbon is notched into the studs or a horizontal ledger and is fastened to the studs at the second floor. Floor joists rest on the ribbon and are fastened to the studs. Fire-stop blocks and fireblocking are installed. Fireblocking impedes the spread of a fire through an otherwise open wall cavity by stopping airflow. Second floor bridging may be installed between the floor joists. The subfloor is fastened to the tops of the second floor joists. Prefabricated trusses are set in place, or ceiling joists and rafters are fastened to the double top wall plate. The roof is sheathed and covered with roof finish materials.

Kolbe & Kolbe Milwork Co., Inc.

Wide expanses of glass in exterior walls, plank ceilings, and heavy exposed beams are key characteristics of post-and-beam framing.

Post-and-Beam Framing

Post-and-beam framing is a system of frame construction in which posts and beams provide the primary structural support. Post-and-beam framing provides for wide expanses of glass in exterior walls and allows for large unobstructed areas inside the building. Plank ceilings and heavy exposed beams are key characteristics of post-and-beam structures. Solid or built-up glued and laminated (glulam) beams used to support the floor and roof are spaced at wide intervals.

Planks of 2″ nominal thickness are used for floors and roofs to span the wider distances and provide structural support. The *nominal size* of a piece of wood is its size before it is planed to finished size. For example, a plank with a 2 × 8 nominal size is $1\frac{1}{2}″ \times 7\frac{1}{2}″$ when planed to finished size. Tongue-and-groove planks are commonly used in post-and-beam framing.

Structural insulated panels may be used to cover roofs and walls. A *structural insulated panel* is a structural member consisting of a thick layer of rigid foam insulation pressed between two OSB or plywood panels. Structural insulated panels require less time to install than planks.

TECHTIPS

Structural insulated panels (SIPs) are available in many standard sizes ranging from 4′ × 6′ to 8′ × 24′.

Balloon Framing

Figure 8-4

RAFTER

CEILING JOIST

DOUBLE TOP PLATE

LET-IN BRACE

PANEL CORNER BRACING

SECOND FLOOR JOISTS

SUBFLOOR

RIBBON

FIRST FLOOR JOISTS

STUDS NOTCHED FOR RIBBON

CROSS BRIDGING

SILL PLATE

FOUNDATION WALL

STUD

SECOND FLOOR JOISTS

FIRESTOP BLOCK

RIBBON

FIREBLOCKING

SECOND FLOOR

FIRESTOP BLOCK

FIRST FLOOR JOISTS

STUD

SILL PLATE

REBAR

SILL CONSTRUCTION

Figure 8-4. Studs in balloon-framed buildings extend from the sill plate to the double top plate.

Posts are usually spaced at equal intervals in exterior walls to support roof or ceiling beams. Posts may also be used at the center of a building, or a load-bearing partition may be used to support the ridge beam.

In post-and-beam framing, the sill plate is also the lowest wood member. The sill plate is fastened to the top of the foundation wall using anchor bolts. **See Figure 8-5.** Header joists and floor beams are fastened to the sill plate and the plank floor is laid. A bottom plate is installed on the plank floor above the header joists to support the posts. The posts are 4 × 4 or larger and extend up from the bottom plate to a 4 × 6 or larger girder. Roof beams are cut to fit the girder and the ridge beam. Structural insulated panels or 2″ planks are then applied as the roof.

Brick Veneer Construction

Brick veneer construction is frame construction with a brick exterior facing. Brick veneer walls may be constructed with platform-framed or balloon-framed structures. An air space is maintained between the brick veneer and the exterior wall sheathing or the exterior wall wrap material to permit both the flow of air and movement between the two walls. Metal ties are set in horizontal mortar joints during construction and fastened to wall studs to attach the brick veneer wall to the frame construction. Weep holes at the base of the brick veneer wall allow moisture to escape.

The foundation wall for brick veneer construction is offset to provide a supporting base for the brick veneer. **See Figure 8-6.** Metal or plastic base flashing extends up at least 6″ behind the housewrap to prevent moisture from penetrating into the structure.

Masonry Construction

Masonry construction is a system of construction in which masonry units such as brick, concrete masonry units, stone, or structural clay tile are formed into walls to carry the load of floor and roof joists. Fire-cut wood joists are set into a notch in a masonry wall and secured with joist anchors that are designed to pull out of the wall in case of fire. A *fire cut* is an angled cut in the end of a wood joist that allows a burnt joist to fall out of the wall structure without disturbing the solid brick wall. Without a fire cut, the falling joist could cause the masonry wall to collapse.

Figure 8-5. Large wood members provide structural support in post-and-beam construction.

Post-and-Beam Framing
Figure 8-5

Figure 8-6. Brick veneer construction is frame construction with brick exterior facing.

Brick Veneer Construction
Figure 8-6

WALL SHEATHING

STUD

BOTTOM PLATE

SUBFLOOR

FLOOR JOIST

HEADER

SILL PLATE

SILL SEALER

FOUNDATION WALL

HOUSEWRAP

METAL TIES FASTENED TO STUDS

WEEP HOLES 4'-0" OC. OMIT MORTAR FROM VERTICAL JOINTS

EXTEND METAL BASE FLASHING AT LEAST 6" BEHIND HOUSEWRAP

Foundation footings and walls sufficient to carry the load serve as the base for solid masonry walls. **See Figure 8-7.** The first floor joists rest on a wythe of concrete masonry units or brick. A *wythe* is a single continuous masonry wall, one unit thick. The balance of the solid masonry wall is two units thick. Upper-story wood ceiling and roof joists are fire cut. Load-bearing partitions through the center of the building are platform framed.

READING SECTIONS

Interior spaces of the Wayne Residence are shown on the sections on Sheet 7. Cutting planes for the section views are shown on Sheet 2. Longitudinal Section A-A is created by the cutting plane passing through the Garage, Dining Room, Entry, Hallway, and Walk-in Closet. Transverse Section B-B is created by the cutting plane passing through the Living Room, Entry, and Entry

door. Both section views are drawn to the scale of $\frac{1}{4}" = 1'-0"$.

Longitudinal Section A-A

Longitudinal Section A-A is created by passing a cutting plane through the long dimension of the Wayne Residence. A W8 × 10 steel beam resting on a 4" diameter steel post is shown in the Family Room. An additional steel column is shown in the Storage Area. The upper portion of the #6 door at the foot of the stairway is visible. Two shelves in the Walk-in Closet of Bedroom 3 are made of 1 × material. Clothes rods are also shown. Doors to the Master Bedroom, Hall Bath, Linen Closet, and the door leading from the Garage to the Kitchen are referenced on the Door Schedule.

Floor-to-ceiling clearances and sizes of framing materials for the roof complete the longitudinal section. Ceiling joists are 2 × 10s and roof rafters are 2 × 8s.

Masonry Construction
Figure 8-7

- BRICK PARAPET WALL
- ROOF JOIST
- CEILING JOIST
- DOUBLE TOP PLATE
- FIRE CUT JOIST
- BEARING PARTITION STUD
- FIRST FLOOR JOIST
- BOTTOM PLATE
- S BEAM
- STEEL COLUMN
- FLOOR SLAB
- COLUMN FOOTING
- FOUNDATION WALL
- FOUNDATION FOOTING

Figure 8-7. Masonry construction uses solid masonry walls to carry the load of floor and roof joists.

Transverse Section B-B

Transverse Section B-B is created by passing a cutting plane through the short dimension of the Wayne Residence. The Stair Detail, also shown on Sheet 7, is directly related to the stairway seen on this section. A wrought iron handrail extends from the Hallway to the Living Room.

An 18″ concrete pier supports a 4″ column at the front of the house. Doors and windows are referenced on the schedules, and floor-to-ceiling heights are provided.

LEARNER RESOURCES

ATPeResources.com/QuickLinks
Access Code: 281467

Name _____ Date _____

Sketching 8-1

In the space provided, sketch a typical section of a platform-framed house from the concrete foundation footing to 24" above the finished first floor. Use the ¾" = 1'-0" scale. Label all parts of the sketch.

1. 10" × 20" foundation footing w/ 2" × 4" keyway and 3 #4 rebar horizontal continuously and #4 rebar horizontal at 2'-0" OC

2. 4" PVC drain tile

3. 10" × 36" foundation wall to 6" above grade level with #4s horizontal continuously at 1'-0" OC and #4s vertical at 2'-0" OC

4. Termite shield

5. 2 × 6 sill plate with ½" Ø × 8" anchor bolts

6. 2 × 10 header joists

7. 2 × 10 floor joists with 1 × 2 wood cross bridging

8. ½" OSB subfloor

9. ¾" oak tongue-and-groove finished floor

10. 2 × 6 bottom plate

11. 2 × 6 studs

12. ½" exterior OSB sheathing

13. 8" vinyl siding

14. ½" gypsum board

15. R-21 batt insulation in walls

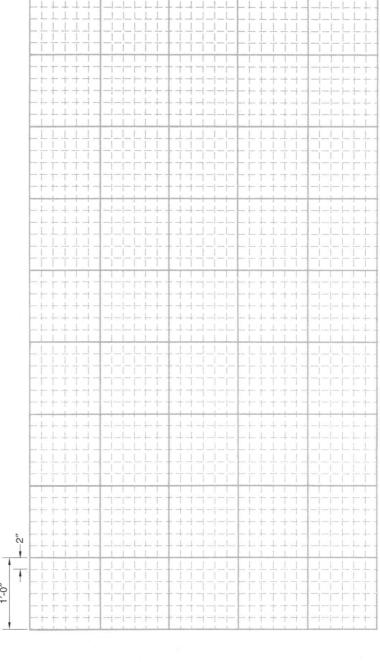

Sketching 8-2

In the space provided, sketch a typical section of a balloon-framed house from the concrete footing to 24" above the finished first floor. Use the ¾" = 1'-0" scale. Label all parts of the sketch.

1. 10" × 20" foundation footing with V-shaped keyway and two #4 rebar horizontal continuously and #4 rebar horizontal at 2'-0" OC

2. 4" PVC drain tile

3. 10" × 30" foundation wall to 4" above grade level with #4s horizontal continuously at 1'-0" OC and #4s vertical at 2'-0" OC

4. Termite shield

5. 2 × 8 sill plate with ½" Ø × 8" anchor bolts

6. 2 × 10 floor joists with solid bridging

7. Batt insulation to 30" in from exterior wall

8. 2 × 10 fire-stop blocking

9. ¾" plywood subfloor

10. Vinyl tile finished floor

11. 2 × 6 studs

12. ½" exterior OSB sheathing

13. 4" wood lap siding

14. ½" gypsum board

15. R-21 batt insulation in walls

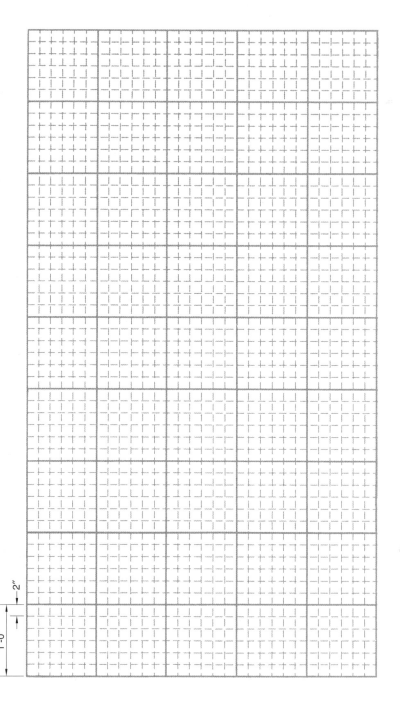

Name _____ Date _____

Identification 8-1

_____ **1.** Floor joist

_____ **2.** Sill plate

_____ **3.** Cross bridging

_____ **4.** Wall double top plate

_____ **5.** Fireblocking

_____ **6.** Ribbon

_____ **7.** Solid bridging

_____ **8.** Partition stud

_____ **9.** Ceiling joist

_____ **10.** Rafter

_____ **11.** Steel beam

_____ **12.** Foundation wall

_____ **13.** Partition double top plate

_____ **14.** Steel post

_____ **15.** Rebar

Completion

Refer to the Typical Wall Section of the Garner Residence on page 191.

_____ **1.** Ties for brick veneer are spaced ___" OC vertically.

_____ **2.** The concrete foundation wall measures ___ from the top of the foundation footing to the bottom of the sill plate.

_____ **3.** Roof trusses are placed ___" OC.

_____ **4.** R-___ batt insulation is placed in exterior walls.

_____ **5.** Floor support is provided by 12" top-bearing floor ___.

_____ **6.** Metal flashing extends ___ below the bottom wythe of brick.

_____ **7.** The foundation footing contains ___ continuous #4 rebar.

_____ **8.** The inside of the exterior wall is finished with ___.

_____ **9.** The eave overhang measures ___ at an 8/12 slope.

_____ **10.** Medium ___ shingles are applied to the roof.

_____ **11.** Anchor bolts are spaced ___" OC in the foundation wall.

_____ **12.** The foundation wall is ___" wide.

_____ **13.** The Typical Wall Section for the Garner Residence is drawn to the scale of ___.

_____ **14.** Batt or ___ insulation may be used above the ceiling.

_____ **15.** The subfloor is ___" plywood.

True-False

T F **1.** Sections are created with cutting planes.

T F **2.** A typical section shows details of material and construction common to that type of construction throughout the building.

T F **3.** Detail 2/6 is found on Sheet 2.

T F **4.** A transverse section is made by passing a cutting plane through the long dimension of a house.

T F **5.** Solid masonry is a type of frame construction.

T F **6.** The most common type of residential construction is platform framing.

T F **7.** The sill plate is the lowest wood member in platform framing.

T F **8.** Studs run full length from the sill plate to the double top plate in balloon framing.

T F **9.** Solid or built-up beams may be used in post-and-beam construction.

T F **10.** The nominal size of a piece of wood is its size after planing.

MEDIUM SHAKE SHINGLES ON 30# FELTS ON 1/2" PLYWD SHEATHING. (15# UNDERLAYMENT FELT)

ROOF PITCHES PER ELEV'S.

2x6 FASCIA HDR

1x8 FASCIA W/EDGE FLASHNG

FREE SPAN ROOF TRUSSES AT 24" OC

8'-1" PL

R19 BATT OR BLOWN INSUL W/ INSUL BAFFLE

2x4 FRAMING AT 24" OC

1x WD TRIM

PLYWD SOFFIT

1'-7" AT 8/12
1'-3" AT 10/12

1/2" INSUL SHEATHING

BRICK VENEER W/TIES 16" OC VERT AND 32" OC HORIZ

R13 BATT INSUL (TYP)

GYP BD

WD BASE

2x6 SILL PLATE IN SILL INSUL

3/4" PLYWD FLR SHEATHING

5 1/4"

FLR LINE

3"

GRADE

1'-0"

2'-9"

12"D TOP BRNG FLR TRUSSES

1/2# DIA A B AT 48" OC
SILL FLASHING

5" 5"

CONC STEM WL W/3 #4 CONTIN HORIZ AND #4 BARS AT 48"OC VERT

#4 DOWELS AT 4'-0" OC

18"
6"

0'-10"

1'-8"

CONC FTG W/3 #4 BARS CONTIN

SCALE: 3/4"=1'-0"

GARNER RESIDENCE

191

Identification 8-2

_____ **1.** Foundation wall
_____ **2.** Rafter
_____ **3.** First floor joist
_____ **4.** Sill plate
_____ **5.** Double top plate
_____ **6.** Partition plate
_____ **7.** Ceiling joist

_____ **8.** Plywood subfloor
_____ **9.** Rebar
_____ **10.** Header Joist
_____ **11.** Ridge board
_____ **12.** Corner post
_____ **13.** Stud
_____ **14.** Cross bridging

Name _____ Date _____

Refer to Wayne Residence—Sections and Detail, Sheet 7.

Multiple Choice

_____ **1.** Regarding the stairway, ___.
    A. 12 risers are shown
    B. 14 risers are shown
    C. treads are 1 × 10 oak
    D. a ½″ nosing is required for each tread

_____ **2.** Regarding roof framing, ___ are required.
    A. 2 × 8 rafters and ceiling joists
    B. 2 × 10 rafters and ceiling joists
    C. 2 × 8 rafters and 2 × 10 ceiling joists
    D. 2 × 10 rafters and 2 × 8 ceiling joists

_____ **3.** Regarding doors, the ___.
    A. #7 doors shown in Longitudinal Section A-A are located in the Living Room
    B. #5 door is 30″ wide
    C. #3 door leads to the Deck
    D. #6 door is located at the top of the stairway

_____ **4.** Regarding concrete work, ___.
    A. an 18″ diameter concrete pier supports the 4″ column at the Front Entry
    B. the basement floor is a 6″ concrete slab
    C. a 10″ concrete footing pad is located under the 3″ diameter steel column
    D. the basement walls are CMUs

_____ **5.** Regarding the roof, the ___.
    A. ridge board is shown in the longitudinal section
    B. roof slope is 1 in 5
    C. roof is finished with asphalt shingles
    D. roof is a hip roof

_____ **6.** Regarding ceiling heights, the ___.
    A. basement ceiling height is 7′-9½″
    B. main level ceiling height is 8′-11⅛″
    C. distance from the basement floor to the main level ceiling is 17′-⅝″
    D. height of the ceiling joists is included in the ceiling height calculation

_____ **7.** The panned ceiling is in the ___.
        A. Living Room
        B. Family Room
        C. Breakfast Area
        D. Dining Room

_____ **8.** Regarding the scale, ___.
        A. both sections are drawn to the same scale
        B. Section A-A is drawn to a full scale
        C. Section B-B is drawn to a 1" = 1'-0" scale
        D. the scale is irrelevant

_____ **9.** Regarding wall finish materials, ___.
        A. the Living Room wall is papered
        B. the Family Room wall is paneled
        C. the bedroom walls are to be finished by the owner
        D. wall finish information is not provided in the sections

_____ **10.** Regarding framing, ___ is shown.
        A. platform framing
        B. balloon framing
        C. solid masonry construction
        D. post and beam framing

True-False

T   F   **1.** The storage area has a concrete slab floor.

T   F   **2.** A cased opening provides a passageway between the Dining Room and Living Room.

T   F   **3.** The Wayne Residence roof is covered with cedar shakes.

T   F   **4.** Two interior stairwells provide a passageway between the basement level and main level.

T   F   **5.** The stair landing is 4'-0" deep.

T   F   **6.** Attic access is provided by a built-in stairway.

T   F   **7.** A wrought iron handrail separates the Living Room from the stairwell.

T   F   **8.** The roof is framed with trusses.

T   F   **9.** Total tread width including the nosing is 10½".

T   F   **10.** The Stair Detail is drawn to a ¼" = 1'-0" scale.

Completion

_____ **1.** The carriages for the stairway are cut from ___.

_____ **2.** The roof slopes ___" in 12".

_____ **3.** The earth symbol is shown only in Section ___.

_____ **4.** The deck handrail is made of ___-treated lumber.

_____ **5.** The stairway landing is constructed with ___" T&G plywood.

DETETAILS

Details are sections, elevations, or plan views drawn at a larger scale to provide additional information about a building. A cutting plane indicates where section details are taken. Identifiers on the cutting plane indicate the applicable section. Details are commonly drawn to show structural, window and door, and trim details.

OBJECTIVES

1. Explain the relationship of details to scales.
2. Discuss dimensions.
3. List and describe the different types of references.
4. Describe details of interior wall elevations.
5. Explain the use of structural details.
6. Explain the use of window and door details.
7. Explain when trim details are used.
8. Describe the details shown on the Wayne Residence plans.

DETAILS

Architects work to include all the graphic information required by everyone involved in the construction process on plan views and elevations. Specifications provide additional written explanations and descriptions. Some features, however, must be drawn at a larger scale since sufficient information cannot be shown for some items at the smaller scale of plans and elevations.

A *detail* is a scaled plan, elevation, or section drawn to a larger scale to show special features. **See Figure 9-1.** Prints for residential construction may include details of interior wall construction, structural parts and special features, windows and doors, and exterior and interior trim. Details are usually drawn to a larger scale than the view from which they are taken.

Scales

Details of sections showing structural construction information for components such as footings and walls, floor systems, and stairways are drawn at a larger scale than the view from which they were taken to provide greater

clarity. Details of special features such as fireplaces, stair trim, and windows are also drawn at a larger scale. Exterior trim details showing cornices, dormers, and entryways and interior trim such as cabinets, bookcases, mantels, and wall trim are drawn at a larger scale as well.

An elevation detail of a plan view may be drawn at the same scale as the plan view. The use of the same scale allows dimensions to be transferred directly from the plan view to the elevation detail.

American Hardwood Export Council

A detail is required to construct built-in features such as a built-in desk or cabinets.

Details

Figure 9-1

Figure 9-1. Details are sections, elevations, or plan views drawn to a larger scale to show more information.

The scale at which a detail is drawn depends on the complexity of the features that need to be shown and take into account the amount of space available on the print sheets. The following are preferred scales for detail views:

- ¾″ = 1′-0″
- 1½″ = 1′-0″
- 3″ = 1′-0″

These scales allow measurements to be worked out on the job site with a tape measure. For example, at a scale of ¾″ = 1′-0″, each ¹⁄₁₆″ on a tape measure represents 1″. At a scale of 1½″ = 1′-0″, each ⅛″ on a tape measure equals 1″. At a scale of 3″ = 1′-0″, each ¼″ on a tape measure equals 1″ and each ¹⁄₁₆″ on the tape measure equals ¼″.

When using a tape measure to calculate dimensions, beginning at the 1″ mark ensures accuracy. **See Figure 9-2.** When scaling critical dimensions on a drawing, the dimensions must be approved by the engineer or architect for the construction project. Scaling critical dimensions is only done when no other means of obtaining the proper dimensions are available.

Full-size details are rarely drawn for residential construction unless the feature is very small or very complex. For example, full-size details may be shown for small features such as moldings or complex parts such as stair handrails.

Dimensions

If dimensions are not shown on plan views and elevations, they will be shown on details. Generally, dimensions are repeated from drawing to drawing only when necessary. Confusion results in the instances where the same feature is unintentionally dimensioned differently on different portions of the drawings. When dimensions are shown only once, it may be necessary to refer to several portions of the prints to determine the dimension.

Sealing Dimensions

Figure 9-2

³/₄″ = 1′-0″   1¹/₂″ = 1′-0″   3″ = 1′-0″

SCALE	TAPE MEASURE
³/₄″ = 1′-0″	¹/₁₆″ = 1″
1¹/₂″ = 1′-0″	¹/₈″ = 1″
3″ = 1′-0″	¹/₄″ = 1″

Figure 9-2. A tape measure may be used to scale detail dimensions on a job site. Critical dimensions must be approved by an engineer or architect.

The two basic types of dimensions are location dimensions and size dimensions. A *location dimension* is a dimension that gives the relationship of a particular component or building feature in relation to another feature. For example, a dimension showing the distance from a building corner to the center of a rough opening for a window is a location dimension. A *size dimension* is a dimension that indicates the length, width, and depth of a particular area or feature. For example, dimensions showing the overall size of a house and dimensions showing the height and width of foundation footings are size dimensions.

Architects place dimensions on the most appropriate view for the construction component or feature being shown. It is often necessary to refer to several prints to identify all dimensions related to a particular component or feature.

References

Details contain notations that refer to the view from which they are taken through cutting plane lines, direction of sight symbols, and notations. These notation references indicate that more information is available on a particular sheet of the prints. Where possible, a detail is placed on the same sheet as its notation reference.

Cutting Planes. Cutting planes are imaginary slices passing through a feature to show its cross section and provide additional construction details. A *cutting plane line* is a line that identifies the exact place where the cutting plane passes through the feature. Arrows on a cutting plane line indicate the direction of sight for the section. When several sections are taken through walls, foundations, or other parts of a building, they are designated with a section notation and an alphabetic identifier, for example, SECTION A-A.

Notations. A notation such as SEE DETAIL is often used to indicate that additional information concerning the referenced feature is shown elsewhere on the prints. Notations with symbols may be used to indicate the direction of sight for interior elevation details. The elevation detail number and the sheet number on which the detail is drawn are shown on the symbol. **See Figure 9-3.**

TECHFACTS

A cutting plane line is a thick line consisting of a long dash and two short dashes.

For example, a symbol with the notation 1/5 refers to DETAIL 1, SHEET 5 and a symbol with the notation 2/5 refers to DETAIL 2, SHEET 5. For typical details, no specific reference is required.

The detail is noted as a typical detail by a notation such as TYPICAL WALL SECTION. This typical wall section drawing is then included on a print sheet with other general detail drawings.

Notations

Figure 9-3

PICTORIAL VIEW

ELEVATION

SECTION DETAIL

PLAN VIEW

ELEVATION DETAIL

Figure 9-3. References for section details are shown using cutting plane lines, direction of sight symbols, and notations. References for elevation details typically include direction of sight symbols and notations.

Interior Wall Elevations

Details of interior wall elevations provide more information than is shown on the plan view. The plan view of a kitchen shows the location of base and wall cabinets, space for the sink and built-in appliances such as dishwashers, and microwave or wall ovens, and any spaces for movable appliances such as refrigerators and ranges. Other information on a plan view indicates the location of windows, doors, and structural parts of the building along with electrical receptacles and outlets.

However, tradesworkers need additional information to build and finish soffits, cabinets, and countertops, and to install lighting, ventilation hoods, fans, and other features. Manufacturer specifications and dimensioned drawings may be included as part of the working drawings.

The plan view of a Kitchen and its elevation details are related. **See Figure 9-4.** The plan view shows that the Kitchen and Breakfast Room measure 11'-8" × 19'-4". L-shaped base and wall cabinets are placed on the south and east walls, and an island cabinet containing a range and grill separates the Kitchen and Breakfast Room. The location of appliances, electrical receptacles, telephone outlet, windows, broom closet, and the cased opening to other rooms of the house are also shown on the floor plan. The three elevations of the kitchen provide additional information on features such as cabinet doors, countertop and full backsplash, paneled broom closet doors, and a brick surround on the island cabinet with a copper hood above. Height dimensions for the cabinets are also given.

TECHFACTS

A kitchen work triangle extends from the refrigerator to the sink to the range. An efficient work triangle should not exceed 21'.

Kitchen Wall Elevations
Figure 9-4

PLAN VIEW

SOUTH WALL ELEVATION DETAIL

EAST WALL ELEVATION DETAIL

WEST WALL ELEVATION DETAIL

Figure 9-4. Kitchen elevation details supplement information shown on the floor plan.

The plan view of a Bath and its elevation details are related. **See Figure 9-5.** The plan view shows a Bath containing a water closet and bathtub with a separate 5'-0" × 6'-0" Powder Room. By relating the plan view to the elevation detail, the tradesworker can see that the double-bowl vanity measures 30" × 6'-0". The vanity has three drawer units and has a shelf running along its length. GFI receptacles are located in walls on both ends of the vanity. A 4'-0" × 5'-11" mirror rests on the 6" vanity backsplash and extends to the 12" soffit. Two #3 doors are shown. The closet on the Powder Room has a pocket door, identified as a #5 door. Additional information concerning the size of doors is given on a Door Schedule included elsewhere on the prints. The closet is illuminated by a pull chain light fixture. Shelves in the Powder Room closet extend from floor to ceiling.

Figure 9-5. Bath elevation details supplement information shown on the floor plan.

Bath Wall Elevation
Figure 9-5

PLAN VIEW

SECTION A-A

ELEVATION

The tub and water closet are located in a 5'-0" × 6'-0" room with ceramic tile from floor to soffit. The tub has a sliding door. The soffit is the same size as the soffit in the Powder Room. A 36" × 42" wall cabinet is hung above the water closet and extends to the soffit.

Illumination for the Bath and Powder Room is provided by ceiling lights controlled by wall switches. A wall switch also controls the ceiling fan above the water closet. The floor for the Bath and Powder Room is ceramic tile.

Other walls throughout a house may have special treatments that also require elevations to show greater detail. For example, fireplaces, bookcases, and special window trim may be shown on elevation details.

Structural Details

A section drawing of the foundation footings and walls provides structural information. Frequently, more structural information is required. For example, more information is required when the foundation footings and walls need to be formed differently in order to meet special conditions, such as grade slopes or varying load requirements. Details are drawn to provide additional construction information. Each detail is labeled with letters that correspond to letters on the plan view. Arrows on a plan view show the direction of sight of the detail. **See Figure 9-6.**

TECHFACTS

To interlock basement walls and footings, a keyway is formed along the top of the footing to improve shear strength.

Stair details provide dimensions and other critical information needed to properly construct a stairway.

Structural Details

Figure 9-6

FOUNDATION PLAN

SECTION A-A
TYPICAL
WALL SECTION

SECTION B-B
TAKEN AT OPENING TO
PATIO GLASS DOORS

SECTION C-C
TAKEN AT WINDOWS
NO MASONRY

SECTION D-D
TAKEN AT FRONT
ENTRANCE

SECTION E-E
SHOWING CARPORT FLOOR

SECTION F-F
UNDER BEARING PARTITION

SECTION G-G
AT CARPORT SCREEN

DETAILS

Figure 9-6. Structural details provide information regarding the foundation footings and walls.

Fireplace details cannot be shown adequately on plan views and small-scale elevations. Details regarding the shape and size of a fireplace are required for construction. The arrangement of the damper, shape and size of the transition to the chimney, and size of the firebox must conform to the dimensions on the plans for the fireplace to have efficient combustion and draft and meet building code requirements. The hearth must be designed so that there is no danger of transmitting heat to the floor joists. **See Figure 9-7.**

Rough framing details for wall and floor openings are generally worked out by the tradesworkers on a construction site. However, an architect will provide details if structural design is involved or if loads must be supported in certain ways. Details showing wall and floor framing or stairway opening framing may be prepared for special situations. Roof framing plans are only shown if the roof has a complex layout. **See Figure 9-8.** Roof trusses are often detailed for installation by the manufacturing facility fabricating the trusses, and a separate shop drawing may be provided to guide in installation.

Window and Door Details

Window and door details are not included on most prints since residential construction commonly uses prehung window and door units. A rough opening of the proper size must be framed to receive each prehung unit. For special applications, details are drawn to show structural elements, installation procedures, and trim. Bay windows or window units composed of several window types may require window details for proper rough construction openings and installation.

Rough framing details may be provided for wall openings when structural design is involved.

Fireplace Details
Figure 9-7

ELEVATION **SECTION** **PLAN VIEW**

Figure 9-7. Details of elevation, section, and plan views provide the information needed to construct a fireplace.

Roof Framing Plans

Figure 9-8

M. BEDRM.

M. BATH

GARAGE

32'-4 1/2"

3-2X10 WOOD
HEADERS W/ 1/2"
PLYWOOD SPACERS

HALL

DINING

KITCHEN

MUD RM.

OFFICE

24'-7"

LIVING RM.

3-2X10 WOOD
HEADERS W/ 1/2"
PLYWOOD SPACERS

STAIR

PORCH

17'-9"

SCALE 1/4"=1'-0"

ROOF FRAMING PLAN

ENTRY

6'-6 1/2"

TYPICAL ALL
OVERHANGS

1'-2"

BEDRM #2

BATH #2

BEDRM #3

11'-7"

LEGEND:

VALLEY, RIDGE AND FASCIA LINE	
WOOD TRUSSES @ 2'-0" O.C.	
VALLEY FRAMING @ 2'-0" O.C.	
2-2X10 WOOD HEADERS W/ 1/2" PLYWOOD SPACER UNLESS NOTED OTHERWISE	

1'-2"

3'-0"

32'-8"

7'-11"

35'-8"

Plan Ahead, Inc.

Figure 9-8. Roof framing plans are provided for roofs with complex layouts.

Window details are drawn as sections through the head, sill, and jamb. The sections through the head and sill are drawn looking directly at the side of the window. A section of a jamb is drawn looking directly down through the window with the cutting plane taken slightly above the sill. Symbols are used to show various members. Rough structural members are shown with an X, and finish members are shown as wood grain. **See Figure 9-9.**

Most windows are delivered to a job site with the glass in place, window in the frame, and all hardware installed. Dimensions are provided so tradesworkers can construct the proper

size rough openings. **See Figure 9-10.** The section of the jamb is revolved 90° and placed in-line with the sections through the head and sill. The height and width of a prehung window unit are used by the tradesworker to determine rough opening size. The size of the rough opening should also allow a small amount of space for shimming the unit to plumb and level. The unit dimension height and width include exterior trim members such as sills and brick mold. The sections through the head and the jamb show the difference between the top and side pieces of the sash and the top and side pieces of the window frame.

TECHFACTS

Coatings on window glass can reduce ultraviolet rays by up to 75%.

Window Details
Figure 9-9

Figure 9-9. Section details through the head, sill, and jamb provide construction information for windows.

Figure 9-10. Section details through the head, sill, and jamb of a window are related. (NOTE: the relationship between the sill and head.)

Window Unit Dimensions

Figure 9-10

LOW-E INSULATING GLASS

SECTION THROUGH HEAD

UNIT WIDTH ¼″

UNIT DIMENSION HEIGHT

ROUGH OPENING HEIGHT

SECTION THROUGH JAMB

LOW-E INSULATING GLASS

SECTION THROUGH SILL

tails (ends) together. The exterior wall is ¾″ plywood siding over ½″ OSB sheathing. The interior wall is finished with ½″ gypsum board.

Moldings for exterior and interior trim are commercially available in a wide range of shapes, sizes, and types of wood. Common moldings include casing, base, shoe, crown, mullion, apron, brick, cove, inside and outside corner, stop, and chair rail. Other moldings are also available.

235# ASPHALT SHINGLES ON 15# ROOFING FELT OVER 1/2" OSB SHTH

12

2 × 8 RAFTER

2 × 10 CLG J

SUBFASCIA

6" BATT INSUL

2x6 DOUBLE TOP PLATE

1 × 10 FASCIA

1 1/8" FRIEZE

5 1/2" R-21 BATT INSUL

3/8" PLYWD

4" CONT AL SCN VENT

1'-6"

2 × 6 STUDS

3/4" PLYWD SDG

1/2" OSB SHTH

1/2" GYP BD

Figure 9-11. A cornice detail shows framing and finish members.

TECHFACTS

Brick details often show the brick bond. The brick bond is the pattern formed by the exposed faces of the brick.

Trim Details

Exterior and interior trim details are usually drawn to a larger scale to clearly show the materials needed. Exterior details are commonly drawn of siding, dormers, doorways, and unique brick patterns. Interior details are commonly drawn of cabinets, stairways, millwork, and trim.

A cornice detail provides framing and finish information. **See Figure 9-11.** The wall is framed with 2 × 6 studs and filled with 5½″ R-21 batt insulation. Ceiling joists are 2 × 10s filled with 6″ batt insulation. Rafters are 2 × 8s covered with ½″ oriented strand board (OSB) and a shingle roof. The rafters are trimmed with a 1 × 10 fascia. A 2 × 8 subfascia ties the rafter

READING DETAILS

Plans for the Wayne Residence contain sheets with details. (Refer to Sheets 5 and 6 of the Wayne Residence.) The Kitchen Plan on Sheet 6 does not include additional details of the floor plan but does indicate cutting planes showing directions of sight for Elevations A-A, B-B, C-C, and D-D. The Stair Detail is shown on Sheet 7.

Panned Ceiling Detail

The Panned Ceiling Detail on Sheet 6 is a section view drawn to the scale of ¾″ = 1′-0″. The ceiling extends 2′-0″ from all walls and then slopes upward at a 45° angle to meet the center portion of the ceiling, which is 1′-0″ above the ceiling near the walls. The ceiling is framed with 2 × 4s and finished with ½″ gypsum board.

Deck Handrail Detail

The Deck Handrail Detail is an elevation view drawn at a ½″ = 1′-0″ scale. Dimensions for the deck are shown on the Floor Plan, Sheet 2. The detail provides dimensions for the handrail.

The deck rests on 2 × 8 joists attached to 4 × 4 pressure-treated posts. The deck floor is made of treated 2 × 6s. Handrail balusters are treated 2 × 2s, mitered at the top and bottom, spaced 6″ on center. Treated 2 × 4s and 2 × 6s form the handrail, which is 3′-2″ above the deck floor.

Fireplace Details

An elevation and a section of the brick fireplace are drawn as details at a ½″ = 1′-0″ scale. The elevation detail shows marble surrounding the firebox with a 2 × 10 × 6′-0″ mantel. The fireplace is 6′-0″ wide.

The section view of the fireplace shows a ceramic tile hearth extending 1′-6″ from the firebox opening. Brick symbols show firebrick around the firebox and face brick elsewhere.

Basement Wall Detail and Walk-out Detail

The Basement Wall and Walkout Details, shown side by side on Sheet 5, are drawn at a ½″ = 1′-0″ scale. The Foundation/Basement Plan on Sheet 1 shows the stepped basement wall and the Plot Plan on Sheet 6 shows the lot slope.

The front and sides of the house are 4″ brick veneer over a 2 × 6 framed wall. The rear of the house is 12″ lap siding over a 2 × 6 framed wall for the portion around the walkout basement. The rear wall below grade is 8″ thick concrete. The 6 on 12 sloped roof is framed with 2 × 8 rafters spaced 16″ OC. Ceiling and floor joists are 2 × 10s spaced 16″ OC. OSB sheathing is covered with felt and cedar shakes.

The brick veneer walls are framed with 2 × 6s over which ½″ insulated sheathing is applied. A ½″ air space separates the face brick from the sheathing. The brick veneer walls are rated R-21. The rear wall is also framed with 2 × 6s that are faced with ½″ foam board insulation. The exterior finish for the rear wall of the house is 12″ lap siding. The rear wall is also rated R-21.

The footing for the 10″ concrete basement wall measures 8″ × 20″. Three #4 rebar are placed continuously in the foundation footing and #4 rebar are placed horizontally every 2′-0″ to reinforce the foundation. The concrete wall contains #4 rebar placed horizontally and vertically at 2′-0″ OC.

The footing for the rear wall of the house is 8″ × 16″ with #4 rebar. A 2′-0″ foundation wall supports the 4″ concrete slab that forms the basement floor. The slab is reinforced with 6 × 6–W1.4 × W1.4 welded wire reinforcement. A 6 mil plastic sheet provides a vapor barrier to resist moisture penetration.

The main floor of the house is supported by 2 × 10 floor joists spaced 16″ OC. Batt insulation is placed 30″ in from all exterior walls. A ¾″ tongue-and-groove plywood deck is nailed to the floor joists, covered with carpet, and trimmed with baseboard molding.

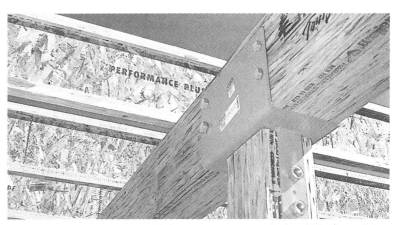

Trus Joist, A Weyerhaeuser Business
Engineered wood products such as wood I-joists and parallel strand lumber (PSL) beams may require specific installation details.

LEARNER RESOURCES

ATPeResources.com/QuickLinks
Access Code: 281467

Name _____   Date _____

Sketching 9-1

Sketch an elevation showing details of the vanity wall in the space provided. Include the following details:

1. 4'-0", two-door vanity, 30" high

2. 12" × 12" × 8'-6" soffit above vanity

3. 6" backsplash on vanity

4. 48" × 48" mirror above vanity

5. Floor-to-ceiling height of 8'-1"

SCALE ¼"=1'-0"

PLAN VIEW

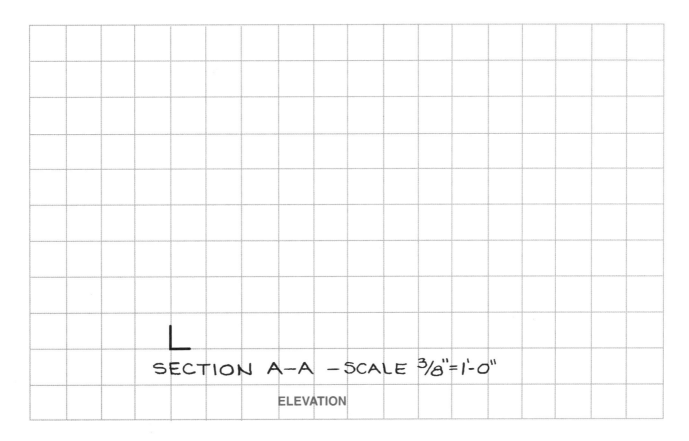

SECTION A–A – SCALE ⅜"=1'-0"

ELEVATION

Name _____ Date _____

Identification 9-1

_____ **1.** Studs

_____ **2.** Siding

_____ **3.** Sash bottom rail

_____ **4.** Apron

_____ **5.** Glass light

_____ **6.** Jamb

_____ **7.** Inside casing

_____ **8.** Sheathing

_____ **9.** Sash top rail

_____ **10.** Sash stile

_____ **11.** Stop

_____ **12.** Outside casing

_____ **13.** Meeting rail

_____ **14.** Sill

_____ **15.** Gypsum board

_____ **16.** Drip cap

_____ **17.** Stool

_____ **18.** Parting strip

_____ **19.** Header

_____ **20.** Screen

Completion

Refer to Details on page 213.

_____ **1.** The fireplace hearth is ___″ above the finished floor level.

_____ **2.** The fireplace opening is ___ high.

_____ **3.** The fireplace hearth is supported by a(n) ___ slab.

_____ **4.** The fireplace chimney is faced with ___ brick.

_____ **5.** The fireplace hearth is a piece of ___.

_____ **6.** The fireplace mantel is made of ___.

_____ **7.** The fireplace mantel is ___ above the finish floor level.

_____ **8.** ___ panel doors are used on Kitchen cabinets.

_____ **9.** The number of wall cabinet doors shown is ___.

_____ **10.** The dishwasher is located to the ___ of the Kitchen sink.

_____ **11.** Pass-through doors from the Kitchen to the breakfast bar are ___ above the finish floor level.

_____ **12.** The Kitchen cabinets are made of ___.

_____ **13.** Wall cabinets are ___″ tall.

_____ **14.** Base cabinets are ___″ tall.

_____ **15.** The number of base cabinet doors shown is ___.

_____ **16.** The number of wall ovens shown is ___.

_____ **17.** A(n) ___ cabinet is placed above the vanity.

_____ **18.** A(n) ___ ceiling is shown over the bathtub.

_____ **19.** ___ tile is 4′-0″ above the finished floor level behind the water closet and vanity.

_____ **20.** The garage roof has a(n) ___ on 12 slope.

_____ **21.** Plywood used to deck the Garage roof is ___″ thick.

_____ **22.** The Garage soffit is covered with ___″ plywood.

_____ **23.** ___ plates are used to tie chords and web members together.

_____ **24.** Web members are made of ___.

_____ **25.** Firecode gypsum board on the Garage ceiling is ___″ thick.

FIREPLACE ELEVATION

WD MANTEL
FLUE
FACE BRK
DMPR
FIRE BRK
ASH PIT DROP
SLATE
4'-4"
2'-6"
10"

BATHROOM ELEVATION

FURRED CLG
LT
MC
GYP BD
SW
CT
4'-0"

KITCHEN ELEVATION 1

3/4" PLYWD DR
BREAKFAST BAR
5'-6"

KITCHEN ELEVATION 2

HOOD R
OVEN
2'-6"
1'-6"
3'-0"

KITCHEN ELEVATION 3

EXH DUCT
FL PNL DR
REFR
DW
WD CAB
8'-0"

CONNECTOR PL
2×4 TOP CHD
12
4
1/2" PLYWD
2×4 WEB MEMBERS
3/4" PLYWD SF
5/8" FIRECODE GYP BD
2×4 CHD

TRUSSED RAFTER DETAIL FOR GARAGE

True-False

T   F   **1.** Details are scaled plans, elevations, or sections drawn to a larger scale to show special features.

T   F   **2.** Details are usually drawn to a larger scale than the view from which they are taken.

T   F   **3.** A preferred scale for details on residential plans is ¼″ = 1′-0″.

T   F   **4.** Generally, dimensions are not repeated on plans unless necessary for clarity.

T   F   **5.** Size dimensions locate a particular feature in relation to another feature.

T   F   **6.** Arrows on a cutting plane line indicate the direction of sight for the section.

T   F   **7.** Specific references are required for typical details.

T   F   **8.** The plan view of a kitchen and its elevations are related.

T   F   **9.** Details of windows are drawn as sections through the head, sill, and jamb.

T   F   **10.** Interior details are commonly drawn of cabinets, millwork, and trim.

Identification 9-2

_____   **1.** Double top plate

_____   **2.** Rafter

_____   **3.** Batt insulation

_____   **4.** Ceiling joist

_____   **5.** Fascia

_____   **6.** Frieze

_____   **7.** Subfascia

Name _____ Date _____

Refer to Sheets 5 and 6 of Wayne Residence.

Multiple Choice

_____ **1.** Regarding the Basement Wall Detail, ___.
   A. 4″ rigid foam insulation board is placed over the foundation wall
   B. the foundation footing is 8″ thick
   C. a 5″ drain tile carries water away from the foundation footing
   D. floor-to-ceiling height in the basement is 7′-0″

_____ **2.** Regarding the Basement Wall Detail, ___.
   A. insulation in the main floor wall is rated R-11
   B. the main floor wall is framed with 2 × 4s at 16″ OC
   C. 2 × 8 floor joists are spaced 16″ OC
   D. 2″ rigid foam insulation is used under the concrete slab

_____ **3.** Regarding the Basement Wall Detail, ___.
   A. the finished main floor is carpet over ½″ plywood
   B. a 2 × 4 truss chord is shown
   C. a ½″ air space is maintained between the brick veneer and sheathing
   D. 2 × 12 ceiling joists are specified

_____ **4.** Regarding the Basement Wall Detail, ___.
   A. the foundation footing is 8″ × 20″
   B. batt insulation is placed to 24″ in from exterior walls
   C. #5 rebar is placed horizontally at 2′-0″ OC in the foundation footing
   D. 235 lb asphalt shingles cover the roof

_____ **5.** Regarding the Walkout Detail, ___.
   A. the roof overhang extends 16″ past the rear wall
   B. the roof has a slope of 6 on 12
   C. the subfloor is ¾″ OSB
   D. a 4″ PVC drain tube carries water away from the foundation footing

_____ **6.** Regarding the Walkout Detail, ___.
   A. the minimum foundation wall height is 2′-0″
   B. 1″ foam board insulation is used
   C. WWR in the concrete slab is 4 × 4, W1.4 × W1.4
   D. the scale is ¾″ = 1′-0″

_____ **7.** Regarding the Fireplace Details, ___.
   A. a 1 × 10 is shown for the mantel
   B. the slate hearth extends 1′-6″ in front of the fireplace
   C. paneling is used to finish the wall above the fireplace
   D. the firebox opening height is 29″

_____ **8.** Regarding the Fireplace Details, ___.

    A. face brick surrounds the firebox

    B. the firebox is 36″ wide

    C. a damper is installed above the smoke shelf

    D. the mantel is made of marble

_____ **9.** Regarding the Panned Ceiling Detail, ___.

    A. the scale is ¾″ = 1′-0″

    B. the panned ceiling slopes up at a 30° angle

    C. 2 × 6s are used to frame the panned ceiling

    D. ⅝″ gypsum board is installed over the framing

_____ **10.** Regarding the Deck Handrail Detail, ___.

    A. the handrail is 3′-0″ above the deck floor

    B. 2 × 10 joists support the deck floor

    C. balusters are spaced 8″ apart

    D. 2 × 2s are used as balusters

Completion

_____ **1.** Fireplace Details are shown in elevations and ___.

_____ **2.** The Deck Handrail Detail is drawn to a(n) ___ scale.

_____ **3.** Roof rafters are spaced ___″ OC.

_____ **4.** ___ fill surrounds the drain tube at the front and sides of the house.

_____ **5.** The Walkout Detail shows ___″ rigid foam insulation within 30″ of the exterior wall.

_____ **6.** All windows are to be double-glazed high ___ glass.

_____ **7.** Posts for the Deck are treated ___.

_____ **8.** The hearth extends ___″ from the fireplace.

_____ **9.** The foundation footing of the Walkout Detail measures ___.

_____ **10.** The concrete slab in the basement is ___″ thick.

_____ **11.** ___ grade plywood is used on the soffit.

_____ **12.** Interior walls on the main floor are finished with ___″ gypsum board.

_____ **13.** The Fireplace Details are drawn to a(n) ___ scale.

_____ **14.** The total width of the fireplace is ___.

_____ **15.** The concrete foundation wall of the basement is ___″ thick.

_____ **16.** ___ molding and carpet finish the main floor.

_____ **17.** The finished ceiling height of the main floor is ___.

_____ **18.** Batt insulation on the rear wall provides an insulation value of ___.

TRADE INFORMATION — FOUNDATIONS, FRAMING, AND FINISHES

Many trade-specific tasks are required to complete the structure of a house in an orderly and efficient manner. The structure of a house includes the foundations, framing, and finishes. Building a foundation involves erecting forms for footings, walls, and slabs or installing structural masonry walls. Framing includes the construction of wood or metal walls, floors, and roofs. Finishes involve the application of exterior and interior materials to complete the structure.

OBJECTIVES

1. Describe the process of developing a concrete foundation system.
2. Describe concrete flatwork for basement floors, garage floors, walkways, driveways, and patios.
3. Discuss a common method of concrete masonry construction.
4. Describe floor, wall, and roof framing in concrete construction.
5. List and describe the common framing components.
6. Identify the different types of insulation.
7. Describe exterior finishes.
8. List the types of masonry exterior finishes.
9. List and describe roof finish materials.
10. List the types of interior finishes.

FOUNDATIONS, FLATWORK, AND MASONRY

The *foundation* is the part of a building that rests on and extends into the ground and provides support for the building above it. Foundations hold the structure in place and provide stability. Concrete is the most popular construction material for residential foundations. Concrete is also used for residential flatwork. *Flatwork* is the forming, placement, and finishing of concrete slabs such as basements, garages, driveways, walkways, and patios. Masonry is another material used in the foundation and structure of a house. *Masonry* is a form of construction involving the assembly of a structure using individual units such as bricks or blocks bonded with mortar.

Concrete Foundation Systems

Concrete foundation work begins by establishing the corners of a building in relation to the point of beginning, which is shown on the plot plan. The building corners are located using a traditional or laser transit level. The building corners must be located accurately because many site measurements are taken from the corner points. Once the building corners have been located, wood stakes are driven at each corner of the building and a nail marking the exact position of the corner is driven into the top of each stake.

TECHFACTS

Specific excavation safety requirements can be found in OSHA 29 CFR 1926.652, Excavations.

Information for the exact dimensions of the foundation is found on the foundation plan or floor plan. After rough excavation of a building lot, batterboards are erected and strings are stretched to indicate the exterior face of the foundation wall. A batterboard is a 1″ or 2″ thick level piece of dimensional lumber formed to hold the building lines and to show the exact boundaries of the building. Batterboards are set back from the excavation and are used for verifying dimensions and elevations at several stages during footing and foundation form construction. **See Figure 10-1.**

Batterboards and Building Lines

Figure 10-1

Figure 10-1. An intersection of building lines stretched between batterboards establishes the exterior face of a foundation wall.

Footings. Concrete for footings is placed first. A *footing* is the portion of a foundation that spreads and transmits loads directly to piles or to the soil. The type and size of footing used depends on the load-bearing capacity of the soil and the type of structure to be built. The footing depth should equal the wall thickness, and the footing width should equal twice the wall thickness. Additionally, the footing should never be less than 6″ thick, and the projection of the footing should be at least one-half the wall thickness to each side of the foundation wall. **See Figure 10-2.** For example, if a wall is 8″ thick, the footing should be 8″ deep, 16″ wide, and extend 4″ on both sides of the foundation wall.

Footing formwork is positioned so that the foundation wall is centered on the footings and the tops of the footings are level and at the proper height. Rebar is placed in the footings when the concrete is placed to increase the tensile strength of the concrete. Information related to rebar installation is shown on section or detail drawings. *Rebar* is a deformed steel bar containing lugs (protrusions) that allow the bars to interlock with concrete. Rebar is used to reinforce concrete structural members. After the concrete for the footings is placed, a keyway is formed in the footings. A *keyway* is a groove formed in fresh concrete that interlocks the footing with concrete from the foundation wall.

Footings

Figure 10-2

Figure 10-2. Footing depth and width are determined by the wall thickness.

Foundations. Foundation wall form-work is erected after the concrete for the footings has set and hardened. T-foundations are a common foundation used in residential and light commercial construction. T-foundations have an inverted T-shaped cross section. A *T-foundation* is a foundation consisting of an independently placed wall above a footing that extends on both sides of the wall. **See Figure 10-3.** Types of T-foundations are full basement, crawl space, and stepped.

T-Foundations

Figure 10-3

Figure 10-3. Types of T-foundations are full basement, crawl space, and stepped.

A *full basement foundation* is a foundation used in residential structures consisting of 9′ high walls to allow space for mechanical systems without sacrificing finished ceiling height in basement areas. Concrete foundation walls for a full basement house are most commonly 8″ thick. Full basement foundations provide an area below the building for living space or storage. The basement area is typically built below ground. **See Figure 10-4.**

Full Basement Foundations
Figure 10-4

Figure 10-4. Full basement foundations are typically built below ground and provide additional living and/or storage space for residential or commercial buildings.

A *crawl space foundation* is a foundation used in residential structures consisting of a short wall built on a spread footing that provides space between the bottom of the floor and the ground. The floor of a crawl space is generally a dirt surface. Building codes typically specify minimum crawl-space-foundation depths ranging from 18″ to 24″. Eighteen inches is the commonly used depth; however, a 24″ crawl space provides more room for utility clearance. The space provided by the crawl space allows access for installing and repairing mechanical, electrical, and plumbing systems.

A *stepped foundation* is a foundation shaped like a series of long steps and is used on steeply sloped lots. A stepped foundation requires less labor, material, and excavation than a level foundation on a sloped lot. Stepped foundations can be constructed to provide either a crawl space or a full basement. Many building codes require that the horizontal distance between two steps be at least 2′. The vertical footing must be at least 6″ thick and no higher than three-fourths the distance between two horizontal steps. The footings of a stepped foundation must be level.

TECHFACTS
Typical concrete is a mixture of portland cement, fine and course aggregate, and water.

Poured concrete foundation walls are formed using job-built or panel forms. **See Figure 10-5.** A *job-built form* is a foundation wall form constructed piece by piece on top of a footing. Bottom plates are fastened to the footing, and studs are erected and properly braced. Sheathing is attached to the studs, and braces are installed to secure the forms. High-density overlay (HDO) plywood, Plyform®, or fiberglass-reinforced-plastic (FRP) plywood is commonly used as sheathing.

A *panel form* is a prefabricated concrete wall form consisting of a metal frame and metal or wood panel facing, or wood studs and plates with wood panel facing. Panel forms are the most common form used in residential construction. Steel wedge form ties or snap ties with spreader cones hold the forms at a uniform distance and maintain proper form wall position when concrete is placed. The end studs are fastened together with duplex nails to form the corner of the foundation wall. A *duplex nail* is a double-headed nail designed to be pulled out easily to facilitate the stripping of forms.

Foundation Wall Forms
Figure 10-5

JOB-BUILT FORMS

PANEL FORMS

Figure 10-5. Job-built or panel forms are used to form foundation walls.

Slab-at-Grade Foundations
Figure 10-6

WARM CLIMATES

COLD CLIMATES

Figure 10-6. Slab-at-grade foundations are common in warm climates and must be properly insulated in cold climates.

Slab-at-grade, or slab-on-grade, concrete foundations are commonly used in warm climates, where the shallow frost line does not present soil heaving and shifting problems. A *slab-at-grade foundation* is a ground-supported foundation system that combines short concrete foundation walls or a thickened concrete edge with a concrete floor slab. The slab rests on a bed of gravel and a vapor barrier placed over the ground. When slab-at-grade foundations are installed in cold climates, additional slab edge insulation is required. **See Figure 10-6.** Residential slabs are commonly 4″ to 8″thick but may be thicker for heavier loads.

Insulating Concrete Forms (ICFs).
Insulating concrete forms (ICFs) are another method of forming concrete foundation walls and exterior residential walls above grade. **See Figure 10-7.** An *insulating concrete form (ICF)* is a type of concrete-forming system that consists of a layer of concrete sandwiched between expanded polystyrene (EPS) foam forms on each side. The forms remain in position after the concrete has been placed and become a permanent part of the walls. Interior walls, floors, and ceilings are then constructed using standard wood or metal framing members. Information for ICF foundations is shown on the foundation plans and section or detail drawings.

Insulating Concrete Forms (ICFs)

Figure 10-7

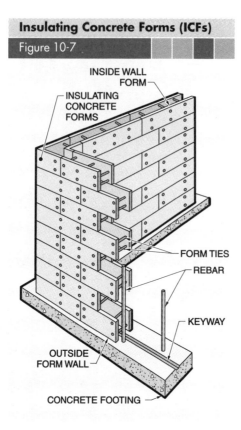

INSIDE WALL FORM

INSULATING CONCRETE FORMS

FORM TIES

REBAR

KEYWAY

OUTSIDE FORM WALL

CONCRETE FOOTING

Figure 10-7. Insulating concrete forms (ICFs) act as the inside and outside form walls into which concrete is placed.

The insulating forms combined with the concrete provide a continuous insulation system and an excellent sound barrier. The forms also serve as backing for gypsum board for the building interior and exterior finish such as wood siding, brick, and stucco. Some building codes, particularly in the South, require that below-grade ICF wall sections be treated to resist the possible infestation of termites and carpenter ants.

A completed ICF building looks the same as a framed structure. ICF construction offers many advantages over traditional wood- or metal-framed buildings, including minimal air infiltration, reduced heating and cooling loads, and better fire resistance. In addition, ICF construction can contribute to LEED® certification since it does not contain formaldehyde, and waste material is 100% recyclable.

Concrete Flatwork

Low forms are erected to allow for concrete flatwork such as basement floors, garage floors, walkways, driveways, and patios. The forms are usually installed and concrete is placed toward the end of a construction project so that the concrete does not become worn or damaged by on-site construction activities prior to occupation. Information about reinforcing is shown in section and detail drawings, floor plans, or the specifications. After finishing, the surface is kept damp for several days to ensure the concrete cures to the required compressive strength.

Basement and Garage Floors. Basement and garage floors may be placed after the foundations have been constructed and are often placed after the building has been framed. This protects the slab from weather damage and other possible damage from construction work.

In basement and garage floors, the perimeter of the floor butts against the foundation walls. The ground area below the basement and garage slabs is excavated to firm undisturbed soil. It is filled and compacted if necessary, and a base course of gravel is laid down. A vapor barrier is placed over the gravel and should extend over the foundation footings. Rebar and welded wire reinforcement are often used to reinforce basement and garage slabs.

Most residential basement slabs are 4″ thick and are often reinforced with welded wire reinforcement. However, basement slabs that support heavy loads have thicker slabs reinforced with rebar. If floor drains are installed, the areas around the drains are slightly pitched down toward the drain to facilitate water removal.

Basement floor information is included in section view drawings of the foundation plans. These drawings show slab thickness, type of reinforcement used, and the distance between the surface of the slab and the ceiling joists above. **See Figure 10-8.**

Specifications for a garage floor elevation are included in a section view of the garage. In a residential structure with an attached garage, the section of the garage floor adjacent to the building is lower than the finish floor elevation of the building. The garage floor is sloped ⅛″ to ¼″ per foot toward the vehicle entry of the garage for proper drainage.

Driveways. Driveway slabs for passenger cars are generally at least 4″ thick. Driveways that must support heavier loads are usually 6″ thick. Reinforcement, such as rebar, welded wire reinforcement, or fiber material, is required for both 4″ and 6″ slabs. Driveway slabs that abut garage floors should have a

finished surface that is ½″ lower than the garage floor to prevent water from entering the garage.

A garage floor should be sloped ⅛″ to ¼″ per foot toward the vehicle entry of the garage for proper drainage.

Basement Floor Information
Figure 10-8

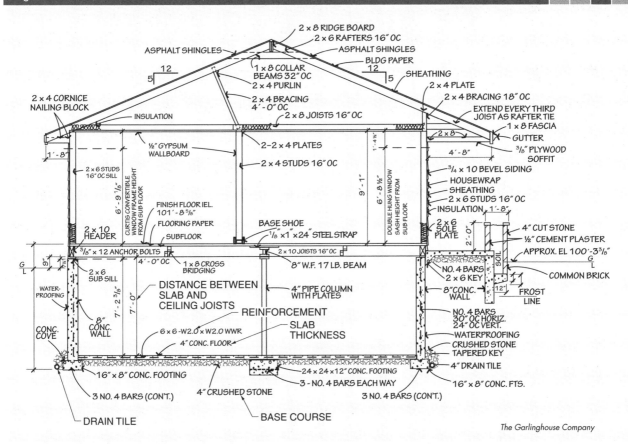

The Garlinghouse Company

Figure 10-8. The section view of a print provides information regarding the location, thickness, and reinforcement of the basement slab.

Walkways. The types of walkways found around buildings are public sidewalks, front walks, and service walks. A public sidewalk is a walkway that runs alongside the street and borders the building lot. Public sidewalks are commonly 4′ to 5′ wide. They are placed next to the street curb or separated from the curb by a planter strip. A front walk is a walkway that extends from a driveway or public sidewalk to the front entrance of a building. Front walks are usually 3′ wide. A service walk is a walkway that extends from a driveway or sidewalk to the rear entrance of a building. Service walks are commonly 2′ to 6′ wide and are set about 2′ away from the foundation. Walkways are commonly 4′ thick and rebar must be placed in sections of the slab over which heavy loads, such as trucks, must cross.

TECHFACTS

A control joint is a groove sawed or hand-tooled into a horizontal or vertical concrete surface to create a weakened plane and control the location of cracking.

Patios. A patio is an exterior concrete slab constructed adjacent to a house and used as an extension of the living areas. Subgrade work is the same as for other slab work. Patios should be at least 4″ thick and pitched ⅛″ to ¼″ per foot away from the structure. Patios are often reinforced with welded wire reinforcement. Expansion joints are formed where the patio slab meets concrete walls or walkways. Control joints should be provided at a maximum of 10′ intervals in both directions on the patio slab. **See Figure 10-9.**

Exterior Flatwork

Figure 10-9

Figure 10-9. Exterior flatwork includes driveways, walkways, and patios. Expansion and control joints are used to control cracking.

Structural Masonry

Masonry materials for the structure of a building include brick and concrete masonry units (CMUs). Elevations and floor plans identify the walls to be built with masonry materials and the types of masonry to be used. Sections through exterior walls, often section details, show masonry information for the walls at windows and doors and the wall finish at the eaves. Floor plans provide dimensions showing the exact location of window and door openings. Structural masonry walls include brick, CMU, and brick/CMU combination. **See Figure 10-10.**

Brick and Concrete Masonry Units. Brick and concrete masonry units (CMUs) are available in a wide range of sizes and shapes. Brick and CMUs are indicated on prints with symbols. Common brick is shown on plan views with 45° lines spaced further apart, while face brick is shown with 45° lines spaced closer together. Horizontal lines indicate brick on elevations. A notation such as FACE

BRICK is generally shown in open spaces between the horizontal lines.

Brick is either standard or modular in size. *Standard brick* is brick classified by its nominal size. For example, the nominal size of a face brick is 2″×4″× 8″, but its actual size is approximately 2¼″× 3¾″ × 8″. *Modular brick* is brick classified by its actual size and designed so that every third horizontal joint falls on a multiple of 4″ (modular measure). Brick is laid in various positions and bonds as noted on the elevations. *Brick bond* is the pattern formed by the exposed faces of the brick. **See Figure 10-11.**

Concrete masonry units are commonly used for foundations. Information on CMUs is shown in elevations with horizontal and vertical lines and a series of dots and small circles or triangles. The standard CMU size is 7⅝″ × 7⅝″ × 15⅝″. When a CMU is laid with ⅜″ mortar joints, it measures 8″ × 8″ × 16″ and conforms to modular measure.

Structural Masonry Walls
Figure 10-10

Figure 10-10. Structural masonry walls include brick, concrete masonry unit (CMU), and brick and CMU.

Brick Bonds

Figure 10-11

BASKET WEAVE   COMMON   ENGLISH   FLEMISH

GARDEN WALL   HERRINGBONE   RUNNING   STACK

Figure 10-11. Brick bonds are noted on elevations.

FLOOR, WALL, AND ROOF FRAMING

Floor, wall, and roof framing can begin after the foundation work has been completed. The first floor is framed first, the subfloor is installed, and then the first floor walls are framed. Subsequent stories are framed in the same manner. After all exterior and load-bearing walls are complete, the roof framing may begin. Roof rafters are constructed and installed on site, while roof trusses are generally prefabricated off site and installed at the building site in sections as completed roof units.

Floor Framing

Floor construction begins after the concrete for the foundation footings and walls is set and hardened and the forms are stripped. Floor plans and section details through exterior walls are referred to in order to determine dimensions and materials to be used. Pressure-treated sill plates are attached to the top of the foundation wall. Floor joists are supported at the ends by the sill plates. Sizes and directions of the floor joists are indicated on the floor plan with notations. Floor joists typically run across the width of a house. Header joists are installed along the ends of the floor joists to maintain proper spacing and joist alignment.

Longer joists require additional support along their span and may be supported with a steel beam or a solid, built-up, or engineered wood beam. Steel or wood posts may be required for intermediate support of beams depending on the length, size, and weight to be supported. **See Figure 10-12.** Floor joists should either butt together or be lapped over the intermediate beam. Butted joists are joined using metal ties. Throughout wood framing operations, a large variety of metal reinforcing ties are available for reinforcing joints such as a butted joint. **See Figure 10-13.** Lapped joists are fastened together by face-nailing.

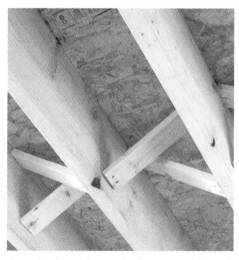

Cross bridging keeps the floor joists aligned and helps distribute the load carried by the floor unit.

Floor Construction

Figure 10-12

FLOOR JOISTS   STEEL BEAM   BUILT-UP BEAM   ENGINEERED WOOD BEAM

Figure 10-12. Notations on floor plans indicate the size and direction of floor joists.

Bridging is often placed between floor joists. *Bridging* is metal or wood cross members or solid wood blocking installed between joists to stiffen the floor unit and prevent joists from twisting. Cross bridging is metal or wood pieces (commonly 1 × 3s or 1 × 4s) attached near the top of one joist and the bottom of the adjacent joist in a cross pattern. Metal cross bridging has nailing flanges driven into place in the faces of the joists. Wood cross bridging is toenailed to the face of the joists. Lumber used for solid bridging is the same width as the floor joists. Solid bridging is placed in a straight line or staggered for easier installation. **See Figure 10-14.**

Wall Framing

After the floor joists are placed, the subfloor is installed and walls are framed. Floor plans and wall details are referred to for proper dimensions. The length and height of walls, size and spacing of studs, and location and size of rough openings for doors and windows are determined. Framed walls are commonly laid out, constructed on the subfloor, and raised into position. The walls are then plumbed, squared, and fastened to the framing members of the floor. **See Figure 10-15.** Lateral bracing for walls is applied to ensure structural integrity. Room layout, particularly for bathrooms and kitchens, is critical, requiring additional reference to the floor plans.

Roof Framing

Roofs are framed after the walls are in place and properly braced. Wall and roof framing sections and details indicate type and size of roofing material and roof overhang. Notations on floor plans indicate the size and direction of ceiling joists. Roof framing plans providing comprehensive roof framing information are included in the prints for houses with complex roof layouts. Elevations indicate the roof slope and finish materials to be applied.

Metal Connectors

Figure 10-13

FACE MOUNT JOIST HANGER

SKEWABLE REINFORCING ANGLE

I-JOIST HANGER

BEAM

JOIST

TAB BENT OVER AND NAILED TO FLANGE

BEAM

I-JOIST

BEAM

JOIST HANGERS AND SUPPORTS

BEAM-TO-COLUMN TIE

TOP FLANGE BEAM HANGER

STANDOFF COLUMN BASE

BEAM

BEAM

COLUMN

BEAM

BEAM

COLUMN

PIER

BEAM HANGER AND POST BASES/CAPS

HURRICANE TIE

BENDABLE FRAMING ANCHOR

RAFTER

TOP PLATE

STUD

BOTTOM PLATE

DOUBLE TOP PLATE

STUDS

FRAMING ANCHORS

Figure 10-13. Metal fasteners are used to tie together members in wood-framed construction.

Bridging

Figure 10-14

OSB SUBFLOOR

FLOOR JOIST

METAL CROSS

OSB SUBFLOOR

FLOOR JOIST

WOOD CROSS

OSB SUBFLOOR

FLOOR JOIST

SOLID WOOD

Figure 10-14. Bridging stiffens a floor unit and prevents joists from twisting.

Framed Walls

Figure 10-15

Figure 10-15. Floor plans and details provide wall-framing dimensions.

Roofs are constructed with trusses or rafters. **See Figure 10-16.** In truss construction, prefabricated trusses are delivered to the job site and commonly installed using a mobile crane. In rafter construction, ceiling joists and rafters are cut and installed individually on the job site. Roof sheathing is applied to provide lateral and structural support for the roof system.

Advanced House Framing

Advanced house framing is a set of framing techniques that reduce both the amount of lumber used and the waste generated in the building of wood-framed homes. The reduction of lumber allows space for more insulation material while maintaining the structural integrity of the home. These techniques help raise energy efficiency. Some advanced framing techniques include the following:

- Designing on two foot modules, which reduces waste and make the best use of sheet sizes
- Spacing wall studs up to 24″ on center
- Spacing floor joists and roof rafters up to 24″ on center
- Using two studs in corners
- Eliminating solid wood headers in non-load-bearing walls
- Using single lumber headers and top plates where appropriate

Trusses vs. Rafters

Figure 10-16

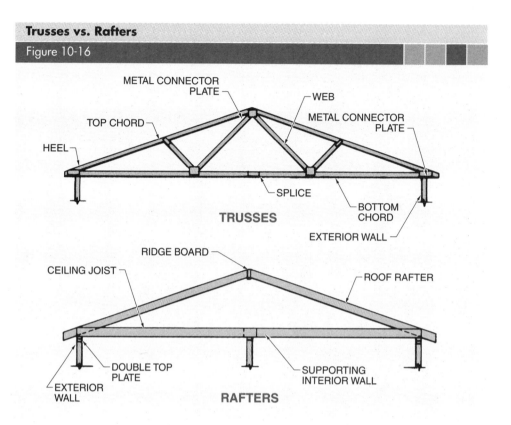

Figure 10-16. Roofs are supported by trusses or rafters.

Use of advanced house framing techniques results in a structurally sound home built with lower material and labor costs than a conventionally framed home. Advanced framing techniques can be used individually or as a complete system. Before using these framing techniques, building codes must be consulted to ensure that advanced framing techniques meet all wind, seismic, and other applicable building code requirements.

Framing Components

Many framing components are available as solid wood members (dimension lumber), engineered wood members (engineered lumber), or metal framing members (steel framing). Solid wood members are cut to size, kiln dried to ensure proper moisture content, and delivered to the job site for installation either as individual units or in prefabricated sections. Engineered wood members such as engineered trusses, joists, and studs are composed of various combinations of wood products that may include solid wood, laminated wood, oriented-strand-board components, or a combination of wood and steel members.

Many of the units are manufactured to specific dimensions based on information obtained from plans and specifications. In some residential construction projects, metal framing members are used in place of solid wood members. Both light-gauge and heavy-gauge metal framing members are available in a variety of sizes, shapes, and metal gauges as necessary to meet structural requirements. Metal framing members are often installed in a similar manner as solid wood members, only with different fastening systems.

Dimension Lumber

Dimension lumber is solid wood framing lumber that is precut to a particular size for the construction industry. Dimension lumber is primarily used for structural load-bearing applications and is graded for its strength. Appearance of dimensional framing lumber is secondary unless the lumber will be visible, as in exposed posts, ceiling beams, and roof beams. Specifications included in a set of construction documents usually provide the species and grade of lumber to be used on a project. Specifications may also include the stress rating and moisture content of the lumber. Unless otherwise indicated, it is assumed that the lumber for a project is surfaced on all four sides (S4S).

Dimension lumber is usually referred to by its nominal size, which differs from its actual, or dressed, size. **See Figure 10-17.** A 2 × 4, for example, is 2″ thick and 4″ wide when it is cut from a log at the sawmill. However, lumber shrinks after being seasoned (air-dried or kiln-dried), and surfacing at the planing mill further reduces its measurements. When a 2 × 4 is placed on the market, its actual size is 1½″ × 3½″. Nevertheless, the lumber is referred to as a 2 × 4 (its nominal size) because its original dimensions were 2″ × 4″. **See Figure 10-18.**

Dimension lumber measurements are stated in the following order: thickness, width, and length. For example, a piece of lumber 2″ (nominal size) thick, 4″ (nominal size) wide, and 16″ long is referred to as a 2 × 4 × 16. Dimension lumber is typically sold in even lengths ranging from 6″ to 24″. An extra (premium) charge is made for lumber over 20″ in length.

Engineered Lumber

Engineered lumber is framing material that is manufactured using solid wood members or veneers; wood strands and fibers; or a combination of solid wood members and wood strand members. Engineered lumber is manufactured using trees from second- and third-growth forests and may also contain recycled wood. **See Figure 10-19.**

Figure 10-17. Dimension lumber is usually referred to by its nominal size, which differs from its actual size due to drying and surfacing.

Laminated veneer lumber (LVL) is produced by combining and bonding wood veneers together. Parallel strand lumber (PSL) and oriented strand lumber (OSL) consist of long wood strands oriented along the length of the lumber and bonded together using an adhesive. Wood I-joists are composed of OSB or plywood webs and dimension lumber or LVL flanges.

Glued Laminated Timber. *Glued laminated (glulam) timber* is an engineered lumber product composed of wood laminations (lams) that are bonded together with adhesives. The grain of the lams runs parallel to the length of the glulam member. Lams are 1⅜″ thick for southern pine species and 1½″ for western wood species. Glulam products are available in standard widths including 3⅛″, 3½″, 5⅛″, 5½″ and 6¾″, although almost any width can be custom produced.

STANDARD LUMBER SIZE				
Type	Nominal Size*		Actual Size*	
	Thickness	Width	Thickness	Width
BOARD	1	2	¾	1½
	1	4	¾	3½
	1	6	¾	5½
	1	8	¾	7¼
	1	10	¾	9¼
	1	12	¾	11¼
DIMENSION LUMBER	2	2	1½	1½
	2	4	1½	3½
	2	6	1½	5½
	2	8	1½	7¼
	2	10	1½	9¼
	2	12	1½	11¼
TIMBER	5	5	4½	4½
	6	6	5½	5½
	6	8	5½	7½
	6	10	5½	9½
	8	8	7½	7½
	8	10	7½	9½

* in in.

Figure 10-18. Nominal board, dimension lumber, and timber sizes noted on prints differ from actual sizes.

Engineered Lumber
Figure 10-19

Trus Joist, A Weyerhauser Business

Figure 10-19. Engineered lumber is used in place of dimensional lumber in residential framing applications.

Glulam timbers are typically manufactured in lengths of up to 20′. Longer glulam timbers are produced by finger-jointing the ends of the lams and gluing them together. Continuous straight beams spanning as much as 140′ have been installed on heavy timber projects. Glulams can be curved or arched.

Laminated Veneer Lumber. *Laminated veneer lumber (LVL)* is an engineered lumber product composed of layered veneers and waterproof adhesive. LVL is commonly used for beams, headers, studs, hip and valley rafters, and flanges for wood I-joists. LVL is available in thicknesses ranging from ¾″ to 2½″, with a 1¾″ thickness commonly used to produce built-up beams. LVL is available in lengths up to 80′, but is most commonly cut into lengths of 48′ and shorter.

Parallel Strand Lumber. *Parallel strand lumber (PSL)* is an engineered lumber product manufactured from strands or elongated flakes of wood that are blended with a waterproof adhesive and cured under pressure. PSL is compatible with common wood-framing materials and is available in standard dimensions. PSL is used for beams and headers, and is frequently used for load-bearing columns. PSL beams are available in $1\frac{3}{4}''$, $2\frac{11}{16}''$, $3\frac{1}{2}''$ $5\frac{1}{4}''$, and $7''$ thicknesses.

Oriented Strand Lumber. Similar to parallel strand lumber, *oriented strand lumber (OSL)* is an engineered lumber product that is made from flaked wood strands that have a high length-to-thickness ratio. The wood strands are combined with a waterproof adhesive, oriented, and formed into a large mat or billet. The mat or billet is pressed and cured in a heated press. OSL is used in a variety of applications ranging from studs to millwork components.

Wood I-Joists. *Wood I-joists* are load-bearing structural members consisting of a web placed between top and bottom flanges. Webs are OSB or plywood panels cut to size. Flanges are made of either dimension lumber or LVL. Wood I-joists are used for floor and ceiling joists and rafters in both residential and commercial construction.

One of the biggest advantages of wood I-joists over dimension lumber products is their high strength-to-weight ratio. Wood I-joists are lighter and easier to handle than solid lumber joists required for the same spans and subjected to similar loads. **See Figure 10-20.** The flanges of wood I-joists provide a wide surface for attachment of sheathing and gypsum board.

Common wood I-joist depths range from $9\frac{1}{2}''$ to $20''$, and depths up to $30''$ can be custom ordered. Wood I-joists

are available in lengths up to 66'. For long wood I-joists, the flanges are finger-jointed. Flanges are typically $1\frac{1}{2}''$ thick with widths varying from $1\frac{3}{4}''$ to $3\frac{1}{2}''$. Web thicknesses range from $\frac{3}{8}''$ to $\frac{1}{2}''$. The upper and lower edges of the webs are butt jointed, toothed, tongue and grooved, or scarfed for fastening to the flanges.

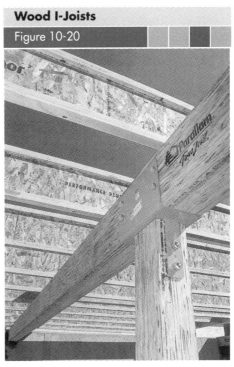

Wood I-Joists

Figure 10-20

Trus Joist, A Weyerhauser Business

Figure 10-20. Wood I-joists are lighter and easier to handle than solid lumber joists required for the same spans and subjected to similar loads.

OSB Rim Boards. OSB rim boards are an engineered wood product used primarily with wood I-joists in floor construction where the ends of the I-joists are fastened to the face of the rim boards. Rim boards fill the space between a sill plate and bottom plate of a wall, or in two-story construction fill the space between the top plate and bottom plate of two wall sections. In addition, rim boards tie together the floor joists. Rim boards serve the same purpose as header joists in traditional solid lumber construction.

Common rim board thicknesses are 1″ and 1⅛″, with depths of 9½″, 11⅞″, 14″, and 16″ to match the depths of wood I-joists and other engineered wood framing products. Rim boards are available in lengths up to 24″ depending on the material used.

Finger-Jointed Lumber. *Finger-jointed lumber* is an engineered lumber product composed of short pieces of dimension lumber joined end-to-end. The ends of the short pieces are machined with a fingerlike profile and glued together. Longer lengths of finger-jointed lumber can be produced that have strength equal to conventional dimension lumber. Structural applications of finger-jointed lumber include studs, plates, joists, and rafters.

Finger-jointed lumber dimensions range from 2 × 2 to 2 × 12 in standard dimension lumber sizes. Finger-jointed lumber with 2 × 4, 2 × 8, and 2 × 10 nominal dimensions is available in common standard lengths but lengths of 32′ or more are also available.

Metal Framing

Metal framing is a method of constructing the framework of a building using light-gauge steel framing members. Metal framing offers some advantages over conventional wood framing. Light-gauge steel framing members are lightweight and straight, allowing a framer to easily cut and install the members. Metal framing members are not affected by insects or decay, and do not shrink or otherwise deform like similar wood framing members. Metal framing is more fire resistant than comparable wood framing members. Metal framing is often specified in sustainable construction since 25% to 35% of metal framing members are manufactured from recycled steel. Light-gauge steel construction is often referred to as "steel for stick" construction since each wood framing member in a typical assembly is replaced with a metal framing member. **See Figure 10-21.**

Steel Framing Members. Light-gauge steel framing members are fabricated from structural-quality sheet steel by cold-forming. The desired shapes of the framing members are achieved through rolling, hammering, or stretching the steel at a low temperature, which may often be room temperature. No additional heat is applied in the manufacture of light-gauge steel framing members.

Light-gauge steel framing members receive a protective coating to prevent corrosion during transportation, storage, and final placement. The protective coating is applied using a hot-dipped steel galvanizing treatment.

Steel Framing Shapes and Dimensions. Light-gauge steel framing members are available in various shapes, thicknesses, and strengths. Common light-gauge steel framing member shapes include the C-shape, track, U-channel, and furring channel. **See Figure 10-22.** The C-shape is the most common shape produced for light-gauge steel framing, and is used for studs and joists. C-shape members consist of a web, flange, and lip. Web depths range from 1⅝″ to 12″. The flanges stiffen the web and provide surfaces for attaching sheathing and gypsum board. The lips extend from the flanges on the open side and stiffen the flanges.

Gauge is the unit of measurement for identifying sheet steel thickness. The higher the gauge number, the thinner the steel. Steel thicknesses also are shown on prints as mils.

A mil is a unit of measurement equal to one thousandth of an inch (1 mil = 0.001″). Metric dimensions (in millimeters) are increasingly being used to express steel thickness. One millimeter is equal to 0.001 meter (1 mm = 0.001 m). **See Figure 10-23.**

Steel Framing Fasteners. Proper fastening systems are crucial for establishing proper connections between steel framing members. Fastening systems include self-tapping screws (including self-drilling and self-piercing screws), welds, and spot clinching. Pneumatically driven pins are commonly used to fasten subfloor and sheathing to steel joists and studs. Powder-actuated fasteners may be used to fasten tracks for non-load-bearing walls to concrete and masonry.

INSULATION

After the house has been completely framed, tradesworkers complete the building envelope, which consists of the exterior wall sheathing, insulation, and exterior finish. *Insulation* is a material used as a barrier to inhibit thermal and sound transmission. *R value* is a measure of the effectiveness of a material to provide thermal insulation. Higher R values indicate greater insulating capabilities.

Insulation is installed between the framing members of the exterior walls, ceilings, attics, and floors of the house. **See Figure 10-24.** Insulation can also be installed in interior wall partitions or ceilings to minimize the transmission of sound between rooms. Insulation is made from a variety of materials. The most common types are rolls and batts, loose-fill, rigid foam, and foam in-place. The type of insulation to be installed in various building areas is shown on floor plans, details, and specifications.

Steel Framing Alliance

Figure 10-21. Light-gauge steel construction is often referred to as "steel for stick" construction since each wood framing member in a typical assembly is replaced with a metal framing member.

Figure 10-22. C-shapes, tracks, U-channels, and furring channels are the most common light-gauge steel framing member shapes.

STEEL GAUGE EQUIVALENTS			
Gauge	Decimal Inch Thickness*	Mils	SI Metric Thickness†
25	0.018	18	0.45
20 (light-duty)	0.033	33	0.85
20 (standard)	0.036	36	0.91
18	0.048	48	1.22
16	0.060	60	1.52
14	0.075	75	1.91
12	0.105	105	2.67

* in in.
† in mm

Figure 10-23. Light-gauge steel thickness is expressed as gauge, mils, and millimeters.

Insulation Location

Figure 10-24

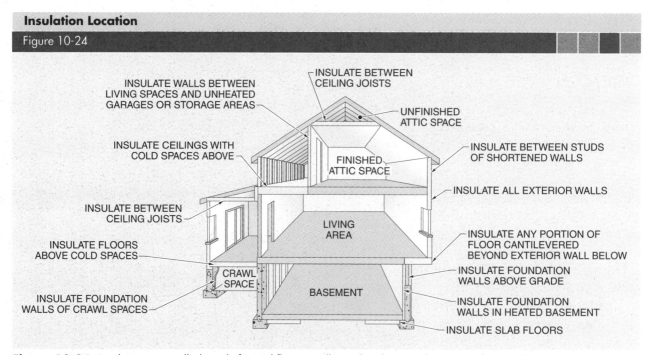

Figure 10-24. Insulation is installed inside framed floors, walls, and ceilings and on the surfaces of foundation walls.

Rolls and Batts Insulation

Rolls and batts (or blankets) are flexible insulation products made from fiberglass. This insulation is made with a vapor barrier material on one side for use in exterior walls, or with no vapor barrier for interior walls or exterior walls where a vapor barrier is not required. It is available in widths that fit the standard spacing of wall studs and attic or floor joists. A 2 × 4 framed wall can hold batt insulation with an R value of R-13 or R-15. A 2 × 6 framed wall can hold R-19 or R-21 batt insulation.

Loose-Fill Insulation

Loose-fill insulation is made of fiberglass, rock wool, or cellulose in the form of loose fibers or fiber pellets. It is blown into place using specialized pneumatic equipment. The blown-in material conforms readily to odd-sized building cavities and attics containing wires, ducts, and pipes. This makes blown-in insulation well suited for places where it is difficult to effectively install other types of insulation.

Rigid Foam Insulation

Rigid foam insulation is typically more expensive than rolls and batts or loose-fill insulation but is very effective in exterior wall sheathing, interior sheathing for basement walls, and special applications such as attic hatches. Foam insulation R values range from R-4 to R-6.5 per inch of thickness, which is up to two times greater than most other insulation materials of the same thickness.

Foam-In-Place Insulation

Foam-in-place insulation is an expansive material made from polyurethane. It is blown onto walls, on attic surfaces, or under floors using specialized spray application equipment to insulate and reduce air leakage. Foam-in place insulation is also available in small pressurized cans for filling in small holes and cracks, such as door and window frames, and electrical and plumbing penetrations. The R value of foam-in place insulations varies per application and ranges from approximately R-3.7 to R-6.2 per inch of thickness.

EXTERIOR AND INTERIOR FINISHES

Specifications and plans provide information needed to finish the exterior and interior of a house. Finish items detailed in the specifications include door and window hardware, bathroom fixtures, electrical fixtures, appliances, wall and floor materials and finishes, and similar items. Tradesworkers fit and apply all trim members, such as window and door casings, various hardware items, and exterior and interior molding.

Exterior Finishes

Exterior finishes are installed after door and window frames have been placed. A variety of materials are used for exterior wall finish including siding, brick, stone, and exterior insulation and finish systems (EIFS). In many cases, more than one material is used for the exterior wall finish of a building. Roofing materials are also part of the exterior finish process. **See Figure 10-25.**

Exterior Wall Finish
Figure 10-25

James Hardie Building Products

Figure 10-25. In many cases, more than one material is used for the exterior wall finish of a building.

The exterior of a building consists of the exterior wall finish and weather barrier or house-wrap material applied over the wall sheathing. The first line of protection against air and water infiltration into a building is the exterior wall finish, which generally includes the finish material, trim, windows, and doors. The second line of defense against air and water infiltration is the weather barrier. Weather barriers must prevent air and water infiltration, yet allow a building to "breathe" to prevent moisture from condensing within the exterior walls.

Siding

Wood is one of the most traditional materials used for exterior wall covering to protect the exterior surface of a building. In addition to solid wood siding, wood panel products, such as plywood and hardboard, are also available for exterior siding. Solid wood and wood panel products used for siding are available in various patterns.

Fiber-Cement Siding. *Fiber-cement siding* is composed of cement, ground sand, and cellulose fiber that are autoclaved (cured with pressurized steam) to increase its strength and dimensional stability. Fiber-cement siding is durable; insect-, water-, and fire-resistant; and is manufactured to resemble traditional wood siding. In addition, fiber-cement siding is environmentally friendly, as recycled materials are used in the manufacture of the siding. Fiber-cement siding is available as planks, panels, and shingles.

Aluminum Siding. Aluminum siding is available with a smooth finish or with an embossed wood grain finish. Whether aluminum siding is smooth or embossed, the siding is prefinished when delivered to the job site. Aluminum siding is produced with or without an insulating backing board. Different styles are available for horizontal and vertical application. Aluminum siding can be applied over sheathing or directly to the stud framing. A weather barrier should be installed beneath the siding.

Vinyl Siding. Vinyl siding is a durable, dent and abrasion resistant, prefinished plastic product. Many styles of vinyl siding are designed to resemble board siding. Many colors and textures are available, including imitation wood grain patterns.

Masonry Exterior Finishes

Masonry exterior finishes involve the use of a non-structural masonry wall comprised of brick veneer, stone veneer, or an exterior insulation and finish system (EIFS) adjacent to a structural wall. The masonry exterior finish is generally directly attached to the structural wall, but in some situations an air space may separate the two walls.

Brick Veneer. Brick veneer is used as an exterior finish on a building over a framed wall. Brick veneer is available in a wide variety of color and finishers and gives the appearance of having solid masonry walls, but the primary structural support is provided by wood or metal structural members.

Stone Veneer. Stone veneer is similar to brick veneer in form and function, but stone veneer emulates rocks or stones rather than brick. Stone veneers consist of manufactured stone units (MSUs) that are available from a variety of manufacturers in many sizes, shapes, and finishes. These materials are shown on exterior elevations with architectural notes and specified by the manufacturers' name and product code. Application varies by material, but stone veneer is most commonly installed in a manner similar to exterior brick veneer materials.

Exterior Insulation and Finish Systems. An exterior insulation and finish system (EIFS) is a multilayer insulating wall system with a base layer of foam insulation. **See Figure 10-26.** EIFS require underlying wood panel sheathing. Polystyrene or polyisocyanurate foam insulation panels are fastened to the substrate using approved adhesives and/or mechanical fasteners. The foam base is covered with a layer of cementious material that bonds reinforcing mesh to the base. Finish layers of cementious and polymer-based materials are applied to create the exterior finish surface providing a waterproof, colorfast, and crack-resistant finish.

Figure 10-26. An exterior insulation and finish system (EIFS) is composed of a layer of exterior sheathing, insulation board, reinforcing mesh, a base coat, and a textured finish.

Roof Finish Materials

Roof finish materials are used to shed water and protect a building from sun, wind, and dust infiltration. Before roof finish materials are applied, the roof must be sheathed, underlayment installed (except under wood shingles), and flashing placed wherever conditions require it. Roof sheathing is usually plywood, OSB, or another non-veneered panel product. Asphalt-saturated felt (tar paper) is used for underlayment. Underlayment should be applied over the entire roof surface as soon as the sheathing installation has been completed.

Composition Shingles. A *composition shingle* is an asphalt or fiberglass shingle coated with a layer of fine mineral granules. **See Figure 10-27.** Composition shingles are less expensive than other types of shingles, are easy to apply, and have a life expectancy of 15 to 25 years. Composition shingles are available in a wide range of styles, textures, and colors. Choosing a light-colored shingle can lower cooling costs compared to a dark-colored shingle. Light-colored shingles keep an attic and upper floor rooms cooler than dark-colored shingles because light-colored shingles absorb less heat and stay cooler than dark-colored shingles.

James Hardie Building Products

Figure 10-27. Composition shingles are less expensive than other types of shingles, are easy to apply, and have a life expectancy of 15 to 25 years.

Wood Shingles and Shakes. Wood shingles and shakes are among the oldest types of roof coverings and are commonly applied when a rustic architectural effect is desired. Most shingles and shakes are produced from western red cedar. Western red cedar has exceptional strength in proportion to its weight, has little expansion and contraction with changes in its moisture content, and is decay resistant.

Roofing Tile. *Roofing tile* is clay, slate, or lightweight concrete material installed as weather-protective finish on a roof. Roofing tile is often heavier than other roofing materials and requires a stronger roof support system. Roofing tile is popular because of its fireproofing qualities.

Metal Roofing. *Metal roofing* is roofing made of steel, aluminum, copper, or various metal alloys. Metal roof covering reflects most of the sun's rays and does not retain as much heat as shingles made from other materials. Metal roofing is much lighter than many other roofing materials, and is fire resistant.

Bituminous Roofing. *Bituminous roofing* is roofing composed of multiple individual layers (plies) of asphalt-impregnated felt or fiberglass material that is fastened to the roof deck and mopped with hot tar to create a waterproof surface. The final layer is coated with gravel, which is embedded in the tar or asphalt. Bituminous roofing is used for flat or low-pitched roofs.

Elastomeric Roofing. *Elastomeric roofing* is composed of continuous sheets of rubberized materials that are rolled out across a flat roof surface. The edges of the sheets are sealed with various mastic materials to create a water-resistant surface. The top of the sheets may be covered with gravel to protect the roof surface. Elastomeric roofing is used on flat roof applications.

Interior Finish Materials

Interior finish materials are used to cover the interior walls and ceilings of a building. Interior finishes include drywall, plaster, or veneer plaster. Drywall is the most popular wall and ceiling finish material in residential construction. The installation of traditional plaster wall and ceiling finish is very labor intensive. Veneer plaster has reduced the labor needed for an equivalent finish.

Drywall. *Drywall* is an interior surfacing material applied to framing members using dry construction methods such as adhesive or mechanical fasteners. **See Figure 10-28.** After installation and finish, drywall is painted, or can be covered by another material, such as wallpaper, tile, or wood. Drywall sheets consist of a gypsum core surrounded by heavy face and back paper. Regular drywall sheets contain a basic core consisting primarily of gypsum, paper pulp, starch, and soap. Fire-resistant drywall sheets contain fiberglass, perlite, or vermiculite, which is added to the basic core materials.

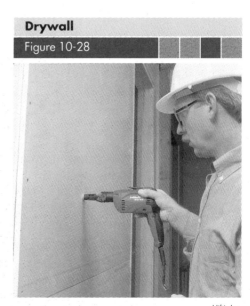

Drywall
Figure 10-28

Hilti, Inc.

Figure 10-28. Drywall is commonly attached to framing using a power drywall screwdriver.

The face of regular and fire-resistant drywall sheets is a multilayer paper that provides a smooth surface for finishing and decorating. The back surface is also a multilayer paper, but is unsuitable for finishing. The face and back paper provide strength to the gypsum core.

The standard width of regular and fire-resistant drywall sheets is 48″. Panel widths of 54″ are available for use on 8′-6″or 9′-0″ high walls. Using 54″ wide panels eliminates the need for a 6″ or 12″ strip of drywall when running the board horizontally. Drywall is available in lengths of 8′, 9′, 10′, 12′, 14′, and 16′ but may be obtained in other lengths from some manufacturers on a special-order basis.

Plaster. Interior surfaces may be coated with a plaster finish. The surface of the plaster is troweled smooth, swirled, or left with a rough finish as noted by the architect in the specifications or as shown on the elevations. Plaster is a mixture of cementitious material (binder), aggregate, and water. A variety of cementitious materials and aggregate are used in various combinations in a plaster mixture to achieve the desired results. Plaster is applied in coats or layers on metal lath to the desired thickness; the total thickness may be up to 2″ thick for solid plaster partitions. Lath is the backing fastened to structural members onto which the plaster is applied. Metal lath is tied, screwed, or clipped to structural members, such as metal studs or furring. Metal lath is available in sheets of diamond mesh or rib expanded metal. Various types of plastering materials are also used to provide sound control, insulation, fireproofing, and ornamentation.

Veneer Plaster. *Veneer plaster* is an interior wall finish that consists of a fire-resistant gypsum board covered by one or two layers of gypsum plaster measuring $\frac{1}{16}''$ to $\frac{1}{8}''$, thick. The baseboard is composed of a gypsum core covered with a special blue face paper that is made specifically to bond with the gypsum plaster. The veneer plaster is troweled and finished similarly to a traditional plaster finish. The advantage of veneer plaster over traditional plaster is that the baseboard is easier and quicker to install than metal lathe, and veneer plaster does not have the long drying time between coats like traditional plaster.

 LEARNER RESOURCES

ATPeResources.com/QuickLinks
Access Code: 281467

Name _____ Date _____

MULTIPLE CHOICE

_____ **1.** Information for the exact dimensions of the foundation may be found on the ___ plan.
   - A. plot
   - B. foundation
   - C. framing
   - D. mechanical

_____ **2.** The footing width should equal ___ the wall thickness.
   - A. one-half
   - B. twice
   - C. four times
   - D. eight times

_____ **3.** Footing formwork is positioned so that the foundation wall is ___ the footings.
   - A. to the left of
   - B. to the right of
   - C. below
   - D. centered on

_____ **4.** A ___ foundation is a foundation consisting of a short wall built on a spread footing that provides space between the bottom of the floor and the ground.
   - A. full basement
   - B. crawl space
   - C. stepped
   - D. slab-at-grad

_____ **5.** Residential slabs are commonly ___″ thick.
   - A. 1″ to 2
   - B. 2″ to 4
   - C. 4″ to 8
   - D. 8″ to 12

6. A garage floor is sloped ___" per foot for proper drainage.
- A. ⅛" to ¼
- B. ¼" to ¾
- C. ¾" to 1
- D. 4

7. Control joints should be provided at a maximum of ___" intervals in both directions on a patio slab.
- A. 1
- B. 5
- C. 10
- D. 20

8. Modular brick is designed so every third horizontal joint falls on a multiple of ___".
- A. 3
- B. 4
- C. 5
- D. 6

9. Regarding masonry walls, ___.
- A. elevations indicate the type of brick to be used
- B. floor plans show the brick bond
- C. brick and CMUs are shown on floor plans with the same symbol
- D. standard brick is classified by actual size

10. Sizes and directions of the floor joists are indicated on the ___ with notations.
- A. elevations
- B. foundation plan
- C. plot plan
- D. floor plan

11. Posts may be required for intermediate support of beams depending on the ___ to be supported.
- A. length
- B. height
- C. depth
- D. joists

12. The actual size of a ___ is 1½" × 3½".
- A. 1 × 4
- B. 2 × 6
- C. 2 × 10
- D. 2 × 4

_____ **13.** ___ lumber is an engineered lumber product composed of short pieces of dimension lumber joined end-to-end.
    A. Laminated veneer
    B. Finger-jointed
    C. Parallel strand
    D. Oriented strand

_____ **14.** Metal framing is often specified in sustainable construction since ___% of metal framing members are manufactured from recycled steel.
    A. 5% to 10
    B. 25% to 35
    C. 50% to 75
    D. 95% to 100

_____ **15.** The ___ is the most common shape produced for light-gauge steel framing.
    A. C-shape
    B. track
    C. U-channel
    D. furring channel

_____ **16.** 1 mil = ___ ″
    A. 0.1
    B. 0.01
    C. 0.001
    D. 0.0001

_____ **17.** ___ is/are a steel framing fastening system.
    A. Nails
    B. Welds
    C. Tongue and groove
    D. Bridging

_____ **18.** ___ roofing is comprised of continuous sheets of rubberized materials that are rolled out across a flat roof surface.
    A. Metal
    B. Elastomeric
    C. Bituminous
    D. Asphalt

_____ **19.** Fire resistant drywall sheets contain ___.
    A. foam
    B. cement
    C. vermiculite
    D. reinforcing mesh

_____ **20.** ___ is the most popular interior finish material in residential construction.
   A. EIFS
   B. Plaster
   C. Veneer plaster
   D. Drywall

True-False

T   F   **1.** The point of beginning is shown on the plot plan.

T   F   **2.** Slab-at-grade foundations are commonly used in warm climates where the frost line presents no heaving and shifting problems.

T   F   **3.** Slabs for residential construction are commonly 2" to 6" thick.

T   F   **4.** Floor joists commonly run along the full length of a house.

T   F   **5.** Straight-line solid bridging is preferred for easier installation.

T   F   **6.** Roofs are framed after exterior and load bearing walls are in place and properly braced.

T   F   **7.** Elevations indicate the roof slope and finish materials.

T   F   **8.** Standard brick is classified by its nominal size.

T   F   **9.** Brick bond is the pattern formed by the exposed faces of brick.

T   F   **10.** Wood is the most popular construction material for residential foundations.

T   F   **11.** A keyway is a groove formed in fresh concrete that interlocks the footing with concrete from the foundation wall.

T   F   **12.** A panel form is a foundation wall form constructed piece by piece on top of a footing.

T   F   **13.** Insulating concrete forms cannot contribute to LEED® certification.

T   F   **14.** Building codes typically specify minimum crawl space foundation depths ranging from 18" to 24".

T   F   **15.** When a 2 × 4 is placed on the market, the actual size is 2" × 4".

T   F   **16.** Light-gauge steel framing members are fabricated from structural-quality sheet steel by hot-forming.

T   F   **17.** The higher the gauge number, the thinner the steel.

T   F   **18.** Brick veneer gives the appearance of having a solid masonry wall, but the primary structural support is provided by wood or metal structural members.

T   F   **19.** EIFS require underlying metal panel sheathing.

T   F   **20.** Asphalt-saturated felt is used for roof underlayment.

TRADE INFORMATION — ELECTRICAL, PLUMBING, AND HVAC

11 CHAPTER

Electrical systems, plumbing systems, and heating, ventilation, and air conditioning (HVAC) systems compose the mechanicals of a residential structure. The electrical system brings in power and distributes the electricity throughout the home. The plumbing system brings in fresh water from outside sources and distributes it to fixtures inside the home. The plumbing system also removes the wastewater from the home. The HVAC system supplies the heat, ventilation, and cooling necessary to provide comfort to occupants of a house.

OBJECTIVES

1. Discuss the importance of the National Electrical Code® (NEC®).
2. Describe service-entrance, feeder circuit, and branch circuit conductors.
3. List and describe common raceway systems used in residential construction.
4. Describe the specifications of the materials and fixtures to be used for an electrical system in a house.
5. List the major components of a plumbing system.
6. List the types of plan views and specifications regarding the location of plumbing fixtures.
7. Describe heating, ventilating, and air conditioning systems.
8. Explain the common methods of sustainable heating systems.
9. Describe sheet metal work.

ELECTRICAL

Supply conductors from a utility company to a piece of property are regulated by the National Electrical Safety Code® (NESC®). Service-entrance conductors and electrical work from the meter base to the service equipment and the dwelling are governed by the current edition of the National Electrical Code® (NEC®). The purpose of the NEC® is the practical safeguarding of persons and property from hazards that may arise from using electricity. The NEC® is published by the National Fire Protection Association (NFPA). The NEC® is advisory; it is adopted by states, counties, and municipalities, and is updated every three years. In addition to the NEC®, local building code ordinances are enforced.

Service

Electrical service is grounded at the service equipment to provide a common grounding terminal for the grounded neutral, equipment grounding conductors, and the grounding electrode conductor. A main bonding jumper grounds the terminal bar to the metal

enclosure connected to the grounding electrode conductor. Feeders and branch circuits are routed from the service equipment to subpanels and loads.

Electrical service to a dwelling unit (house) is commonly 120/240 V, 1φ (phase) and is provided by an overhead service drop or an underground service lateral. Clearances for overhead drops are regulated by subsection 230.24 of the NEC® and Table 232.1 of the NESC. Burial depths for service laterals are regulated by Table 300.5 of the NEC®. Local building code ordinances may amend these clearances and depths. A power line is shown on a plot plan using a line consisting of a series of intermittent long and short dashes. **See Figure 11-1.**

TECHFACTS

The National Electric Code was first created in 1897. In 1911, the National Electric Code® was transferred to the Electrical Committee of the National Fire Protection Association. Since 1959, the NEC® has been updated every three years.

247

Power Lines

Figure 11-1

Figure 11-1. The location of power lines is shown on a plot plan.

Conductors

Copper (Cu) and/or aluminum (Al) conductors are used to wire dwellings. Copper conductors are more expensive than aluminum conductors but have less resistance (for the same size conductor) to current flow. Aluminum conductors in larger sizes are commonly used for service-entrance conductors and feeders to supply power to subpanels. Table 310.15(B)(16) of the NEC® identifies conductor sizes and ampacities for copper and aluminum or copper-clad aluminum conductors according to temperature ratings.

Service-Entrance Conductors. Service-entrance conductors shall have at least a 100 A (amp) rating where the calculated load is 10 kVA (kilovolt amps) or greater. A 100 A service shall be provided if there are six or more two-wire branch circuits. The minimum size for service-entrance conductors for any dwelling is #6.

Service-entrance conductors are routed in a raceway or service-entrance cable. Insulation is THW, THWN, XHHW, RHW, or other types listed for wet locations. (See Article 310 of the NEC® for conditions of use for each type of insulation.)

Service-entrance conductors are sized from the total volt-amp rating of the dwelling unit. The formula $I = {}^{VA}\!/_V$ is used to calculate amps, where I = amps, VA = volt-amps, and V = volts. Volt-amps are divided by volts to obtain ampacity ($I = {}^{VA}\!/_V$). For example, a calculated load of 36,000 VA on a 240 V, 1φ service has an ampacity of 150 A (36,000 VA ÷ 240 V = 150 A). Per Table 310.15(B)(16) of the NEC, #1/0 THWN Cu conductors are required.

Feeder and Branch Circuit Conductors. Feeder circuits include all conductors between the service equipment and subpanels. Branch circuits include all conductors from the last overcurrent protective device to the load.

Feeder circuits can be any size required to supply a subpanel or taps to individual loads. The minimum-size feeder circuit conductor is #10 per section 215.2 of the NEC®. Wiring methods for feeder circuits include conductors in raceways, service-entrance (SE) cable, or metal-clad (MC) cable. Feeder circuit conductors are selected from the VA rating of the load served. For example, a subpanel on a 240 V, 1φ supply circuit with a connected load of 20,400 VA requires #4 THWN Cu conductors. The formula, $I = {}^{VA}\!/_{V}$, is used to find the ampacity of the conductors (20,400 VA ÷ 240 V = 85 A). The conductors are then selected from Table 310.15(B)(16) of the NEC® based on ampacity. An ampacity of 85 A requires #4 THWN Cu conductors at 75°C.

The minimum-size branch circuit for a dwelling unit is 15 A. Branch circuits can be any size required to supply the load and can supply one load or a number of loads. Typical branch circuits in dwellings supply combination or single loads. General lighting and receptacle outlets are combination loads. An air conditioner, heating unit, food waste disposer, compactor, and other similar appliances are a single load.

A 15 A branch circuit commonly has 10 outlets to supply power to lighting fixtures and general-purpose receptacles. A 20 A branch circuit commonly has 13 outlets to supply power to lighting fixtures and general-purpose receptacles. **See Figure 11-2.**

Branch Circuits

Figure 11-2

Figure 11-2. The number of outlets permitted on a branch circuit is determined by dividing the rating of the overcurrent protective device (OCPD) by 1.5 A. The NEC® does not limit the number of outlets.

Raceway Systems

A *raceway* is an enclosed channel designed to protect electrical conductors. Raceways are made of metal or insulating material. The types of raceway systems used for specific dwelling units are indicated in the print specifications and governed by electrical codes adopted for local use. Many cities permit nonmetallic-sheathed cable (commonly called Romex®) to be used for wiring dwelling units. Other cities may require that all conductors in residential construction be routed in metal conduit.

The most common raceway systems used in residential construction are electrical metallic tubing (EMT), electrical nonmetallic tubing (ENT), rigid nonmetallic conduit (PVC), and multiple-conductor cable assemblies such as AC armored cable and non-metallic-sheathed cable. In addition, service-entrance cable (SE, ASE, and USE) is used in applications requiring protection from severe mechanical abuse. **See Figure 11-3.**

Electrical Metallic Tubing (EMT). Electrical metallic tubing (EMT), also known as thin-wall, is similar to rigid metal conduit but is approximately 40% lighter. Thin-wall is used in exposed and concealed work. Thin-wall may be used in most locations, but because of its light weight, thin wall, and compression or set screw couplings and connectors, it cannot be used where it could be subjected to severe physical damage. Thin-wall is available in 10′ lengths from ½″ to 4″ in diameter with ½ ″ and ¾″ sizes most commonly used in residential construction.

Raceway Systems
Figure 11-3

Figure 11-3. Raceway systems for single-family dwelling units include electrical metallic tubing, electrical nonmetallic tubing, rigid nonmetallic conduit, AC armored cable, nonmetallic sheathed cable, and service entrance cable.

Thin-wall must be supported every 10' and within 3' of each outlet box, junction box, cabinet, or fitting. The total number of degrees in all bends in any run shall not exceed 360°. Studs and joists may be notched or drilled to accommodate EMT. Notches, which are preferred, should be as narrow as possible and no deeper than necessary to minimize weakening of the structural members.

Electrical Nonmetallic Tubing (ENT). Electrical nonmetallic tubing (ENT) is a flexible corrugated plastic raceway. Sizes of ½" to 1" diameter are available for installation in walls, floors, and ceilings, and above suspended ceilings with a 15-minute fire rating. ENT may be bent by hand to a radius of not less than 4" for a ½" diameter and not less than 5¾" for a 1" diameter. The total number of degrees in all bends in any run shall not exceed 360°.

Electrical nonmetallic tubing must be supported every 3' and within 3' of each outlet box, junction box, cabinet, or fitting. All cut ends must be trimmed, and bushings or adapters must be used to prevent abrasion.

Rigid Nonmetallic Conduit (RNMC). Rigid nonmetallic conduit (RNMC), also known as polyvinyl chloride (PVC), is waterproof, rustproof, and decay resistant. Types of rigid nonmetallic conduit are Schedule 40 and Schedule 80. Schedule 40 (thin-wall) does not have the strength of metal conduit and should not be used where it may be subjected to severe physical damage. Schedule 80 (heavy wall) may be installed in most locations where rigid metal conduit may be used.

Polyvinyl chloride conduit can be cut with a handsaw and glued together with couplings and connectors. The total number of degrees in all bends in any run shall not exceed 360°.

All field bends must be made with bending equipment. Supports shall be provided within 3' of each box, cabinet, or connection. The maximum spacing between supports is based upon the diameter of the RNMC. For example, the 3' maximum spacing between supports is permitted in runs of ½" to 1" diameter RNMC.

AC Armored Cable (AC). AC armored cable (AC) is a fabricated assembly of insulated conductors in a flexible metallic enclosure. AC may be used in dry locations where it is not exposed to physical damage. An integral grounding conductor ensures a good path for fault current to return from the point of fault to the grounded conductor connected to the grounded busbar in the main service panel.

AC must be supported every 4'-6"and within 12" of outlets and fittings and may be run through holes or notches in the studs. Holes must be at least 1¼" from the edge of the stud so that the cable is not penetrated when fastening gypsum board or other items to the wall. Notches must be covered with ¹⁄₁₆" thick steel protector plates. Bends are permitted but shall be no less than five times the diameter of the cable when measured along the inside edge. For example, the minimum bending radius of ½" cable is 2½".

Nonmetallic-Sheathed Cable (NM and NMC). Nonmetallic-sheathed cable, also known as Romex®, has two, three, or four conductors with a separate bare ground wire. Romex is used to economically wire dwelling units and small commercial buildings. Romex is installed with staples or connectors and must be supported every 4'-6"and within 12" of outlets and fittings. Metal or nonmetallic boxes may be used with Romex.

The letters NM and NMC indicate specific types of nonmetallic cable and the characteristics of the cable. *Type NM cable* is a nonmetallic-sheathed cable where the conductors are enclosed within a nonmetallic jacket, and is the type typically used for dry interior wiring. *Type NMC cable* is a nonmetallic-sheathed cable where the conductors are enclosed within a corrosion-resistant, nonmetallic jacket that can be used for interior or exterior wiring. NM and NMC shall not be buried in concrete.

Romex may be run through the centers of studs, joists, and rafters. Romex may be installed in notched studs when covered by a ¹⁄₁₆″ thick steel protector plate.

Service-Entrance Cable (SE, ASE, and USE). Service-entrance cable is used for service-entrance wiring or general interior wiring. The neutral may be insulated or bare when used for service-entrance wiring. An insulated neutral is required when used for general interior wiring. SE cable has a flame-retardant and moisture-resistant outer covering. SE cable is unarmored and will not withstand severe physical abuse. ASE cable has an armored coating for additional protection. USE cable is moisture-resistant with an unarmored coating and is designed for underground installation.

TECHFACTS

Conductors are sized using the American Wire Gauge (AWG) numbering system. The smaller the AWG number, the larger the diameter of the conductor.

Service-entrance cables may be routed through studs, joists, and rafters. Holes drilled in wood members must not be closer than 1¼″ to the edge. Notched members shall be covered with a ¹⁄₁₆″ thick steel protector

plate. Bends in unarmored cable shall not have a radius less than five times the diameter of the cable. The cable shall be supported at intervals not exceeding 4′-6″ and within 12″ of outlets and fittings.

Plans and Schedules

Specifications describe the materials and fixtures to be used for an electrical system in a house. Specific manufacturers' trade names and catalog numbers are often provided as well. Floor plans or electrical shop drawings directly related to the floor plans show locations for lighting outlets, receptacles, switches, and other electrical devices. Branch-circuit schedules provide information for lighting outlets, receptacles, and switches. Lighting fixture schedules provide information regarding the type and location of lighting fixtures required. Low-voltage systems such as security systems or communications systems are installed according to floor plans, schedules, or electrical shop drawings found in the construction documents.

Dimensions are not indicated on floor plans to locate receptacles and outlets. Long dashed lines on a floor plan representing circuits connect receptacles, outlets, and switches to show outlet controls, not specific locations. Individuals installing the electrical systems determine the exact locations of the outlets, receptacles, and switches, and install them according to the applicable electrical code requirements. No point along the floor line in any wall 2′-0″ or more in length shall be more than 6′-0″ from a receptacle in that wall space. Corners unbroken along the floor line by doorways, fireplaces, and similar openings are included. Receptacles, in general, should be spaced equal distances apart.

In kitchens, receptacles are installed in each countertop space of 12″ or more. Receptacles for fastened-in-place appliances, such as disposals, or receptacles for appliances occupying dedicated space, such as refrigerators, are not included. In bathrooms, at least one wall receptacle is installed adjacent to the basin. In addition, one receptacle each is required for the laundry area, basement, garage, and exterior of the house. All 15 A and 20 A, 125 V receptacles in bathrooms, in garages, and outdoors (with grade-level access) and receptacles serving countertops of kitchens shall have ground-fault circuit interrupter (GFCI) protection per subsection 210.8(A) of the NEC®. Also, receptacles in unfinished basements and within 6'-0"of wet bar sinks shall have GFCI protection.

Provisions must be made for the proper placement and installation of electrical receptacles, switches, and similar items for people with disabilities. ANSI/ICC A117.1, Accessible and Usable Buildings and Facilities, contains specifications to make buildings accessible and usable for people with disabilities. For example, ANSI/ICC A117.1 specifies the side-reach height range of a wheelchair-bound individual as 15″ to 48″. Outlets and switches should not be installed below 15″ or above 48″ from the finished floor.

Branch circuit schedules and lighting fixture schedules supplement information shown on the floor plan. **See Figure 11-4.** The service drop is located on the northwest corner of the house. Service-entrance conductors run in rigid galvanized conduit to the meter and then to the main power panel. All branch circuits are protected by fuses or circuit breakers. Circuits 1 through 8 are shown. Circuit 1 includes all receptacles and lighting outlets for BR 1 and BR 2. The arrow with the number 1 indicates a home run to circuit 1 on the main power panel. In BR 1, one type-A ceiling outlet is controlled by a single-pole wall switch.

Four wall receptacles are installed per section 210.52 of the NEC®. In BR 2, one type-A ceiling outlet is controlled by a single-pole wall switch and four wall receptacles are shown.

VDV Systems

Voice/data/video systems are becoming increasingly common in residential construction. A *voice/data/video (VDV) system* is a low-voltage electrical system designed for use with various types of information technology equipment, including telephone systems, computer systems and networks, television video systems for cable and/or satellite dish systems, and security and fire alarm systems. These systems are typically detailed and installed by specialty contractors or suppliers familiar with these systems.

Voice/data/video drawings show connections to information sources such as incoming telephone lines and video feeds. Locations for connections to the systems in various rooms and locations throughout the house are shown with symbols on a floor plan. Security and alarm system suppliers not only install and maintain the wiring and connections at the residence, but also provide monitoring services to alert police and fire departments in case of a breach of the systems.

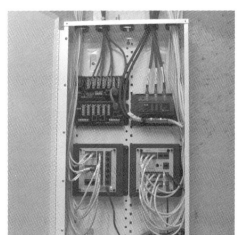

Distribution modules are used in a VDV system to route information to and from different areas of a house.

Figure 11-4. Floor plans show receptacles, outlets, and switches. Schedules provide additional information.

PLUMBING

Plumbing is a system of pipes, fittings, and devices within a building that supplies fresh water and removes waterborne waste and stormwater. Plumbing is installed according to information provided on plan views, specifications, and piping drawings. This information is used in conjunction with applicable building code ordinances to determine installation requirements and procedures.

Recently, model codes have been changed to include the adoption and installation of fire suppression systems in residential construction. This piping installation is installed in a manner similar to plumbing for fresh water and wastewater systems. The house design and structural configuration are considered when installing plumbing lines. For example, the direction of joists and the location of plumbing fixtures have a bearing on pipe locations.

Installation of plumbing occurs during many stages of the construction process. Connections to the water supply, sanitary sewer, and stormwater drainage systems are completed following initial excavation. Basement drains are placed before the concrete for the basement slab is placed. Slab-at-grade foundations require water supply and wastewater piping to be installed before concrete is placed.

Rough-in plumbing work is completed after rough framing is completed. The insides of walls can be easily accessed for installation of supply, wastewater, and vent piping. These systems are inspected by the local building code enforcement officials to ensure compliance with the plans and specifications prior to application of interior finish materials. Plumbing fixtures for the finish plumbing work are installed after the walls are covered.

Piping

The major components of a plumbing system are water supply piping, sanitary drainage and vent piping, and stormwater drainage piping. **See Figure 11-5.** In some regions, natural gas piping and fire prevention system piping may also be installed.

Plumbing Systems

Figure 11-5

Figure 11-5. Water supply piping and sanitary drainage and vent piping are the primary components of residential plumbing systems.

Water Supply Piping. Water supply piping conveys potable water to the points of use in the house. *Potable water* is water free from impurities in amounts that could cause disease or harmful effects.

The water supply is under pressure as it enters the house from a city water main or a well pump. The water flows through a water meter that measures the amount of water used. The cold water supply is piped throughout the house to points of use. One branch of the cold water supply is diverted to a water heater, where the temperature of the water is raised to a predetermined amount. Hot water is piped from the outlet side of the water heater to points of use throughout the house, often parallel to the cold water line. Fixtures at each hot and cold water outlet control the flow of water.

Supply pipes may be of copper or plastic materials. **See Figure 11-6.** Copper systems include various pipe diameters and fittings that are fastened by soldering or other mechanical means. Plastic systems are comprised of various materials, pipe diameters, and fittings that are fastened with adhesives or mechanical fittings. The three main types of plastic systems are polyvinyl chloride (PVC), chlorinated polyvinyl chloride (CPVC), and cross-linked polyethylene (PEX).

Polyvinyl chloride (PVC) is a rigid plastic pipe that is used for water mains and water service lines. *Chlorinated polyvinyl chloride (CPVC)* is a rigid plastic pipe that can withstand greater pressure and higher temperatures than PVC. *Cross-linked polyethylene (PEX)* is flexible tubing that allows directional changes to be made with minimal fittings, has resistance to high temperatures and high pressures, and is fastened in sections with crimping or compression connections. PEX can be installed using conventional plumbing in which water distribution pipes and branches convey water to fixtures, or can be installed in a home run system that uses centrally located manifolds to distribute water to each fixture with dedicated hot and cold water lines.

Copper Supply Piping
Figure 11-6

Figure 11-6. Copper piping is the most-used supply piping in residential construction.

Fire Suppression Piping. A *fire protection system* is a safety system that detects and suppresses a fire using a system of alarms, sensors, valves, pipes, and delivery devices. A residential fire protection system uses water as the primary extinguishing method. Residential fire suppression systems are comprised of a main feeder pipe, distribution piping to the various living areas of the structure, and sprinkler heads to deliver water to the areas of combustion. **See Figure 11-7.** Piping must meet code requirements that keep all piping and fittings intact in conditions of extreme heat. Metal or CPVC pipe is used in residential fire protection systems.

Residential Fire Suppression Systems

Figure 11-7

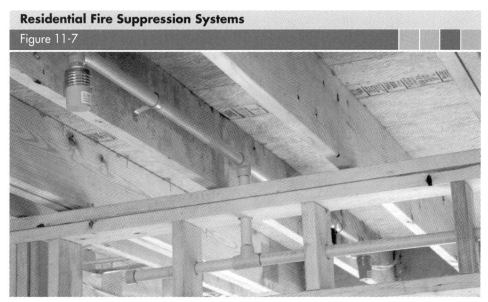

Rapid Response® Home Fire Sprinkler System by Tyco Fire Suppression & Building Products

Figure 11-7. Some jurisdictions require fire suppression systems in new residential construction.

Wet pipe and dry pipe systems are the two primary types of fire suppression systems. In wet pipe systems, water is constantly maintained within the entire piping system and is released by an activated sprinkler head immediately at the point of combustion. In dry pipe systems, the piping is filled with compressed air or nitrogen that holds closed the dry pipe valve. When the excessive heat from the fire melts the thermal linkage on the sprinkler head, the air escapes the system, opening the dry pipe valve. Water enters the pipe and is delivered through the open sprinkler head onto the fire.

Sanitary Drainage and Vent Piping.
The sanitary drainage system conveys wastewater and waterborne waste from plumbing fixtures to the sanitary sewer or septic system. Sanitary sewers receive wastewater that must be treated before being released into the fresh water supply.

A water seal is provided on waste piping at each plumbing fixture using a plumbing trap to prevent sewer gas from entering a house. **See Figure 11-8.** Local building codes may require pressurized testing of the waste piping

before inspection approval and issuance of an occupancy permit.

Figure 11-8. Traps provide a water seal on waste piping to prevent sewer gas from entering a house.

In a city or municipal sanitary sewer system, waste piping is routed directly from the house to the sewer system. In rural areas, a municipal sewer system may not be available. Wastewater and waterborne waste is routed to a septic tank and an absorption (leach) field. Solid waste collects in the septic tank and is broken down by chemical action. Wastewater flows from the septic tank and is distributed into the soil of the absorption field.

Vent piping provides air circulation within the sanitary drainage system to equalize pressure in the system and permit the proper flow of wastewater and waterborne waste. In addition, vent piping allows gases and odors to flow from the plumbing system through roof vents.

Stormwater Drainage Piping. Stormwater drainage piping carries rainwater and other precipitation to a storm sewer or other place of disposal. Proper stormwater drainage systems prevent the accumulation of stormwater around a house and leakage into the house. When the house has a basement or there is a likelihood of stormwater backing into the house around the perimeter, stormwater is collected and routed away from the house using drain tile placed around the foundation. Stormwater must be distributed and absorbed in the soil according to local ordinances. Many local ordinances prohibit stormwater from being directed to storm sewers.

In some areas, water is collected and routed to a sump well installed in the basement floor of a house. A sump pump mounted in the sump well ejects the stormwater from the well through a pipe extending through the foundation wall to the outside, away from the building.

For some sustainable construction, stormwater may be collected in a retention tank or other storage system. This water, often called gray water because it has not been treated as potable water, can be used for various non-potable water applications, such as landscape sprinkler systems or toilet systems.

Roughed-in Piping. *Rough-in* is the installation of pipes and plumbing fittings that will be concealed after construction is complete. Knowing the exact location of roughed-in piping is critical to ensuring that fixtures are installed in the proper final location. Specifications provide the manufacturer name and model numbers of fixtures to be installed. Dimensions for water supply and sanitary drainage and vent piping required for proper installation of plumbing fixtures are provided on rough-in sheets from the manufacturer. **See Figure 11-9.** Specifications state that a Kohler K-3310-4 stainless steel kitchen sink is to be installed. The rough-in sheet shows that sink drains are 11⅞″ from the back edge of the sink top and the sink is 7½″ deep. A 1½″ outlet pipe extends through the wall 12¹³⁄₁₆″ below the top edge of the sink.

In some cases, a rough-in sheet will not include water supply and sanitary drainage rough-in dimensions. The variety of faucet selections or job conditions prohibits listing the exact rough-in dimensions. Where these dimensions are unavailable, standard rough-in dimensions are commonly used. For example, standard dimensions for roughing in a double-bowl sink specify the waste opening at approximately 14″ above the finished floor and the hot and cold supply water through the wall at approximately 16″ above the finished floor.

Drainage piping must be properly graded so water and waterborne waste flows to the point of disposal.

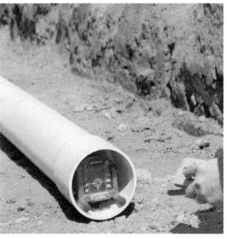

Topcon Laser Systems, Inc.

Rough-In Sheets

Figure 11-9

ROUGH-IN NOTES

FIXTURE DIMENSIONS ARE NOMINAL AND CONFORM TO TOLERANCES IN ASME/ANSI STANDARD A112.19.3M.	
(T) DRAIN TYPICALLY 12-13/16″.	
CUTOUT	32½″ x 20-¾″ WITH ½″ RADIUS CORNERS.

Kohler Co.

Figure 11-9. Manufacturer rough-in sheets provide dimensions for the proper installation of plumbing fixtures.

Plans and Specifications

Plan views provide information regarding the location of plumbing fixtures, waste piping, sanitary drains, and stormwater drains. **See Figure 11-10.**

Plumbing fixtures such as lavatories, water closets, and bathtubs are shown using symbols. Hose bibbs are located on exterior walls to provide connections for garden hoses.

Plan Views

Figure 11-10

Figure 11-10. Symbols are used on plan views to indicate the location of plumbing fixtures.

Basement and foundation plans provide the location of floor drains and drain tile. Plot plans provide information regarding drainage fields and connections to the supply water and sanitary sewer lines. Sections and interior elevation details supplement information provided on plan views.

Specifications provide information such as fixture manufacturers, model numbers, and number of plumbing fittings required. Some specifications are included on the prints as notations. Other specifications may be sheets bound in a separate document or forms supplied by the contractor or a government agency. If there is a discrepancy between the specifications and the prints, the specifications take precedence.

To accommodate people with physical disabilities, ADA-compliant plumbing fixtures may be required. Water closets must be positioned to provide adequate clearance for a wheelchair-bound individual to maneuver within the bathroom. The top edges of lavatories and kitchen sinks must be 34″ maximum from the finished floor and provide adequate knee and toe clearance. Grab bars may need to be installed along the bathtub or water closet.

Piping Drawings. Piping drawings show the layout of a plumbing system. Piping drawings are more common for larger or custom-built houses and may not be provided in a set of prints for smaller dwellings. An architect, contractor, subcontractor, or supplier may provide piping drawings, depending on the size of the job and local code requirements.

Piping drawings are not drawn to scale, but the general location of plumbing components is shown on the drawings. Different line types are used to indicate the difference between waste and vent piping and between hot and cold water supplies. The lines are also used with symbols to show the installation of required plumbing fittings. A piping drawing can be drawn as an elevation view or as an isometric drawing. **See Figure 11-11.**

Piping Drawings

Figure 11-11

ELEVATION

ISOMETRIC

Figure 11-11. Piping drawings may be furnished by the architect, contractor, or plumber.

An elevation piping drawing is drawn in sections with interior walls hidden from view. Plumbing fixtures and piping are shown in cross section in the installed position. Isometric piping drawings are three-dimensional drawings showing piping and plumbing fixtures drawn with vertical and 30° lines. Vertical lines represent vertical pipes, while 30° lines represent horizontal pipes. A comprehensive isometric piping drawing includes all piping and fittings for a plumbing system. Piping drawings are useful when ordering the pipe and fittings required for a job.

HEATING, VENTILATING, AND AIR CONDITIONING

Heating, ventilating, and air conditioning (HVAC) systems supply the heating, ventilation, and cooling necessary to provide comfort to occupants of a house. An HVAC system also controls humidity, introduces fresh air, and cleans and circulates air throughout the house to provide maximum comfort.

Installation occurs after rough framing but before wall finish materials are applied. Installation of an HVAC system involves installation of ductwork; piping for hot and cold water; heating and cooling systems and gas lines; and electrical wiring for the HVAC system.

Two common types of residential heating systems are forced warm air and radiant heating systems. Radiant heating systems are classified as either hot water (hydronic) systems or electric systems. Alternate heating systems, such as solar or geothermal systems, may also be used to efficiently heat homes.

Forced Warm Air Heating Systems

A *forced warm air heating system* is a residential heating system that uses a blower to draw air (return air) from rooms through return air grilles and ductwork. The return air passes through a furnace system where it is filtered and then heated by any number of a variety of energy sources. The heated air (supply air) passes through the plenum and is distributed to the desired rooms through supply ductwork and registers.

Supply air ducts are commonly installed between floor joists, ceiling joists, or under slab-at-grade floors. Supply air ducts branch from a trunk supply line centrally located in the house. Supply air registers are generally located close to the exterior walls of the house with return air grilles and ductwork located near the center of the house. This arrangement of supply registers and return air grilles allows the proper circulation of return air from rooms to the furnace, and allows the return of supply air back to the rooms. **See Figure 11-12.**

The major components of a forced warm air heating system are the furnace, blower, ductwork, and unit controls. A *furnace is* a piece of equipment that heats the air circulating in a forced warm air heating system. Furnaces differ in design and operation based on the method used to generate heat. Electricity or fuels such as natural gas, fuel oil or wood are used to generate heat in a furnace. Furnaces using fuel have a burner, combustion chamber, heat exchanger, and unit controls. The burner is the heat-producing element of the furnace. The combustion process occurs in the combustion chamber. Heat is transferred to the heat exchanger where the air is heated as it passes through. Electric furnaces have resistance heating elements in place of the burner, combustion chamber, and heat exchanger.

Forced Warm Air Heating System

Figure 11-12

Figure 11-12. Supply air registers and return air grilles are located strategically to provide maximum comfort in a forced warm air heating system.

A *blower* is a piece of equipment that draws air from various living spaces and moves it through the furnace, where it is heated before being conveyed back into the rooms. The most common blower is the centrifugal blower with a blower wheel that rotates rapidly within a sheet metal enclosure. As the blower wheel rotates, air is drawn through the center and discharged out the side to the plenum. Ductwork directs supply air from the furnace into rooms to be heated, and return air from building spaces to the furnace. Supply air registers and return air grilles are located at the ends of the ductwork runs.

Supply air ductwork must be sized to carry the proper amount of air to the supply air registers. The design of the ductwork system is selected for economy and efficiency. Furnaces, blowers, and ductwork are all sized by the cubic feet of air per minute (cfm) required to properly condition the air in the living space. **See Figure 11-13.**

A perimeter radial ductwork system is the simplest and most cost-effective ductwork system for residential construction. An extended plenum duct work system is useful in long house designs such as ranch-style houses. A perimeter loop ductwork system is commonly used in cold climates.

TECHFACTS

Duct size is expressed in inches of diameter for round ducts and in inches of width and height for rectangular ducts.

Ductwork is made from galvanized sheet metal, fiberglass, or reinforced aluminum-faced materials. All ductwork must comply with applicable building codes. Supply air registers are installed on supply ducts. Supply air registers are sized to supply and direct the proper amount of heated air to a desired room. **See Figure 11-14.** Return air grilles in forced warm air heating systems are located and sized to return as much air from building spaces as supplied. Fewer return air grilles are generally installed than supply air registers. However, return air grilles are usually larger and more centrally located than supply air registers.

Ductwork Systems

Figure 11-13

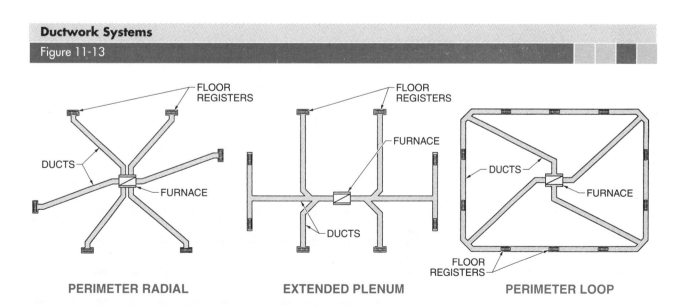

PERIMETER RADIAL   EXTENDED PLENUM   PERIMETER LOOP

Figure 11-13. Ductwork systems must be sized to carry the proper amount of air to the living space.

HVAC Plans

Figure 11-14

AIR REGISTER SIZE

12 x 16
LW
S-8

DINING ROOM

12 x 16
LW
S-9

REF.

BREAKFAST BAR

KITCHEN

DN

RETURN
AIR GRILLES

R-2
18"
BB

R-3
18"
BB

UP

DN

R-1
18"BB

ENTRY

RETURN AIR
GRILL SIZES

R-4
18"BB

S-11

12 x 16
LW

OVEN

RANGE

KIT. EXH.
FAN

LAV

12 x 16
LW

CL

LINEN
CL

BROOM
CL

Figure 11-14. Sizes of supply air registers and return air grilles are specified on HVAC plans.

Unit controls are a set of controls installed on a furnace by the manufacturer or installer to maintain safe and efficient operation of the furnace. Unit controls are classified as power controls, operating controls, and safety controls. *Power controls* are controls located in the electrical conductors leading to the furnace and blower. Power controls include the conductors, overcurrent protective devices, overload protective devices, and disconnecting means to the heating unit. Power controls must be installed by a licensed electrician according to provisions of the NEC®.

Operating controls are controls that cycle equipment on and off as required. Operating controls include a step-down transformer (in a low-voltage control system), a thermostat, a blower control, and operating relays or contactors that turn components on or off. A step-down transformer reduces the voltage available for use in the control system. A thermostat is a temperature-sensing electrical switch that turns the furnace on and off. Thermostat controls may be manually or computer controlled. The blower control operates the blower used to circulate air through the furnace and to the desired rooms.

Safety controls are controls that prevent injury to personnel or damage to equipment in the event of equipment malfunction. Safety controls include limit and combustion safety controls, such as thermocouples. Motor overloads may also be required in some furnaces.

Radiant Heating Systems

A *radiant heating system* is a series of pipes utilized to transfer heat to the living space by being filled with hot water or a series of electrical cables embedded in the floor or ceiling. Radiant heating systems are hot water (hydronic) and electric systems.

Hot Water Radiant Heating. A *hot water radiant heating (hydronic) system* utilizes water that is heated in a boiler at a central location and then distributed to the desired rooms through tubing. Hot water heating systems consist of a boiler, compression tank, circulating pump, piping, terminal devices, and unit controls. Water is heated in the boiler, distributed through supply water piping to terminal devices, and flows through the return water piping to the boiler to be reheated and redistributed. **See Figure 11-15.**

Hot Water Heating System

Figure 11-15

SUPPLY WATER PIPING

TERMINAL DEVICES

COMPRESSION TANK

RETURN WATER PIPING

BOILER

CIRCULATING PUMP

Figure 11-15. A circulating pump is located in return water piping and provides the pressure required to pump heated water through a system.

A *boiler* is a closed tank connected to an energy source that heats water to a high temperature. Boilers are classified according to the method of heat generation. Fuels commonly used include natural gas and fuel oil. Electric heating elements are also used

if other fuels are unavailable or less cost efficient. If feasible, water heated by the sun (solar energy) can be used, or water that is temperature conditioned by passing it through a series of pipes below the ground (geothermal energy) can also be used.

A *compression tank* is a tank that absorbs and relieves pressure caused by water expansion when heated. A compression tank is installed on the supply side of the boiler.

A *circulating pump* is a device that moves water through the supply water piping in a hot water heating system. A circulating pump is commonly located in the return water piping close to the boiler. Circulating pump size is determined by the volume of water in the system. *Piping* is tubing used to distribute hot water from the boiler to terminal devices and to return water back to the boiler to be reheated.

In the rooms to be heated, the hot water passes through terminal devices. A *terminal device* is a device that extracts heat from hot water to heat the air in the desired rooms. Terminal devices include radiators, convectors, blower coils, and radiant panels. A fan or blower may be used to circulate the heated air efficiently. The water returns to the boiler through return water piping. Unit controls control the boiler, circulating pump, and terminal devices and are similar to unit controls for a forced warm air heating system.

Piping for hot water radiant floor heating systems is installed in frame buildings or in slab-at-grade floors. In a frame building, flexible plastic tubing is placed between sleepers below the subfloor. Care is taken to ensure that the tubing is not punctured when the subfloor is installed. For slab-at-grade floors, tubing is set in place before the concrete is placed. **See Figure 11-16.** Heat from the hot water is radiated through the concrete and into the living area.

Radiant Floor Heating Systems
Figure 11-16

Figure 11-16. Tubing for a hot-water radiant floor heating system is installed before concrete is placed for a slab-at-grade foundation.

Hot water heating systems in residential construction are commonly one-pipe systems. In a one-pipe system, hot water is distributed to the desired rooms using branches and risers. The amount of hot water flowing through each terminal device is controlled by a valve setting or a thermostat. Two-pipe systems use separate pipes for supply and return water. Two-pipe systems provide a more consistent water temperature to all terminal devices as cooled water is returned in a separate pipe to the boiler. The two-pipe system requires additional piping and often is not cost effective for residential construction.

Electric Radiant Heating. An *electric radiant heating system* generates heat through electricity meeting resistance as it flows through embedded heating cables or baseboard units. Electric radiant heating is used in panel systems and baseboard units. Panel systems have thin wires embedded in prefabricated floor, wall, or ceiling panels. The amount of electricity flowing through the wires in the panels is controlled by a programmable or nonprogrammable thermostat. **See Figure 11-17.** Baseboard units are installed after the walls are finished and are mounted to the wall or floor. Air is heated as it contacts the heated electric coils. Some baseboard units contain water

or another heat-retaining fluid to extend the time that heat is retained and transferred to the air.

Electric Radiant Heating Panels
Figure 11-17

2 x 8 CEILING JOISTS 16″ OC

6″ BATT INSULATION

CONDUCTORS

PANEL STAPLED TO JOISTS

½″ GYPSUM BOARD

Figure 11-17. Electric radiant heating panels have embedded within each panel thin wires that radiate heat.

Whole-House Systems Approach

The *whole-house systems approach* is a system for home building or remodeling used by the homeowner, architect, and builder to optimize home energy efficiency. This approach takes into consideration the individual elements of a house and the ways in which these elements affect the house as a complete system. Some elements that are considered in the whole-house systems approach include site conditions, local climate conditions, insulation and air sealing, lighting and daylighting, space heating and cooling, water heating, and appliances. There are several benefits of using this approach when designing and building a house including reduced utility and maintenance costs, increased comfort, reduced noise, and a healthier indoor environment.

Sustainable Energy Systems

Sustainable energy systems use available natural sources to eliminate or reduce the amount of combustion or electricity necessary to produce heat or power. *Solar energy* and geothermal heat are two types of sustainable energy sources. Solar energy is the energy available from the sun in the form of sunlight. Solar energy can be changed to thermal or electrical energy. A *solar thermal energy system* is a sustainable energy system that collects and stores solar energy and is used to heat air and water in a residential structure. Well-designed solar thermal energy collection and storage systems maximize the amount of thermal energy received. **See Figure 11-18.**

Proper solar design focused on the locations of windows and skylights can increase direct solar heat in living spaces and have an impact on the amount of illumination required by lighting systems.

Solar energy can also be converted to electrical energy for use in a residence. *Photovoltaics* is a solar energy technology that uses crystalline silicon wafers that are sensitive to sunlight in order to directly convert solar radiation into electricity. A group of wafers, or cells, are combined to form a larger arrangement called a module or solar panel. A group of modules, or solar panels, called a photovoltaic (PV) array, produces an appreciable amount of electrical power with no moving parts, noise, or emissions. The PV array is usually mounted on the roof or nearby on the ground and may include battery storage or may feed the power back into direct use or feed the power back into the electrical utility grid. A *photovoltaic system* is an electrical system consisting of a PV module array and other electrical components needed to convert solar energy into electricity usable by loads. The most common residential photovoltaic system is a utility-connected system that operates a PV array in parallel with and connected to the electric utility grid. **See Figure 11-19.**

Solar Thermal Energy System
Figure 11-18

Figure 11-18. A solar thermal energy system converts solar energy to thermal energy. The thermal energy created is then used to heat air and water.

Typical Utility-Connected PV System
Figure 11-19

Figure 11-19. A utility-connected PV system is the most common system configuration. Various electrical components control, condition, and distribute the power to on-site loads.

Geothermal heat is heat derived from the heat contained within the earth. Heat contained within the earth is maintained at a constant temperature (50°F to 70°F) in the soil and rock below the frost line. With geothermal heating systems, ground-source heat pumps pull heat energy from the earth and convey it through a house. **See Figure 11-20.** A typical ground-source heat pump uses flexible tubing filled with water, refrigerant, or an antifreeze solution. As the fluid flows through the tubing in the ground, it absorbs heat energy from the earth. The warmed fluid is pumped into and provides heat for the living space. As the energy is transferred to the living space, the fluid flows through return tubing into the earth to repeat the heating process. Geothermal systems may be used in combination with other piped heating systems to augment their heating capacity and minimize the amount of fuel or electricity required to bring the circulating water up to the necessary temperature prior to recirculation.

Air Conditioning

Air conditioning is the process used to control humidity, temperature, and/or cleanliness of air within a house. An *air conditioner* is a piece of equipment used to control humidity and temperature, and remove airborne impurities in a house. An air conditioner consists of a cooling coil or an evaporator, an electric compressor, and a condenser that work together to cool the air. Cooled air is circulated through the desired rooms where it absorbs heat and is returned to the air conditioner. Two types of air conditioning systems used in residential construction are split systems and package systems. **See Figure 11-21.**

In a split system, also known as central air conditioning, the condenser and evaporator are in separate locations. The condenser is typically located on a concrete or PVC slab outside the house. The evaporator is installed on the discharge side of the furnace blower. Heat is absorbed from the air as it passes through the fins of the evaporator. A condensate drain line directs water that has condensed to the drain. The ductwork of the forced air system conveys the cooled air throughout the house. When designing and sizing a split HVAC system, additional flow resistance caused by the evaporator must be considered.

Package systems have the condenser and evaporator installed in the same unit. Supply air and return air are ducted to the unit. The unit can be mounted in the attic, in the garage, or through foundation walls. Some package air conditioning systems have integral heating system components.

Large homes may utilize a piped system for cooling similar to a piped system for heating. A chiller replaces the boiler, and chilled water is piped through to terminal units to cool living spaces. Geothermal piping can also be utilized with this type of cooling system, using the constant temperature of cooled water passed below ground to minimize the amount of energy required to recool the circulated water.

Plans and Specifications

The plot plan, foundation plan, and floor plan are commonly used for HVAC installation. The plot plan shows the location of the air conditioner and the electrical power source and natural gas supply if required. Locations for geothermal piping may also be indicated. The foundation plan gives information regarding ventilation fan locations; furnace, boiler, and air conditioning equipment locations; and ductwork. The floor plan indicates the sizes and locations of supply and return ducts. If required, furnace, boiler, and air conditioning information is also provided on the floor plan. The direction of floor joists, ceiling joists and studs in partitions and walls must be determined before piping or ductwork can be planned and installed. Information regarding the HVAC system is shown using dimensions and symbols.

Additional information may be provided on mechanical schedules, shop drawings, and ductwork layouts provided by the architect, HVAC contractor, or specifications. An engineer may be contracted by the architect or contractor to determine the specific equipment, ductwork, and/or piping requirements of the system.

Specifications for an HVAC system include information that is not included in other parts of the prints. Heating, ventilating, and air conditioning equipment is described in the specifications by the manufacturer name, model number, and type of system. The output capacity and materials used for piping and supports are also included.

SHEET METAL WORK

Sheet metal products and other sheet materials are applied on both the exterior and interior of a house. Sheet metal products used on the exterior of the house provide protection against weather and moisture infiltration. Stormwater is routed away from the house by gutters, flashing, and trim. The majority of sheet metal work required on the interior of the house is associated with the HVAC ductwork system. Most sheet metal components are prefabricated. However, some sheet metal applications require a product to be fabricated on site.

Information regarding sheet metal work is included on foundation plans, exterior elevations, floor plans, and details. Additional information may also be provided in the specifications or by the architect or contractor.

Sheet metal is commonly installed during the roofing application to ensure moisture protection and proper flow of stormwater. Flashing and crickets prevent stormwater from seeping under roofing materials. **See Figure 11-22.** Flashing is required at any change in direction of a roof, including along adjacent walls and roof projections. Step flashing is overlapped on the sides of a chimney or adjacent wall. Flashing is also used on built-up roofing as a transition between adjacent vertical and horizontal surfaces. A sheet metal cricket (saddle) is fabricated and placed along the upper edge of a chimney to prevent ice and debris from accumulating. The dimensions of a cricket are determined by the location of the chimney and the pitch of the roof. Custom sheet metal gutters or special ornamental vents may also be fabricated and installed at the job site.

Sheet Metal Flashing

Figure 11-22

Figure 11-22. Sheet metal flashing provides moisture protection and proper flow of stormwater.

LEARNER RESOURCES

ATPeResources.com/QuickLinks
Access Code: 281467

Name _____ Date _____

MULTIPLE CHOICE

_____ **1.** The NEC® is published by the ___.
  A. ICC
  B. IEEE
  C. USGBC
  D. NFPA

_____ **2.** Service-entrance conductors shall have at least a ___ A rating where the calculated load is 10 kVA or greater.
  A. 10
  B. 25
  C. 100
  D. 500

_____ **3.** Romex® is another name for ___.
  A. NM
  B. RNMC
  C. AC
  D. EMT

_____ **4.** Regarding electrical conductors, ___.
  A. copper conductors have more resistance than aluminum conductors of the same size
  B. service-entrance conductors are sized from the total volt-amp rating of the dwelling
  C. branch-circuit conductors run from the meter base to the subpanel
  D. Table 310.16 of the NEC® gives conductor sizes and ampacities based on conductor length

_____ **5.** A 15 A branch circuit commonly has ___ outlets to supply power to lighting fixtures and general-purpose receptacles.
  A. 5
  B. 10
  C. 13
  D. 20

_____ **6.** A major component of a plumbing system is ___ piping.
      A. water supply
      B. duct
      C. hydronic
      D. conduit

_____ **7.** ___ are the two primary types of residential fire suppression systems.
      A. Hot and cold
      B. CO_2 and foam
      C. Wet pipe and dry pipe
      D. Electric and liquid

_____ **8.** ___ provide information regarding connections to the supply water and sanitary sewer lines.
      A. Plan views
      B. Foundation plans
      C. Sections
      D. Plot plans

_____ **9.** Regarding the plumbing system, ___.
      A. vent piping allows gases to flow through drain lines
      B. return water is under pressure
      C. stormwater drainage piping conveys rainwater
      D. fixtures at each hot and cold water inlet control the flow of water

_____ **10.** On isometric piping drawings, vertical lines represent vertical pipes, while ___° lines represent horizontal pipes.
      A. 15
      B. 30
      C. 45
      D. 90

_____ **11.** Along with providing heating, ventilation, and cooling, an HVAC system also ___.
      A. eliminates humidity
      B. removes fresh air
      C. cleans and circulates air
      D. controls air pressure

_____ **12.** Furnaces, blowers, and ductwork are all sized by the ___ required to properly condition the air in the living space.
      A. cubic feet per minute (cfm)
      B. pounds per square inch (psi)
      C. voltage (V)
      D. gallons per minute (gpm)

_____ **13.** In a hot water radiant heating system, a ___ is a closed tank connected to an energy source that heats water to a high temperature.

      A. compression tank
      B. circulating pump
      C. terminal device
      D. boiler

_____ **14.** Regarding furnaces, ___.

      A. supply air registers of a forced warm air heating system are generally located near the center of the house
      B. a perimeter radial ductwork system is the simplest and most cost effective
      C. operating controls cycle the furnace ON or OFF
      D. it is common to have more return air grilles than supply air registers

_____ **15.** A typical ground-source heat pump uses flexible tubing filled with ___.

      A. air
      B. fuel oil
      C. antifreeze solution
      D. thin wires

_____ **16.** Regarding alternate heating systems, ___.

      A. no combustion process is required to produce heat
      B. solar energy can be converted to geothermal energy
      C. geothermal systems derive cooling from heat contained within the earth
      D. the most common residential photovoltaic system is a self-contained system

TRUE-FALSE

T   F   **1.** A power line is shown on a plot plan using two continuous lines.

T   F   **2.** A lateral electrical service is run from a pole to a dwelling.

T   F   **3.** The minimum size service-entrance conductor for a dwelling is #6.

T   F   **4.** The minimum size branch circuit for a dwelling is 20 A.

T   F   **5.** EMT must be supported every 10' and within 3' of each outlet box, junction box, cabinet, or fitting.

T   F   **6.** Raceways for electrical conductors are always made of metal.

T   F   **7.** Romex® has a separate bare ground wire.

T   F   **8.** Schedule 40 (heavy wall) may be installed in most locations where rigid metal conduit may be used.

T   F   **9.** Bends in AC armored cable are permitted but shall be no greater than five times the diameter of the cable when measured along the inside edge.

T	F	**10.** Slab-at-grade foundations require water supply and wastewater piping to be installed before concrete is placed.
T	F	**11.** Potable water is free of impurities in amounts that could cause harm.
T	F	**12.** Piping drawings are commonly drawn to the same scale as the floor plans.
T	F	**13.** Only metal pipe is used in residential fire protection systems.
T	F	**14.** Two common types of residential heating systems are forced warm air and radiant heating systems.
T	F	**15.** Hot water heating systems in residential construction are commonly two-pipe systems.
T	F	**16.** A residential fire protection system uses water as the primary extinguishing method.
T	F	**17.** Split systems have the condenser and evaporator installed in the same unit.
T	F	**18.** Unit controls are a set of controls installed on a furnace by the manufacturer or installer to maintain safe and efficient operation of the furnace.
T	F	**19.** Ductwork is made from galvanized sheet metal, fiberglass, or reinforced aluminum-faced materials.
T	F	**20.** Geothermal energy is the energy available from the sun in the form of sunlight.

COMPLETION

_____ **1.** Supply conductors from a utility company to a piece of property are regulated by the ___.

_____ **2.** ___ conductors have less resistance to current flow than aluminum conductors of the same size.

_____ **3.** ___ schedules provide information for lighting outlets, receptacles, and switches.

_____ **4.** A(n) ___ system is a low-voltage electrical system designed for various types of information technology equipment.

_____ **5.** Plumbing fixtures for the ___ plumbing work are installed after the walls are covered.

_____ **6.** Water supply piping conveys ___ water to the points of use in the house.

_____ **7.** ___ is a rigid plastic pipe that can withstand greater pressure and higher temperatures than PVC.

_____ **8.** A(n) ___ ductwork system is the simplest and most cost effective ductwork system for residential construction.

_____ **9.** ___ heat is heat derived from the heat contained within the earth.

_____ **10.** A sheet metal ___ is fabricated and placed along the upper edge of a chimney to prevent ice and debris from accumulating.

FINAL REVIEW AND EXAMS

Plans for residential construction consist of plot plans, floor plans, elevations, details, and sections. Plot plans provide information about the building lot. Floor plans show the overall shape and size of the house and provide location and size dimensions. Elevations show the exterior of the house. Details and sections provide specific structural information. Various plans within a set of prints relate to each other to provide comprehensive information.

PRINTREADING

Plans for residential construction are drawn following accepted drafting practices using traditional methods or CAD. Prints are produced from the working drawings. The prints and specifications are used by contractors and subcontractors to determine bids. Tradesworkers refer to the prints throughout construction to determine materials, location dimensions, and size dimensions.

Symbols and abbreviations are used to standardize plans and conserve space. Plot plans show the size and shape of the building lot and the location of the house on the lot. Utilities and streets are also shown. Plot plans are drawn to smaller scales. For example, a common scale for residential plot plans is 1" = 20'-0". Floor plans are generally the first drawings to be completed. The most commonly used scale for floor plans is ¼" = 1'-0". Elevations show the exterior of the house. The most commonly used scale for elevations is also ¼" = 1'-0". Cutting planes on plan views refer to sections and details. Sections provide additional information that cannot be easily shown on

plan views. Details are drawn to larger scales than plan views to clearly show the type and size of construction materials required to complete the house. Window and door schedules identify the specific type and size of windows and doors required. Windows and doors are referenced in schedules.

Tasks performed by tradesworkers are coordinated to facilitate efficient construction. Many tasks require the completion of rough-in work and return follow-up finish work to complete the job. For example, electrical work requires a rough-in of all circuits after stud walls are erected and installation of receptacles, switches, and fixtures after finished walls are in place.

A general contractor secures a building permit, and local building officials inspect the work of the various trades during construction. The house must pass a final inspection before occupancy is permitted.

The Final Review for *Printreading for Residential Construction* should be completed before taking the exams based on the Stewart Residence. The Final Review is based on the contents of the text.

TECHTIPS

Review prints in the order in which a building is constructed — site plan, foundation plan, floor plan(s), and exterior elevations.

STEWART RESIDENCE

The Stewart Residence is a contemporary house on a sloping lot located on Leawood Drive in Columbia, Missouri. The house was designed by Hulen & Hulen Designs and the plans were drawn by Pam Hulen. The complete set of plans contains eight sheets. The Stewart Residence includes the following plans:

Sheet 1
> Basement Level Floor Plan
> Plot Plan

Sheet 2
> Floor Plan
> Door Schedule
> Window Schedule
> Electrical Symbols Legend

Sheet 3
> South Elevation
> East Elevation
> Roof Plan

Sheet 4
> North Elevation
> West Elevation
> Typical Wall Detail

Sheet 5
> Kitchen Plan Detail
> Elevation Detail 1/5

> Elevation Detail 2/5
> Elevation Detail 3/5
> Elevation Detail 4/5
> Elevation Detail 5/5
> Section 6/5

Sheet 6
> Section 1/6
> Section 2/6
> Elevation Detail 3/6

Sheet 7
> Basement Level Mechanical Plan
> Section A-A

Sheet 8
> Main Level Mechanical Plan
> Cold and Hot Water Piping Diagram
> Sanitary and Vent Piping Diagram

Exams for the Stewart Residence include the following:
- Plot Plans
- Floor Plans
- Elevations
- Details
- Sections
- Mechanical Plans and Plumbing Diagrams
- Final Exam

 LEARNER RESOURCES

ATPeResources.com/QuickLinks
Access Code: 281467

Name _____ Date _____

_____ **1.** A township contains ___.
  - A. 36 sq mi
  - B. 36 quarter sections
  - C. 6 furlongs
  - D. 6 sections

_____ **2.** The denominator of a fraction is the number ___ the fraction bar.
  - A. to the left of or above
  - B. to the right of or below
  - C. above
  - D. below

T   F   **3.** The size and direction of floor joists is generally indicated on elevations.

T   F   **4.** Rebar increases the strength of concrete.

T   F   **5.** Elevations are pictorial drawings showing interior views of a building.

_____ **6.** A dimension showing the distance from a building corner to the center of a rough opening for a window is a(n) ___ dimension.

_____ **7.** The abbreviation 7 R DN refers to the number of ___ descending to a lower floor level.

T   F   **8.** A true blueprint has white lines on a blue background.

_____ **9.** Studs in ___ framing run full length from the sill plate to the double top plate.

_____ **10.** The North Elevation is the ___.
  - A. elevation facing north
  - B. direction a person faces to see the north side of the house
  - C. elevation facing south
  - D. front of the house

_____ **11.** Solid bridging is placed in a straight line or ___ to facilitate nailing.

T   F   **12.** Cutting planes for floor plans are taken 6′-0″ above the finished floor.

T   F   **13.** True North is designated on a plot plan to show house orientation on the lot.

_____ **14.** The window size is indicated ___.
   A. on sections
   B. in a window schedule
   C. with the height stated first
   D. on plot plans

T   F   **15.** Roof slope is shown on exterior elevations.

_____ **16.** Details are ___ drawn to a larger scale to show additional information.
   A. sections
   B. cutting planes
   C. scales
   D. prints

_____ **17.** The ___ size of a piece of wood is its size before planing.

T   F   **18.** Quadrilaterals are three-sided plane figures.

_____ **19.** _____ printers use print heads that contain small nozzles that spray ink onto the paper.
   A. Laser
   B. LED
   C. Inkjet
   D. Electrostatic

T   F   **20.** The radius of a circle is twice its diameter.

_____ **21.** The ___ is the lowest member in a platform-framed structure.

_____ **22.** Regarding CAD, ___.
   A. drawings cannot be shared on the Internet
   B. layering facilitates the drawing of plans for specific trades
   C. a mouse is an output system
   D. drawings cannot be easily modified

T   F   **23.** Floor plans show the shapes, sizes, and relationships of rooms.

_____ **24.** Detail 4/7 is found on Sheet ___.

T   F   **25.** A riser is the vertical portion of a stair step.

T   F   **26.** A two-story house with finished basement requires two floor plans.

_____ **27.** Regarding angles, a(n) ___.
   A. right angle contains 90°
   B. straight line contains 270°
   C. acute angle contains more than 90°
   D. obtuse angle contains less than 90°

_____ **28.** The footing width should equal ___ the wall thickness.
   A. one-half
   B. twice
   C. four times
   D. eight times

T   F   **29.** An isosceles triangle contains 3 different angles.

T   F   **30.** Exterior doors must be at least 1¾" thick.

_____ **31.** C size paper is ___.
    A. 8½" × 11"
    B. 11" × 17"
    C. 17" × 22"
    D. 18" × 24"

_____ **32.** In an oblique ___ drawing, receding lines are drawn at one-half scale.

_____ **33.** The locations of streets, easements, and utilities are shown on ___.
    A. sections
    B. details
    C. elevations
    D. plot plans

T   F   **34.** GFCI receptacles must be placed adjacent to kitchen sinks.

T   F   **35.** A gable roof has a double slope in two directions.

_____ **36.** A(n) ___ scale is used to draw plot plans.
    A. architect's
    B. civil engineer's
    C. mechanical engineer's
    D. site

T   F   **37.** Air conditioning units remove moisture from air in the house.

T   F   **38.** In regard to roofs, unit rise is the horizontal increase in height per foot of run.

_____ **39.** Natural grade is ___.
    A. the slope of the lot before rough grading
    B. the slope of the lot after rough grading
    C. shown on plot plans with solid lines
    D. shown on the survey plat

_____ **40.** A(n) ___ section is made by passing a cutting plane through the short dimension of a house.

_____ **41.** Dimension lines may be terminated with ___.
    A. extension lines
    B. slashes
    C. dimensions
    D. the outside faces of studs

T   F   **42.** The preferred method of dimensioning framed walls is to dimension to the outside face of stud corner posts.

T   F   **43.** Roof slope is the relationship of unit rise to unit run.

T   F   **44.** All triangles contain 180°.

_____ **45.** The architect's scale ___.
        A. is graduated in decimal units
        B. contains a ruler and nine scales
        C. may be triangular in shape
        D. is used when creating maps and survey drawings

T   F   **46.** A lateral electrical service is run underground.

T   F   **47.** The minimum size branch circuit for a dwelling is 15 A.

_____ **48.** Size dimensions for rooms are most clearly shown on ___.
        A. plot plans
        B. floor plans
        C. sections
        D. details

_____ **49.** ___ framing is the most common type of framing for residential construction.

T   F   **50.** A light is a pane of glass.

T   F   **51.** Floor joists may be lapped.

T   F   **52.** Concrete masonry unit partitions are generally dimensioned to the face of the finish material.

_____ **53.** A line 2¼″ long on a plan drawn at the scale of ¾″ = 1′-0″ represents a dimension of ___ in the finished house.

T   F   **54.** The apex of a triangle drawn on a window on an elevation points to the hinged side.

T   F   **55.** Termite shields or treated wood serves as a barrier against termites.

T   F   **56.** A 15 A, 120 V circuit contains 8 VA.

T   F   **57.** Supply air registers of a forced warm air heating system are generally located near the center of a house.

_____ **58.** The scale most commonly used on floor plans is ___.
        A. ⅛″ = 1′-0″
        B. ¼″ = 1′-0″
        C. ⅜″ = 1′-0″
        D. ½″ = 1′-0″

_____ **59.** Compass directions are commonly used to ___.
        A. name exterior elevations
        B. locate dimensions for rough openings of doors and windows
        C. denote roof slope
        D. determine swale on building lots

_____ **60.** Horizontal lines of isometric drawings are drawn ___° above the horizon.
        A. 15
        B. 30
        C. 45
        D. 90

_____ **61.** A flat roof must slope at least ___" per foot for proper water runoff.
   A. ¹⁄₁₆
   B. ⅛
   C. ½
   D. ¾

T   F   **62.** A dimension line indicates size or location.

T   F   **63.** The abbreviation for bedroom is BDR.

T   F   **64.** A wood stud partition with ⅜" drywall on each side of 2 × 4 studs is 4½" thick.

_____ **65.** A(n) ___ is a strip of privately owned land set aside for placement of public utilities.
   A. set aside
   B. planter strip
   C. right-of-way
   D. easement

T   F   **66.** Standard brick is classified by its nominal size.

T   F   **67.** Copper conductors are more expensive than aluminum conductors.

T   F   **68.** A cornice detail provides framing and finish information.

Identification 12-1

_____ **1.** Concrete (elevation)

_____ **2.** Glass (elevation)

_____ **3.** Rough framing member

_____ **4.** Sliding doors (plan view)

_____ **5.** Pedestal lavatory

_____ **6.** Common brick (plan view)

_____ **7.** Ceiling light

_____ **8.** Hose bibb

_____ **9.** Brick veneer (plan view)

_____ **10.** Switch

Identification 12-2

_____ **1.** Isosceles triangle

_____ **2.** Hexagon

_____ **3.** Acute angle

_____ **4.** Square

_____ **5.** Equilateral triangle

_____ **6.** Eccentric circles

_____ **7.** Concentric circles

_____ **8.** Rectangle

_____ **9.** Rhombus

_____ **10.** Octagon

Identification 12-3

_____ **1.** Baseboard

_____ **2.** Vertical rebar

_____ **3.** Horizontal rebar

_____ **4.** Sill plate

_____ **5.** Floor truss

_____ **6.** Brick

_____ **7.** Foundation footing

_____ **8.** Brick tie

_____ **9.** Foundation wall

_____ **10.** Earth

Completion

_____ **1.** ¼″ = 1′-0″

_____ **2.** ¼″ = 1′-0″

_____ **3.** ¼″ = 1′-0″

_____ **4.** ¼″ = 1′-0″

_____ **5.** ⅜″ = 1′-0″

Identification 12-4

_____ **1.** Interior door

_____ **2.** Exterior door

_____ **3.** Casement window

_____ **4.** Double-hung window

_____ **5.** Earth

_____ **6.** Steel

Ⓐ   Ⓑ   Ⓒ

Ⓓ   Ⓔ   Ⓕ

285

Name _____ Date _____

Refer to Stewart Residence.

T   F   **1.** The Plot Plan is drawn to the scale of ¼" = 1'-0".

_____ **2.** The lot for the Stewart Residence generally slopes down from ___ to ___.
     A. southeast; northwest
     B. northeast; southwest
     C. northwest; southeast
     D. north; south

T   F   **3.** PH drew the Plot Plan for the Stewart Residence.

_____ **4.** The lot for the Stewart Residence contains ___ sq ft.
     A. 514
     B. 11,025
     C. 15,960
     D. 23,104

_____ **5.** The front of the Stewart Residence faces ___.

_____ **6.** The finish floor elevation of the main level is ___ above the finish floor elevation of the garage.

T   F   **7.** A 24' existing pine tree in the front yard has a 20'-0" diameter drip.

_____ **8.** The southeast corner of the garage is ___ from the point of beginning and ___ from the east property line.
     A. 15'-0"; 40'-0"
     B. 40'-0"; 15'-0"
     C. 40'-0"; 96'-0"
     D. 105'-0"; 152'-0"

_____ **9.** The general shape of the lot for the Stewart Residence is a ___.
     A. rhombus
     B. rhomboid
     C. trapezoid
     D. trapezium

T   F   **10.** The Den is located on the south side of the Stewart Residence.

T   F   **11.** Leawood Drive is parallel to the east property line of the Stewart Residence.

_____ **12.** The northeast corner of the lot is approximately ___ above the point of beginning.
     A. 6'-0"
     B. 8'-0"
     C. 10'-0"
     D. 12'-0"

_____ **13.** The lot for the Stewart Residence is ___ wide and ___ deep measured along the property lines.
     A. 84'-0"; 96'-0"
     B. 96'-0"; 105'-0"
     C. 105'-0"; 152'-0"
     D. 105'-0"; 144'-0"

_____ **14.** The finish floor elevation of the Den is ___.

_____ **15.** A(n) ___ on the finish grade diverts surface water away from the northwest corner of the Stewart Residence.

_____ **16.** A Deck is located on the ___ side of the Stewart Residence.

_____ **17.** The driveway slopes approximately ___ from the Garage entrance to Leawood Drive.
     A. 2'-0"
     B. 4'-0"
     C. 6'-0"
     D. 8'-0"

_____ **18.** An easement for utilities is located along the ___ property line.

    T   F   **19.** Three existing trees are shown on the lot for the Stewart Residence.

_____ **20.** The elevation for the point of beginning is ___.

_____ **21.** The lot for the Stewart Residence is steepest near the front ___.

_____ **22.** The finish floor elevation of the garage is ___.

_____ **23.** The west property line is ___ long.

_____ **24.** The south and east property lines meet at an angle of ___.

_____ **25.** The Stewart Residence is set back ___ from the front property line.

Identification

_____ **1.** Tree

_____ **2.** Property line

_____ **3.** Finish grade

_____ **4.** Utility easement

_____ **5.** Point of beginning

Ⓐ   Ⓑ   Ⓒ

14'   • ELEV 0'-0"

Ⓓ   Ⓔ

Name _____ Date _____

Refer to Stewart Residence.

_____ **1.** The overall dimensions of the Stewart Residence, not including the Deck, are 42'-5" × ___.

_____ **2.** Floor plans for the Stewart Residence are drawn to the scale of ___.

_____ **3.** The main electrical panel is located in the ___.

_____ **4.** The Future Bath is stubbed in for a ___, ___, and ___.
      A. lavatory; water closet; shower
      B. lavatory; water closet; bathtub
      C. double-bowl vanity; water closet; bathtub
      D. lavatory; water closet; laundry

_____ **5.** Notations on the Basement Level Floor Plan indicate that floor joists for the main level are ___.

    T   F   **6.** The incandescent fixture in the dining room is controlled by three-way switches.

_____ **7.** Regarding the bedrooms, ___.
      A. Bedroom 3 has a walk-in closet
      B. Bedroom 2 is larger than Bedroom 3
      C. fluorescent fixtures are located in each bedroom
      D. the Master Bedroom has four recessed can fixtures

_____ **8.** Regarding the Den, ___.
      A. bypass doors separate the Den from the Entry
      B. bay windows are located in the west wall
      C. overall room dimensions are 13'-0" × 15'-8½"
      D. six duplex outlets are located 12" above the finish floor

_____ **9.** Regarding the Kitchen, ___.
      A. a 3' square skylight is located in the panned ceiling
      B. the refrigerator is located on the north wall
      C. casement windows provide a view of the front yard
      D. the cooktop is mounted in the island cabinet

_____ **10.** Regarding the Living Room, ___.
      A. built-in cabinets and shelves flank the fireplace
      B. all duplex outlets are located 12" above the finish floor
      C. ceiling lighting is controlled by three-way switches
      D. casement windows with a circle top are located in the east wall

_____ **11.** Regarding the Dining Room, ___.
  A. sliding glass doors lead to the Deck
  B. a ceiling fan with light fixture is controlled by a wall switch
  C. all electrical receptacles are GFCI protected
  D. the overall size is 11'-0" × 10'-0"

_____ **12.** Regarding the Entry, ___.
  A. a coat closet is to the right of the front door
  B. a stairway with 7 R UP leads to the main level
  C. four skylights provide natural light
  D. a 12" sidelight is located on the hinged side of the door

_____ **13.** Regarding the bathrooms, ___.
  A. both bathrooms on the main level are the same size
  B. the Master Bath contains a linen closet
  C. the Master Bath has a pull chain fixture
  D. the Hall Bath has one light

_____ **14.** Regarding the Future Family Room, ___.
  A. a full glass door leads to the Deck
  B. a telephone outlet is adjacent to the fireplace
  C. the overall size is 14'-9½" × 17'-4½"
  D. no windows are shown in the west wall

_____ **15.** Regarding the future Workshop, ___.
  A. casement windows provide natural light
  B. floor joists above run east to west
  C. all duplex outlets are 42" above the finish floor
  D. there is direct access to the Garage

_____ **16.** Regarding the Garage, ___.
  A. a 7'-0" × 16'-0" overhead door is shown
  B. the lower level of the house is three steps up
  C. an overhead steel beam is supported by 3" diameter steel columns
  D. overall dimensions are 13'-1½" × 23'-2½"

T   F   **17.** A low storage area is located beneath the Den.

T   F   **18.** Two cutting planes on the Floor Plan refer to sections shown on Sheet 6.

_____ **19.** A total of ___ telephone outlets is installed in the Stewart Residence.

_____ **20.** The hallway on the main level is ___ wide.

_____ **21.** ___ lighting fixtures in the kitchen are controlled by three-way switches.

T   F   **22.** The walk-in closet in the Master Bedroom has two shelves with rods.

T   F   **23.** The lighting fixture in the storage closet of the Future Family Room is controlled by a pull chain.

T   F   **24.** The concrete slab beneath the stairway is thickened to support the additional weight.

_____ **25.** The finish floor level of the low storage area is ___" above the finish floor level of the garage.

_____ **26.** A(n) ___ fixture near the fireplace in the Future Family Room is controlled by a wall switch.

_____ **27.** The attic is entered through a scuttle measuring ___.

_____ **28.** The Deck measures 10'-0" × ___.

_____ **29.** Closets in Bedrooms 2 and 3 are ___ deep.

_____ **30.** The hall linen closet is ___ wide.

_____ **31.** A panned ceiling is shown in the ___.

_____ **32.** The ceiling in the ___ Room is vaulted.

_____ **33.** The concrete foundation wall beneath the den is ___" thick.

T   F   **34.** The water heater is located in the Laundry Room.

_____ **35.** The north wall of the Kitchen projects ___ beyond the rest of the north wall of the Stewart Residence.

T   F   **36.** The Hall Bath contains two GFI outlets.

T   F   **37.** Bay windows are located in the Living Room.

T   F   **38.** The front stairs contain 12 risers.

T   F   **39.** The linen closet in the Master Bath has no lighting fixture.

T   F   **40.** Two Garage door opener outlets are shown on the Garage ceiling.

_____ **41.** A total of ___ duplex outlets are located 12" above the finish floor in the walls of the Future Family Room.

_____ **42.** H windows in the Future Family Room are centered ___ from the northwest corner of the house.

_____ **43.** E windows in the Workshop are centered ___ from the northeast corner of the house.

T   F   **44.** A floor drain is shown in the center of the Garage floor.

T   F   **45.** Two H windows provide natural light in the Laundry Room.

T   F   **46.** The hallway on the main floor is 21'-1¼" long.

T   F   **47.** Ceiling fixtures on the Kitchen ceiling are fluorescent.

_____ **48.** The service-entrance conductors enter the house on the ___ side.

_____ **49.** Bedroom 3 contains approximately ___ sq ft.
  A. 93
  B. 103
  C. 133
  D. 153

_____ **50.** The Master Bedroom contains approximately ___ sq ft.
  A. 117
  B. 137
  C. 157
  D. 177

_____ **51.** The storage closet beneath the stairway measures 3'-5¾" × ___.

_____ **52.** D windows in the Den are centered ___ from the framed southwest corner.

T   F   **53.** A cased opening with arch leads from the Kitchen to the Dining Room.

_____ **54.** The main entry is ___ wide.

_____ **55.** The bay for A windows in the Den is ___ wide.

_____ **56.** Four recessed can lighting fixtures are shown in the ___.
  A. Den
  B. Living Room
  C. Master Bath
  D. Kitchen

T   F   **57.** Wrought iron handrails are shown for the entry steps.

T   F   **58.** Refrigerator space in the Kitchen is provided on the east wall.

T   F   **59.** All bedroom closets have bypass doors.

T   F   **60.** The wall receptacle on the north wall of the Living Room is split-wired.

Identification

_____ **1.** Ceiling fixture

_____ **2.** Floor drain

_____ **3.** Ceiling fan with light

_____ **4.** Wall sconce fixture

_____ **5.** Casement window

_____ **6.** Telephone

_____ **7.** Single-pole switch

_____ **8.** 120 V receptacle

_____ **9.** Brick

_____ **10.** Concrete

Name _____ Date _____

Refer to Stewart Residence.

_____ **1.** All elevations are drawn to the scale of ___.

_____ **2.** The ___ Elevation shows the front of the Stewart Residence.

_____ **3.** Regarding the South Elevation, ___.
    A. the fireplace chimney is centered on the bay windows
    B. sidelights flank the entry door
    C. all exterior walls are brick veneer
    D. one skylight is centered on the entry door

_____ **4.** Regarding the East Elevation, ___.
    A. the roof slopes 4 in 12
    B. an ACQ-treated handrail leads to the entry door
    C. exterior walls are brick veneer and 4″ lap siding
    D. a 3′-0″ diameter glass block window and one-half glass door provide natural light in the Garage

_____ **5.** Regarding the North Elevation, ___.
    A. the Deck extends completely across the back side of the Stewart Residence
    B. 4 × 4 treated posts set in 12″ diameter concrete piers support the Deck
    C. exterior walls are brick veneer and 8″ lap siding
    D. the roof is finished with cedar shakes

_____ **6.** Regarding the West Elevation, the ___.
    A. Den floor and Basement floor are at the same level
    B. chimney is brick veneer with a 4″ limestone cap
    C. roof slope is 5 in 12
    D. the Basement ceiling height is 6′-1½″

T   F   **7.** The Deck floor level is level with the main floor level.

T   F   **8.** Overhead Garage doors are vinyl-clad metal.

_____ **9.** A total of ___ C windows are shown on the East Elevation.

_____ **10.** Exterior walls are either brick veneer or ___″ vinyl siding.

_____ **11.** The O window has a(n) ___ top.

_____ **12.** The roof has a total of ___ skylights.

T   F   **13.** Front entry steps contain a landing.

T   F   **14.** Deck steps are attached to the rear wall.

_____ **15.** The front entry has a(n) ___-panel, insulated metal door.

T   F   **16.** All concrete foundation footings are at the same level.

_____ **17.** Regarding the deck, ___.
                A. four 12" diameter concrete piers are shown
                B. stairs are straight run with two handrails
                C. stairs are located on the west end of the Deck
                D. the handrail is 3'-0" above the deck floor

T   F   **18.** A combination of gable and shed roofs is shown for the Stewart Residence.

T   F   **19.** Glass blocks are shown on the North and East Elevations.

_____ **20.** The Basement has a clear ceiling height of ___.

_____ **21.** B windows are 4'-9" × ___.

_____ **22.** The front entry steps are made of ___.

_____ **23.** Exterior wall finish above the Garage roof is ___.

_____ **24.** Each Garage door is 9'-0" wide × ___ high.

_____ **25.** The K skylight is visible on all elevations except the ___ Elevation.

Matching

_____ **1.** Pitch symbol

_____ **2.** Finished wood

_____ **3.** Brick veneer

_____ **4.** Batt insulation

_____ **5.** Centerline

_____ **6.** Diameter

_____ **7.** Finish grade

_____ **8.** Gravel fill

_____ **9.** Dimension line

_____ **10.** Rigid foam insulation

Name _____ Date _____

Refer to Stewart Residence.

_____ **1.** Elevation Detail 2/5 shows the ___ wall of the Kitchen.

_____ **2.** Kitchen base cabinets contain a total of ___ drawers.

_____ **3.** The refrigerator cabinet has an opening ___" wide.

    T   F   **4.** Wall countertops have a 4" backsplash.

    T   F   **5.** Soffits over the wall cabinets are 14" deep.

    T   F   **6.** A full glass, insulated metal door leads to the Deck.

_____ **7.** Regarding the wall cabinets, ___.
    A. two 21" × 30" cabinets are required
    B. three 33" × 30" cabinets are required
    C. all wall cabinets are 12" deep
    D. all wall cabinets are the same height

_____ **8.** Regarding the base cabinets, ___.
    A. the drawer base is 14" wide
    B. all base cabinets are 3'-0" high
    C. an 8" backsplash is attached to the countertop
    D. all base cabinets have doors

    T   F   **9.** Elevation 3/5 shows details of the oven cabinet.

_____ **10.** Kitchen cabinet elevation details are drawn to the scale of ___.

_____ **11.** The Kitchen Plan is drawn to the scale of ___.

_____ **12.** Regarding the Kitchen Plan, ___.
    A. the panned ceiling is shown with dashed lines
    B. Detail 3/5 shows the sink
    C. the refrigerator is centered between the oven and broom pantry
    D. Detail 5/5 shows the cut through the skylight

_____ **13.** Regarding the section detail of the skylight, ___.
    A. the skylight is 3'-0" in diameter
    B. 6" batt insulation surrounds the skylight shaft
    C. the scale is ⅜" = 1'-0"
    D. galvanized sheet metal is used as flashing

    T   F   **14.** The broom pantry is placed between the lazy Susan pantry and the cooktop.

_____ **15.** The breakfast bar is ___" lower than the island counter.

_____ **16.** All wall cabinets, except for the hood cabinet, are ___ high.

_____ **17.** The soffit over the broom pantry is ___ deep.

T   F   **18.** The microwave is placed in the oven cabinet above the oven.

_____ **19.** Vertical clearance between the base cabinet countertops and wall cabinets is ___.

T   F   **20.** The sink base cabinet is 36" wide.

_____ **21.** Soffits over the wall cabinets are ___ high.

T   F   **22.** The lazy Susan pantry is shown on Elevation Detail 1/5.

_____ **23.** Regarding the section detail of the skylight, ___.
   A. panned ceiling framing is 2 × 6s
   B. the cutting plane for the section is shown on the Kitchen Plan
   C. 12" batt insulation surrounds the skylight framing
   D. the blown insulation is R-19

_____ **24.** The opening for the oven is ___" wide.

T   F   **25.** The vertical clearance between the countertops and wall cabinets is 1'-6".

Matching

_____ **1.** Cabinet door hinged on left

_____ **2.** Cabinet door hinged on right

_____ **3.** Rough wood

_____ **4.** Cutting plane line

_____ **5.** Batt insulation

Name _____ Date _____

Refer to Stewart Residence.

_____ **1.** The cutting plane for Section 1/6 is shown on Sheet(s) ___.

_____ **2.** Sections are drawn to the scale of ___.

T   F   **3.** Sections are shown on Sheet 6 of 7.

T   F   **4.** Roof slope for the Stewart Residence is 5 in 12.

_____ **5.** The finish floor level of the Den is ___ below the finish floor level of the Living Room.

_____ **6.** Floor-to-ceiling height of the Dining Room is ___.

T   F   **7.** The Workshop is directly below the Master Bedroom.

_____ **8.** Section 1/6 is a(n) ___ section.

_____ **9.** Section 2/6 is a(n) ___ section.

_____ **10.** Regarding the chimney, ___.
     A. face brick is used in the Future Family Room and the Living Room
     B. native stone is used in the Living Room
     C. a 12" × 48" mantle is installed over the fireplace
     D. a stone hearth is shone

_____ **11.** Regarding the Workshop, ___.
     A. two hollow-core doors are shown
     B. six-panel exterior doors lead to the backyard
     C. one steel-clad door is shown
     D. there is low storage below

T   F   **12.** Door 8 provides an entrance to the Master Bedroom.

_____ **13.** The finish floor level of the low storage area is ___ below the finish floor level of the Future Family Room.

T   F   **14.** North and south walls of the living room are 10'-0" high.

T   F   **15.** The Living Room contains a vaulted ceiling.

T   F   **16.** Sections of the Stewart Residence were drawn by PH.

_____ **17.** The stairway from the Garage to the lower level contain ___ risers.

_____ **18.** A(n) ___ beam in the Garage supports floor joists above.

T   F   **19.** The floor-to-ceiling height of the Future Family Room is 7'-9½".

T   F   **20.** Two casement windows are shown on the section of the Dining Room.

_____ **21.** Regarding the fireplaces, one is located on the ___.
  A. south wall of the Living Room
  B. east wall of the Future Family Room
  C. east wall of the Living Room
  D. north wall of the Future Family Room

_____ **22.** Closet doors for Bedroom 3 are ___ doors.

T   F   **23.** The size for Dining Room windows is 4'-9" × 5'-0⅜".

T   F   **24.** The circletop window in the living room contains six pie-shaped lights.

T   F   **25.** The floor-to-ceiling height in all bedrooms is 8'-1⅛".

Matching

_____ **1.** Concrete

_____ **2.** Native stone

_____ **3.** Brick veneer

_____ **4.** Steel beam

_____ **5.** Pitch symbol

Name _____ Date _____

Refer to Stewart Residence.

T   F   **1.** The Mechanical Room does not contain a floor drain.

_____ **2.** The air conditioner condenser coil is ___.
  A. shown on Sheet 8
  B. attached to the furnace with a flex connection
  C. indicated by a circle on the north wall
  D. located directly above the furnace

T   F   **3.** The flue is 30″ × 8″.

_____ **4.** The diameter of the waste vent from the Master Bath to the main vent is ___″.
  A. 1½
  B. 2
  C. 3
  D. 4

_____ **5.** The flue in the outside wall of the Master Bath is connected to the ___.
  A. furnace
  B. hot water tank
  C. air conditioner
  D. vent piping for the Master Bath double sink

_____ **6.** There are ___ air outlets from the HVAC system in the Den.

_____ **7.** The main water service pipe is ___″ diameter.

_____ **8.** The water supply line to the dishwasher is ___″ diameter.

_____ **9.** The size of the return air duct at the point where it drops to enter the furnace is ___.
  A. 15 × 15
  B. 23 × 12
  C. 18 × 8
  D. 22 × 19

_____ **10.** The abbreviation CO on the sanitary and vent piping diagram designates ___.

_____ **11.** The duct at the north wall of the Future Family Room is ___.
  A. 12″ high × 8″ wide
  B. 12″ high × 6″ wide
  C. 8″ high × 12″ wide
  D. 6″ high × 12″ wide

T F **12.** One 10 × 6 duct in the Future Family Room is capped for future use.

T F **13.** No ducts extend to the upper floors from the wall between the Future Family Room and the low storage area.

T F **14.** The gas line is attached to the furnace on the west side of the furnace.

_____ **15.** The liquid and suctions lines shown on the north wall are related to the ___.
    A. hot water tank
    B. floor drain
    C. air conditioner
    D. furnace

T F **16.** All air supply ductwork shown is 8″ high.

T F **17.** Ductwork must be lowered between the Workshop and Garage to extend under the supporting beam.

_____ **18.** The 8 × 4 duct at the east end of the Garage supplies air to the ___.
    A. Garage
    B. Master Bedroom
    C. Bedroom 2
    D. Bedroom 3

_____ **19.** The floor condensate drain from the air conditioning coil is ___″ in diameter.

_____ **20.** The gas meter is on the ___ wall.
    A. north
    B. south
    C. east
    D. west

_____ **21.** The capacity of the furnace is ___ cfm.

T F **22.** There are three hose bibbs shown on the water piping diagram.

T F **23.** Both bathtub waste drain pipes are 2″ in diameter.

_____ **24.** In the note 5 TONS CLG CAP, the abbreviation CLG is ___.

T F **25.** A ½″ water supply line is provided for the refrigerator.

T F **26.** A funnel drain is located in the basement floor.

_____ **27.** The cold water supply connection to the hot water tank is ___″.
    A. ½
    B. ¾
    C. 1
    D. 1½

_____ **28.** The abbreviation WC on the cold and hot water piping diagram designates ___.

_____ **29.** The abbreviation VTR on the sanitary and vent piping diagram designates ___.

Name _____ Date _____

Refer to Stewart Residence.

T   F   **1.** Plans for the Stewart Residence contain six sheets.

T   F   **2.** PH of Hulen & Hulen Designs drew all plans for the Stewart Residence.

T   F   **3.** The scale for each sheet of the Stewart Residence plans is given in a title block on each sheet.

_____ **4.** The Stewart Residence is a ___.
- A. one-story house with full basement
- B. two-story house with full basement
- C. one-and-one-half story house with living space in the attic
- D. contemporary house on a sloping lot

_____ **5.** The building corner from which horizontal measurements begin is located ___ of the point of beginning.
- A. 40'-0" south and 15'-0" west
- B. 40'-0" north and 15'-0" east
- C. 40'-0" south and 15'-0" east
- D. 40'-0" north and 15'-0" west

_____ **6.** The front of the Stewart Residence is finished with ___.
- A. 8" vinyl siding and wood shingles
- B. 4" vinyl siding, brick veneer, and wood shingles
- C. 8" vinyl siding, brick veneer, and asphalt shingles
- D. brick veneer

T   F   **7.** The native stone chimney is south of the ridge board.

T   F   **8.** Casement windows in the Kitchen provide a view of Leawood Drive.

T   F   **9.** One #3 door is required.

_____ **10.** Regarding the floor plans, ___.
- A. the Stewart Residence has four bedrooms
- B. a separate Breakfast Area adjoins the Kitchen
- C. the Den and Future Family Room are on the same level
- D. the Master Bedroom measures 12'-9" × 13'-6"

T   F   **11.** Two hose bibbs are shown for the Stewart Residence.

T   F   **12.** Four 1⅜" × 2'-8" × 6'-8" hollow-core, six-panel birch doors are required.

T   F   **13.** Six telephone outlets are to be installed during construction.

T   F   **14.** Glass block windows for the Stewart Residence are custom made.

_____ **15.** Skylights in the entry measure ___.

_____ **16.** Duplex outlets in the Stewart Residence are placed either 12" or ___" above the finished floor.

T   F   **17.** Floor joists for the main floor run north to south.

_____ **18.** All roofs of the Stewart Residence have a(n) ___ in 12 slope.

_____ **19.** Roof overhang at exterior walls measures ___.

_____ **20.** Regarding typical concrete foundations, ___.
       A. two #4 horizontal rebar are continuous
       B. 4" rigid insulation is placed around foundation walls
       C. a 16" × 8" concrete footing supports the foundation wall
       D. foundation walls are 10" thick

_____ **21.** Regarding typical exterior walls, ___.
       A. 2 × 6 studs are 16" OC
       B. ½" diameter ABs are 2'-0" OC
       C. insulation is blown in all exterior walls
       D. sill plates are 2 × 8s

_____ **22.** Regarding doors, ___.
       A. all are flush panel
       B. #11 is an exterior door
       C. a full glass door leads to the deck
       D. all are 6-panel wood doors

_____ **23.** Regarding windows, ___.
       A. Andersen C15 casement windows are shown in Bedrooms 2 and 3
       B. the vertical dimension for Den windows is 5'-0⅜"
       C. all windows in the residence are the same type
       D. all the windows are casement

_____ **24.** Four ___ can fixtures are installed in the Den ceiling.

T   F   **25.** The hall closet has a pull chain lighting fixture.

T   F   **26.** The deck and handrail are ACQ treated.

T   F   **27.** Perforated PVC drain tile is placed around foundation walls.

T   F   **28.** Elevation details of the kitchen are drawn to the scale of ¼" = 1'-0".

T   F   **29.** An 8' utility easement runs along the north side of the lot.

_____ **30.** All receptacles near vanities are ___ protected.

_____ **31.** The Laundry Room is entered through the ___.

_____ **32.** The Garage measures ___ × 26'-2½".

_____ **33.** N windows are shown on the ___ Elevation.

T   F   **34.** The Stewart Residence contains gable and shed roofs.

T   F   **35.** The exterior wall finish of the Stewart Residence is 8" vinyl siding and brick veneer.

APPENDIX

ARCHITECTURAL SYMBOLS . . .

Material	Elevation	Plan	Section
Earth			
Brick	WITH NOTE INDICATING TYPE OF BRICK (COMMON, FACE, ETC.)	COMMON OR FACE FIREBRICK	SAME AS PLAN VIEWS
Concrete		LIGHTWEIGHT STRUCTURAL	SAME AS PLAN VIEWS
Concrete Masonry Unit		OR	OR
Stone	CUT STONE RUBBLE	CUT STONE RUBBLE CAST STONE (CONCRETE)	CUT STONE CAST STONE (CONCRETE) RUBBLE OR CUT STONE
Wood	SIDING PANEL	WOOD STUD REMODELING	ROUGH MEMBER TRIM MEMBER PLYWOOD
Plaster		METAL LATH AND PLASTER SOLID PLASTER	LATH AND PLASTER
Roofing	SHINGLES	SAME AS ELEVATION	
Glass	OR GLASS BLOCK	GLASS GLASS BLOCK	SMALL SCALE LARGE SCALE

. . . ARCHITECTURAL SYMBOLS

Material	Elevation	Plan	Section
Facing Tile	CERAMIC TILE	FLOOR TILE	CERAMIC TILE LARGE SCALE CERAMIC TILE SMALL SCALE
Structural Clay Tile			SAME AS PLAN VIEW
Insulation		LOOSE FILL OR BATTS RIGID SPRAY FOAM	SAME AS PLAN VIEWS
Sheet Metal Flashing		OCCASIONALLY INDICATED BY NOTE	
Metals Other Than Flashing	INDICATED BY NOTE OR DRAWN TO SCALE	SAME AS ELEVATION	SMALL SCALE · STEEL · CAST IRON · ALUMINUM · BRONZE OR BRASS
Structural Steel	INDICATED BY NOTE OR DRAWN TO SCALE	OR	REBARS LI SMALL SCALE · LI LARGE SCALE L-ANGLES, S-BEAMS, ETC.

PLOT PLAN SYMBOLS

NORTH	FIRE HYDRANT	WALK	E OR	ELECTRIC SERVICE
POINT OF BEGINNING (POB)	MAILBOX	IMPROVED ROAD	G OR	NATURAL GAS LINE
UTILITY METER OR VALVE	MANHOLE	UNIMPROVED ROAD	W OR	WATER LINE
POWER POLE AND GUY	TREE	BUILDING LINE	T OR	TELEPHONE LINE
LIGHT STANDARD	BUSH	PROPERTY LINE		NATURAL GRADE
TRAFFIC SIGNAL	HEDGE ROW	PROPERTY LINE		FINISH GRADE
STREET SIGN	FENCE	TOWNSHIP LINE	+ XX.00′	EXISTING ELEVATION

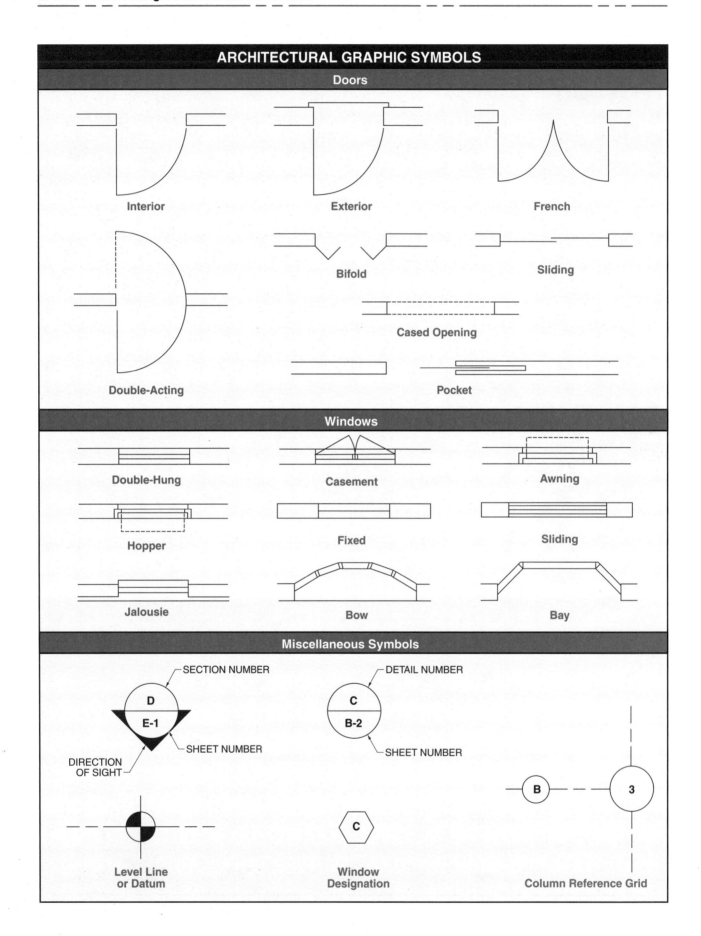

ARCHITECTURAL GRAPHIC SYMBOLS

Doors

Interior

Exterior

French

Double-Acting

Bifold

Sliding

Cased Opening

Pocket

Windows

Double-Hung

Casement

Awning

Hopper

Fixed

Sliding

Jalousie

Bow

Bay

Miscellaneous Symbols

SECTION NUMBER
D
E-1
DIRECTION OF SIGHT
SHEET NUMBER

DETAIL NUMBER
C
B-2
SHEET NUMBER

B — — 3

Level Line or Datum

C
Window Designation

Column Reference Grid

ELECTRICAL SYMBOLS...

Lighting Outlets

OUTLET BOX AND INCANDESCENT LIGHTING FIXTURE
CEILING   WALL

INCANDESCENT TRACK LIGHTING

BLANKED OUTLET (B) (B)

DROP CORD (D)

EXIT LIGHT AND OUTLET BOX. SHADED AREAS DENOTE FACES.

OUTDOOR POLE-MOUNTED FIXTURES

JUNCTION BOX (J) (J)

LAMPHOLDER WITH PULL SWITCH (L)PS (L)PS

MULTIPLE FLOODLIGHT ASSEMBLY

EMERGENCY BATTERY PACK WITH CHARGER

INDIVIDUAL FLUORESCENT FIXTURE

OUTLET BOX AND FLUORESCENT LIGHTING TRACK FIXTURE

CONTINUOUS FLUORESCENT FIXTURE

SURFACE-MOUNTED FLUORESCENT FIXTURE

Panelboards

FLUSH-MOUNTED PANELBOARD AND CABINET

SURFACE-MOUNTED PANELBOARD AND CABINET

Convenience Outlets

SINGLE RECEPTACLE OUTLET

DUPLEX RECEPTACLE OUTLET– 120 V

TRIPLEX RECEPTACLE OUTLET– 240 V

SPLIT-WIRED DUPLEX RECEPTACLE OUTLET

SPLIT-WIRED TRIPLEX RECEPTACLE OUTLET

SINGLE SPECIAL-PURPOSE RECEPTACLE OUTLET

DUPLEX SPECIAL-PURPOSE RECEPTACLE OUTLET

RANGE OUTLET R

SPECIAL-PURPOSE CONNECTION DW

CLOSED-CIRCUIT TELEVISION CAMERA

CLOCK HANGER RECEPTACLE (C)

FAN HANGER RECEPTACLE (F)

FLOOR SINGLE RECEPTACLE OUTLET

FLOOR DUPLEX RECEPTACLE OUTLET

FLOOR SPECIAL-PURPOSE OUTLET

UNDERFLOOR DUCT AND JUNCTION BOX FOR TRIPLE, DOUBLE, OR SINGLE DUCT SYSTEM AS INDICATED BY NUMBER OF PARALLEL LINES

Busducts and Wireways

SERVICE, FEEDER, OR PLUG-IN BUSWAY B B B

CABLE THROUGH LADDER OR CHANNEL C C C

WIREWAY W W W

Switch Outlets

SINGLE-POLE SWITCH S

DOUBLE-POLE SWITCH S2

THREE-WAY SWITCH S3

FOUR-WAY SWITCH S4

AUTOMATIC DOOR SWITCH SD

KEY-OPERATED SWITCH SK

CIRCUIT BREAKER SCB

WEATHERPROOF CIRCUIT BREAKER SWCB

DIMMER SDM

REMOTE CONTROL SWITCH SRC

WEATHERPROOF SWITCH SWP

FUSED SWITCH SF

WEATHERPROOF FUSED SWITCH SWF

TIME SWITCH ST

CEILING PULL SWITCH S

SWITCH AND SINGLE RECEPTACLE S

SWITCH AND DOUBLE RECEPTACLE S

A STANDARD SYMBOL WITH AN ADDED LOWERCASE SUBSCRIPT LETTER IS USED TO DESIGNATE A VARIATION IN STANDARD EQUIPMENT a,b a,b Sa,b

...ELECTRICAL SYMBOLS

Commercial and Industrial Systems

PAGING SYSTEM DEVICE

FIRE ALARM SYSTEM DEVICE

COMPUTER DATA SYSTEM DEVICE

PRIVATE TELEPHONE SYSTEM DEVICE

SOUND SYSTEM

FIRE ALARM CONTROL PANEL — FACP

Signaling System Outlets for Residential Systems

PUSHBUTTON

BUZZER

BELL

BELL AND BUZZER COMBINATION

COMPUTER DATA OUTLET

BELL RINGING TRANSFORMER — BT

ELECTRIC DOOR OPENER — D

CHIME — CH

TELEVISION OUTLET — TV

THERMOSTAT — T

Underground Electrical Distribution or Electrical Lighting Systems

MANHOLE — M

HANDHOLE — H

TRANSFORMER-MANHOLE OR VAULT — TM

TRANSFORMER PAD — TP

UNDERGROUND DIRECT BURIAL CABLE

UNDERGROUND DUCT LINE

STREET LIGHT STANDARD FED FROM UNDERGROUND CIRCUIT

Above-Ground Electrical Distribution or Lighting Systems

POLE

STREET LIGHT AND BRACKET

PRIMARY CIRCUIT

SECONDARY CIRCUIT

DOWN GUY

HEAD GUY

SIDEWALK GUY

SERVICE WEATHERHEAD

Panel Circuits and Miscellaneous

LIGHTING PANEL

POWER PANEL

WIRING – CONCEALED IN CEILING OR WALL

WIRING – CONCEALED IN FLOOR

WIRING EXPOSED

HOME RUN TO PANEL BOARD
Indicate number of circuits by number of arrows. Any circuit without such designation indicates a two-wire circuit. For a greater number of wires indicate as follows: —///— (3 wires) —////— (4 wires), etc.

FEEDERS
Use heavy lines and designate by number corresponding to listing in feeder schedule

WIRING TURNED UP

WIRING TURNED DOWN

GENERATOR — G

MOTOR — M

INSTRUMENT (SPECIFY) — I

TRANSFORMER — T

CONTROLLER

EXTERNALLY-OPERATED DISCONNECT SWITCH

PULL BOX

PLUMBING, PIPING, AND VALVE SYMBOLS

Plumbing

Corner Bathtub
Recessed Bathtub
Sitz Bath
Bidet
Shower Stall
Shower Head ....(Plan) (Elev.)
Overhead Gang Shower ...... (Plan) (Elev.)
Pedestal Lavatory
Wall Lavatory
Corner Lavatory
Handicapped Lavatory
Dental Lavatory ...... DENTAL LAV
Standard Kitchen Sink
Kitchen Sink, R & L Drain Board
Kitchen Sink, L H Drain Board
Combination Sink & Dishwasher
Combination Sink & Laundry Tray
Service Sink
Wash Sink (Wall-Type)
Wash Sink
Laundry Tray (Single)
Laundry Tray (Double)
Water Closet (Tank-Type)
Water Closet (Integral Tank)
Water Closet (Flush Valve, Floor Outlet)
Water Closet (Flush Valve, Wall-Hung)
Urinal (Wall-Hung)
Urinal (Stall)
Urinal (Trough-Type) ...... TU
Drinking Fountain (Recessed)
Drinking Fountain (Semi-Recessed)

Plumbing (continued)

Drinking Fountain (Projecting-Type)
Hot Water Tank ...... HWT
Water Heater ...... WH
Meter ...... M
Hose Rack ...... HR
Hose Bibb ...... HB
Gas Outlet ...... G
Vacuum Outlet
Drain ...... D
Grease Separator ...... G
Oil Separator
Cleanout
Garage Drain
Floor Drain with Backwater Valve
Roof Sump

Piping

Soil and Waste, Above Grade
Soil and Waste, Below Grade
Vent
Cold Water
Hot Water
Hot Water Return
Fire Line ...... F F
Gas Line ...... G G
Acid Waste ...... ACID
Drinking Water Supply
Drinking Water Return
Vacuum Cleaning ...... V V
Compressed Air ...... A

Pipe Fittings

Fitting	Screwed	Soldered
Joint		
Elbow–90°		
Elbow–45°		
Elbow–Turned Up		
Elbow–Turned Down		

Pipe Fittings (continued)

Fitting	Screwed	Soldered
Elbow–Long Radius		
Side Outlet Elbow–Outlet Down		
Side Outlet Elbow–Outlet Up		
Base Elbow		
Double Branch Elbow		
Single Sweep Tee		
Double Sweep Tee		
Reducing Elbow		
Tee		
Tee–Outlet Up		
Tee–Outlet Down		
Side Outlet Tee–Outlet Up		
Side Outlet Tee–Outlet Down		
Cross		
Concentric Reducer		
Eccentric Reducer		
Lateral		
Expansion Joint		

Valves

Valve	Screwed	Soldered
Gate Valve		
Globe Valve		
Angle Globe Valve		
Angle Gate Valve		
Check Valve		
Angle Check Valve		
Stop Cock		
Safety Valve		
Quick-Opening Valve		
Float Valve		
Motor-Operated Gate Valve		

HVAC SYMBOLS

Equipment Symbols	Ductwork	Heating Piping
EXPOSED RADIATOR	DUCT (1ST FIGURE, WIDTH; 2ND FIGURE, DEPTH) — 12 X 20	HIGH-PRESSURE STEAM —HPS—
RECESSED RADIATOR	DIRECTION OF FLOW	MEDIUM-PRESSURE STEAM —MPS—
FLUSH ENCLOSED RADIATOR	FLEXIBLE CONNECTION	LOW-PRESSURE STEAM —LPS—
PROJECTING ENCLOSED RADIATOR	DUCTWORK WITH ACOUSTICAL LINING	HIGH-PRESSURE RETURN —HPR—
UNIT HEATER (PROPELLER) – PLAN	FIRE DAMPER WITH ACCESS DOOR — FD / AD	MEDIUM-PRESSURE RETURN —MPR—
UNIT HEATER (CENTRIFUGAL) – PLAN	MANUAL VOLUME DAMPER — VD	LOW-PRESSURE RETURN —LPR—
UNIT VENTILATOR – PLAN	AUTOMATIC VOLUME DAMPER	BOILER BLOW OFF —BD—
STEAM	EXHAUST, RETURN OR OUTSIDE AIR DUCT – SECTION — 20 X 12	CONDENSATE OR VACUUM PUMP DISCHARGE —VPD—
DUPLEX STRAINER	SUPPLY DUCT – SECTION — 20 X 12	FEEDWATER PUMP DISCHARGE —PPD—
PRESSURE-REDUCING VALVE	CEILING DIFFUSER SUPPLY OUTLET — 20" DIA CD 1000 CFM	MAKEUP WATER —MU—
AIR LINE VALVE	CEILING DIFFUSER SUPPLY OUTLET — 20 X 12 CD 700 CFM	AIR RELIEF LINE —V—
STRAINER	LINEAR DIFFUSER — 96 X 6-LD 400 CFM	FUEL OIL SUCTION —FOS—
THERMOMETER	FLOOR REGISTER — 20 X 12 FR 700 CFM	FUEL OIL RETURN —FOR—
PRESSURE GAUGE AND COCK	TURNING VANES	FUEL OIL VENT —FOV—
RELIEF VALVE	FAN AND MOTOR WITH BELT GUARD	COMPRESSED AIR —A—
AUTOMATIC 3-WAY VALVE		HOT WATER HEATING SUPPLY —HW—
AUTOMATIC 2-WAY VALVE	LOUVER OPENING — 20 X 12-L 700 CFM	HOT WATER HEATING RETURN —HWR—
SOLENOID VALVE		

Air Conditioning Piping

REFRIGERANT LIQUID	—RL—
REFRIGERANT DISCHARGE	—RD—
REFRIGERANT SUCTION	—RS—
CONDENSER WATER SUPPLY	—CWS—
CONDENSER WATER RETURN	—CWR—
CHILLED WATER SUPPLY	—CHWS—
CHILLED WATER RETURN	—CHWR—
MAKEUP WATER	—MU—
HUMIDIFICATION LINE	—H—
DRAIN	—D—

ALPHABET OF LINES

Name and Use	Conventional Representation	Example
Object Line Define shape. Outline and detail objects.	THICK	OBJECT LINE
Hidden Line Show hidden features.	$\frac{1}{8}''$ (3 mm) THIN $\frac{1}{32}''$ (0.75 mm)	HIDDEN LINE
Centerline Locate centerpoints of arcs and circles.	$\frac{1}{16}''$ (1.5 mm) THIN $\frac{1}{8}''$ (3 mm) $\frac{3}{4}''$ (18 mm) TO $1\frac{1}{2}''$ (36 mm)	CENTERLINE CENTERPOINT
Dimension Line Show size or location. **Extension Line** Define size or location.	DIMENSION LINE DIMENSION THIN 2'-6" EXTENSION LINE	DIMENSION LINE $1\frac{3}{4}$ EXTENSION LINE
Leader Call out specific features.	OPEN ARROWHEAD THIN X CLOSED ARROWHEAD 3X	$1\frac{1}{2}$ DRILL LEADER
Cutting Plane Show internal features.	THICK $\frac{1}{8}''$ (3 mm) $\frac{1}{16}''$ (1.5 mm) A A $\frac{3}{4}''$ (18 mm) TO $1\frac{1}{2}''$ (36 mm)	A A LETTER IDENTIFIES SECTION VIEW CUTTING PLANE LINE
Section Line Identify internal features.	$\frac{1}{16}''$ (1.5 mm) THIN	SECTION LINES
Break Line Show long breaks. **Break Line** Show short breaks.	$\frac{3}{4}''$ (18 mm) TO $1\frac{1}{2}''$ (36 mm) THIN FREEHAND THICK	LONG BREAK LINE SHORT BREAK LINE

ENGLISH-TO-METRIC CONVERSION

Quantity	To Convert	To	Multiply By
Length	inches	millimeters	25.4
	inches	centimeters	2.54
	feet	centimeters	30.48
	feet	meters	0.3048
	yards	centimeters	91.44
	yards	meters	0.9144
Area	square inches	square millimeters	645.2
	square inches	square centimeters	6.452
	square feet	square centimeters	929.0
	square feet	square meters	0.0929
	square yards	square meters	0.8361
Volume	cubic inches	cubic millimeters	1639
	cubic inches	cubic centimeters	16.39
	cubic feet	cubic centimeters	2.832
	cubic feet	cubic meters	0.02832
	cubic yards	cubic meters	0.7646

METRIC-TO-ENGLISH CONVERSION

Quantity	To Convert	To	Multiply By
Length	millimeters	inches	0.03937
	centimeters	inches	0.3937
	meters	feet	3.281
	meters	yards	1.0937
Area	square millimeters	square inches	0.00155
	square centimeters	square inches	0.1550
	square centimeters	square feet	0.0010
	square meters	square feet	10.76
	square meters	square yards	1.196
Volume	cubic centimeters	cubic inches	0.06102
	cubic meters	cubic feet	35.31
	cubic meters	cubic yards	1.308

ABBREVIATIONS . . .

Term	Abbreviation	Term	Abbreviation	Term	Abbreviation
A		below	BLW	circuit breaker	CB or CIR BKR
above	ABV	bench mark	BM		
access	ACS	beveled wood siding	BWS	circuit interrupter	CI
access panel	AP	bituminous	BIT	circumference	CRCMF
acoustic	AC or ACST	blocking	BLKG	cleanout	CO
acoustical plaster ceiling	APC	blueprint	BP	clear glass	CL GL
acoustical tile	AT. or ACT.	board	BD	closet	C, CL, CLO, or CLOS
adjacent	ADJ	board foot	BF or BD FT		
adjustable	ADJT or ADJ	boiler	BLR	coaxial	COAX.
aggregate	AGG or AGGR	bookcase	BC	cold air	CA
air circulating	ACIRC	book shelves	BK SH	cold-rolled	CR
air conditioner	AIR COND	boulevard	BLVD	cold-rolled steel	CRS
air conditioning	A/C or AIR COND	boundary	BDRY	cold water	CW
		brass	BRS	collar beam	COL B
alloy	ALY	breaker	BRKR	color code	CC
alloy steel	ALY STL	brick	BRK	combination	COMB.
alternate	ALTN	British thermal unit	BTU	combustible	COMBL
alternating current	AC	bronze	BRZ	combustion	COMB.
aluminum	AL	broom closet	BC	common	COM
ambient	AMB	building	BLDG or BL	composition	COMP
American National Standard	AMER NATL STD	building line	BL	concrete	CONC
		built-in	BLTIN	concrete block	CCB or CONC BLK
American National Standards Institute	ANSI	built up roofing	BUR	concrete floor	CCF, CONC FLR, or CONC FL
American Steel Wire Gauge	ASWG	**C**			
American Wire Gauge	AWG	cabinet	CAB.	concrete masonry unit	CMU
ampere	A or AMP	cable	CA	concrete pipe	CP
anchor	AHR	canopy	CAN.	concrete splash block	CSB
anchor bolt	AB	caulking	CK or CLKG	condenser	COND
appearance	APP	cantilever	CANV	conductor	CNDCT
apartment	APT.	cased opening	CO	conduit	CND
approximate	APX or APPROX	casing	CSG	construction	CONSTR
		cast iron	CI	construction joint	CJ or CONSTR JT
architectural	ARCH.	cast-iron pipe	CIP		
architecture	ARCH.	cast steel	CS	continuous	CONT
area	A	cast stone	CST or CS	contour	CTR
area drain	AD	catch basin	CB	contract	CONTR or CONT
as drawn	AD	caulked joint	CLKJ		
asphalt	ASPH	cavity	CAV	contractor	CONTR
asphalt roof shingles	ASPHRS	ceiling	CLG	control joint	CJ or CLJ
asphalt tile	AT.	cellar	CEL	conventional	CVNTL
automatic	AUTO.	cement	CEM	copper	CU
auxiliary	AUX	cement floor	CF	corner	COR
avenue	AVE	cement mortar	CEM MORT	cornice	COR
azimuth	AZ	center	CTR	corrugate	CORR
		centerline	CL	counter	CNTR
		center matched	CM	county	CO
		center-to-center	C TO C	cubic	CU
B		central	CTL	cubic feet	CFT or CU FT
barrier	BARR	ceramic	CER	cubic foot per minute	CFM
barrier, moisture vapor-proof	BMVP	ceramic tile	CT	cubic foot per second	CFS
		ceramic-tile base	CTB	cubic inch	CU IN.
barrier, waterproof	BWP	ceramic-to-metal (seal)	CERMET	cubic yard	CU YD
basement	BSMT	chamfer	CHAM or CHMFR	current	CUR
bathroom	B			cutoff	CO
bathtub	BT	channel	CHAN	cutoff valve	COV
batten	BATT	check valve	CV	cut out	CO
beam	BM	chimney	CHM	**D**	
bearing	BRG	chord	CHD	damper	DMPR
bearing plate	BPL or BRG PL	cinder block	CINBL	datum	DAT
bedroom	BR	circle	CIR	decibel	DB
		circuit	CKT		

. . . ABBREVIATIONS . . .

Term	Abbreviation	Term	Abbreviation	Term	Abbreviation
degree	DEG	excavate	EXCA or EXC	general contractor	GEN CONT
depth	DP	exchange	EXCH	girder	G
design	DSGN	exhaust	EXH	glass	GL
detail	DTL or DET	exhaust vent	EXHV	glass block	GLB or GL BL
diagonal	DIAG	existing	EXST	glaze	GLZ
diagram	DIAG	expanded metal	EM	glued laminated	GLULAM
diameter	DIA or DIAM	expansion	EXP	grade	GR
dimension	DIM.	expansion joint	EXP JT	grade line	GL
dimmer	DIM. or DMR	exterior	EXT	gravel	GVL
dining room	DR or	exterior grade	EXT GR	grille	G
	DNG RM			gross weight	GRWT
direct current	DC	**F**		ground	GRD
direction	DIR			ground (outlet)	G
disconnect	DISC.	face brick	FB	ground-fault circuit	
disconnect switch	DS	faceplate	FP	interrupter	GFCI
dishwasher	DW	Fahrenheit	F	ground-fault interrupter	GFI
distribution panel	DPNL	fiberboard, solid	FBDS	gypsum	GYP
divided	DIV	finish	FIN. or FNSH	gypsum board	GYP BD
door	DR	finish all over	FAO	gypsum-plaster ceiling	GPC
door stop	DST	finish grade	FG	gypsum-plaster wall	GPW
door switch	DSW	finish one side	FIS	gypsum sheathing board	GSB
dormer	DRM	finish two sides	F2S	gypsum wallboard	GWB
double-acting	DA or	finished floor	FIN. FLR,		
	DBL ACT		FIN. FL, or	**H**	
double-hung window	DHW		FNSH FL	hardboard	HBD
double-pole double-throw	DPDT	firebrick	FBRK or FBCK	hardware	HDW
double-pole double-		fireplace	FPL or FP	header	HDR
throw switch	DPDT SW	fireproof	FP or FPRF	heat	HT
double-pole single-		fire resistant	FRES	heated	HTD
throw	DPST	fixed transom	FTR	heater	HTR
double-pole single-		fixed window	FX WDW	heating	HTG
throw switch	DPST SW	fixture	FIX. or FXTR	heating, ventilating, and	
double-pole switch	DP SW	flashing	FLG or FL	air conditioning	HVAC
double-strength glass	DSG	floor	FLR or FL	height	HGT
down	DN or D	floor drain	FD	hexagon	HEX.
downspout	DS	flooring	FLR or FLG	high density overlay	HDO
dozen	DOZ	fluorescent	FLUR or FLUOR	high point	HPT
drain	D or DR	flush	FL	highway	HWY
drain tile	DT	foot or feet	FT	hinge	HNG
drawer	DWR	footing	FTG	hollow-core	HC
drawing	DWG	foundation	FND or FDN	hollow metal door	HMD
dressed and matched	D & M	frame	FR	honeycomb	HNYCMB
drip cap	DC	frostproof hose bibb	FPHB	horizontal	HOR or HORZ
drop in pipe	D.I.P.	full scale	FSC	horsepower	HP
dryer	D	full size	FS	hose bibb	HB
drywall	DW	furnace	FURN	hot air	HA
dwelling	DWEL	furred ceiling	FC	hot water	HW
		furring	FUR	hot water tank	HWT
E		fuse	FU	humidity	HMD
each	EA	fuse block	FB		
east	E	fusebox	FUBX	**I**	
elbow	ELB	fuseholder	FUHLR	illuminate	ILLUM
electric or electrical	ELEC	fusible	FSBL	incandescent	INCAND
electrical metallic tubing	EMT			inch	IN.
electric operator	ELECT. OPR	**G**		inch per second	IPS
electric panel	EP	gallon	GAL.	inside diameter	ID
electromechanical	ELMCH	gallon per hour	GPH	install	INSTL
elevation	ELEV or EL	gallon per minute	GPM	insulation	INS or INSUL
enamel	ENAM	galvanized	GV or GALV	interior	INT
end-to-end	E to E	galvanized iron	GI or GALVI	iron	I
entrance	ENTR or ENT	galvanized steel	GS or		
equipment	EQPT		GALVS	**J**	
equivalent	EQUIV	garage	GAR.	jamb	JB or JMB
estimate	EST	gas	G	joint	JT
example	EX	gate valve	GTV	joist	
		gauge	GA	**K**	
				kiln dried	KD
				kitchen	K, KT, or KIT.

... ABBREVIATIONS ...

Term	Abbreviation	Term	Abbreviation	Term	Abbreviation
L		National Electrical Safety Code	NESC	property line	PL
laminate	LAM	natural grade	NG	pull switch	PS
laminated veneer lumber	LVL	negative	(–) or NEG	pump	PMP
landing	LDG	noncombustible	NCOMBL		
lateral	LATL	north	N	**Q**	
lath	LTH	nosing	NOS	quadrant	QDRNT
laundry	LAU	not to scale	NTS	quarry tile	QT
laundry tray	LT			quarry tile base	QTB
lavatory	LAV	**O**		quarry tile floor	QTF
leader	L	obscure glass	OBSC GL	quarter	QTR
left hand	LH	octagon	OCT	quarter-round	¼RD
length	L, LG, or LGTH	on center	OC		
		one-pole	SP	**R**	
level	LVL	opening	OPG or OPNG	radiator	RAD or RDTR
library	LIB			raised	RSD
living room	LR	open web joist	OJ, OW J, or OW JOIST	random	RDM
light	LT			range	R
light switch	LT SW	opposite	OPP	receptacle	RCPT
limestone	LMS or LS	optional	OPT	recessed	REC
linen closet	L CL	ordinance	ORD	rectangle	RECT
lining	LN	oriented strand board	OSB	redwood	RWD
linoleum	LINO	outlet	OUT.	reference	REF
linoleum floor	LF or LINO FLR	outside diameter	OD	reference line	REFL
		out-to-out	O TO O	reflected	REFLD
lintel	LNTL	overall	OA	refrigerator	REF or REFR
living room	LR	overcurrent	OC	register	REG or RGTR
local	LCL	overcurrent relay	OCR	reinforce or reinforcing	RE or REINF
louver	LVR or LV	overhead	OH or OVHD	reinforced concrete	RC
low point	LP			reinforcing steel	RST
lumber	LBR	**P**		reinforcing steel bar	REBAR
		paint	PNT	required	REQD
M		panel	PNL	retaining	RETG
main	MN	pantry	PAN.	revision	REV
makeup	MKUP	parallel	PRL	revolution per minute	RPM
manufactured	MFD	parallel strand lumber	PSL	revolution per second	RPS
marble	MRB or MR	partition	PTN	right hand	RH
masonry	MSNRY	passage	PASS.	riser	R
masonry opening	MO	penny (nails, etc.)	d	road	RD
material	MTL or MATL	perimeter	PERIM	roof	RF
maximum	MAX	perpendicular	PERP	roof drain	RD
median	MDN	per square inch	PSI	roofing	RFG
medicine cabinet	MC	phase	PH	room	RM or R
medium	MDM	piping	PP	rough	RGH
medium density overlay	MDO	plaster	PLAS or PL	rough opening	RO or RGH OPNG
meridian	MER	plastered open	PO		
metal	MET.	plate	PL	rough-sawn	RS
metal anchor	MA	plate glass	PG, PL GL, or PLGL	round	RND
metal door	METD			rubber	RBR
metal flashing	METF	platform	PLAT	rubber tile	RBT or R TILE
metal threshold	MT	plumbing	PLBG	rustproof	RSTPF
mineral	MNRL	plywood	PLYWD		
minimum	MIN	point	PT	**S**	
mirror	MIR	point of beginning	POB	safety	SAF
miscellaneous	MISC	polyvinyl chloride	PVC	sanitary	S
miter	MIT	porch	P	S-beam	S
mixture	MIX.	pound	LB	scale	SC
modular	MOD	power	PWR	schedule	SCH or SCHED
molding	MLD or MLDG	power supply	PWR SPLY	screen	SCN, SCR, or SCRN
		precast	PRCST		
mortar	MOR	prefabricated	PFB or PREFAB	screen door	SCD
N				screw	SCR
National Electrical Code®	NEC®	prefinished	PFN	scuttle	S
		property	PROP.	section	SEC or SECT.
				select	SEL

. . . ABBREVIATIONS

Term	Abbreviation	Term	Abbreviation	Term	Abbreviation
self-cleaning	SLFCLN	standard	STD	vent hole	VH
self-closing	SELF CL	steel	ST or STL	ventilate	VEN
service	SERV or SVCE	steel sash	SS	ventilating equipment	VE
		stone	STN	vent pipe	VP
sewer	SEW.	storage	STO or STG	vent stack	VS
sheathing	SHTH or SHTHG	street	ST or STR	vertical	VERT
		structural	STRL	vestibule	VEST.
sheet	SHT or SH	Structural Clay Products		vinyl tile	VT or V TILE
sheeting	SH	Research Foundation	SCR	vitreous tile	VIT TILR
sheet metal	SM	structural clay tile	SCT	void	VD
shelf and rod	SH&RD	structural glass	SG	volt	V
shelving	SH or SHELV	supply	SPLY	voltage	V
shingle	SHGL	survey	SURV	voltage drop	VD
shower	SH	suspended	SUSP	volt amp	VA
shower and toilet	SH & T	switch	SW or S	volume	VOL
shower drain	SD				
shutter	SHTR	**T**		**W**	
sidelight	SI LT	telephone	TEL	wainscot	WSCT, WAIN., or WA
sill cock	SC	television	TV		
single-phase	1PH	temperature	TEMP	walk in closet	WIC
single-pole	SP	tempered plate glass	TEM PL GL	wall	W
single-pole double-throw	SPDT	terra cotta	TC	wallboard	WLB
single-pole double throw switch	SPDT SW	terazzo	TZ or TER	wall receptacle	WR
		thermostat	THERMO	warm air	WA
single-pole single-throw	SPST	thick	THK	washing machine	WM
		threshold	TH	water	WTR or W
single-pole single-throw switch	SPST SW	tile base	TB	water closet	WC
		tile drain	TD	water heater	WH
single-pole switch	SP SW	tile floor	TF	water line	WL
single-strength glass	SSG	timber	TMBR	water meter	WM
single-throw	ST	toilet	T	waterproof	WTRPRF
sink	SK or S	tongue-and-groove	T & G	water-resistant	WR
skylight	SLT	township	T	watt	W
sliding door	SLD or SL DR	tread	TR or T	weatherproof	WTHPRF or WP
		typical	TYP		
slope	SLP			weather-resistant	WR
soffit	SF	**U**		weather stripping	WS
soil pipe	SP	underground	UGND	weep hole	WH
soil stack	SSK	unexcavated	UNEXC	welded wire reinforcement	WWR
solid core	SC	unfinished	UNFIN or UNF	west	W
soundproof	SNDPRF			white pine	WP
south	S	unit heater	UH	wide	W
specific	SP	unless otherwise specified	UOS	wide flange	W or WF
specification	SPEC			window	WDO
splash block	SB	untreated	UTRTD	wood	WD
square	SQ	utility	U or UTIL	wood frame	WF
square feet	SQ FT	utility room	UR or U RM	wrought iron	WI
square inch	SQ IN.				
square yard	SQ YD	**V**		**Y**	
stack	STK	vacuum	VAC	yard	YD
stained	STN	valley	VAL	yellow pine	YP
stainless steel	SST	valve	V	**Z**	
stairs	ST	variance	VAR	Zone	Z
stairway	STWY	vent	V		

GLOSSARY

A

abbreviation: Letter or series of letters of words denoting a complete word.

acronym: Abbreviated word formed from the first letter of each word that describes the article.

acute triangle: Triangle that has no 90° angles.

addition: Process of combining two or more whole numbers to obtain a total.

air conditioner: Piece of equipment used to control humidity and temperature and remove airborne impurities in a house.

air conditioning: Process used to control humidity, temperature, and/or cleanliness of air within a house.

alkaline copper quaternary: A wood preservative used to prevent decay and make the wood suitable for exterior use.

arc: Portion of the circumference of a circle.

architect's scale: Drafting scale used when producing drawings of buildings and structural parts.

area: Two-dimensional surface measurement.

B

balloon framing: System of frame construction in which one-piece exterior wall studs extend from the first floor line or sill plate to the double top plate.

baseline: East-West line that defines a group of townships on a grid.

benchmark: Stake driven into the ground or a fixed point in the street or along the curb that is used as the point of beginning.

bituminous roofing: Roofing composed of multiple individual layers (plies) of asphalt-impregnated felt or fiberglass material that is fastened to the roof deck and mopped with hot tar to create a waterproof surface.

blower: Piece of equipment that draws air from various living spaces and moves it through the furnace, where it is heated before being conveyed back into the rooms.

boiler: Closed tank connected to an energy source that heats water to a high temperature.

brick bond: Pattern formed by exposed faces of brick.

brick veneer construction: Frame construction with brick exterior facing.

bridging: Metal or wood cross bridging or solid wood blocking installed between joists to stiffen a floor unit and prevent joists from twisting.

building information modeling (BIM): Integrated, electronically managed system that aligns all working drawings, structural drawings, and shop drawings into a consistent system.

built-up beam: Structural member made of laminated wood members, designed to carry heavy loads.

C

chlorinated polyvinyl chloride (CPVC): Rigid plastic pipe that can withstand greater pressure and higher temperatures than PVC.

chord: A line from circumference to circumference that does not pass through the centerpoint of a circle.

circle: Plane figure generated around a centerpoint.

circulating pump: Device that moves water through the supply water piping in a hot water heating system.

circumference: Perimeter (outside edge) of a circle.

civil engineer's scale: Drafting scale used when creating maps and survey drawings.

compass: Drafting instrument used to draw arcs and circles.

317

composition shingle: Asphalt or fiberglass shingle coated with a layer of fine mineral granules.

compression tank: Tank that absorbs and relieves pressure caused by water expansion when heated.

computer: Device that receives information from an input device, processes it, and displays the results on a monitor.

contemporary design: Architectural design that reflects current trends and may include more complex rooflines, geometric windows, and curved or angled walls.

contour line: Dashed or solid line on a plot plan that passes through points having the same elevation.

cross-linked polyethylene (PEX): Flexible tubing that allows directional changes to be made with minimal fittings, has resistance to high temperatures and high pressures, and is fastened in sections with crimping or compression connections.

cutting plane line: Line that identifies the exact place where a cutting plane passes through a feature.

D

decimal fraction: Fraction with a denominator of 10, 100, 1000, 10,000, and so on.

denominator: Part of a fraction that indicates the total number of parts or divisions of a whole number.

detail: Scaled plan, elevation, or section drawn to a larger scale to show special features.

diameter: Distance from circumference to circumference passing through the centerpoint of a circle.

dimension lumber: Solid wood framing lumber that is precut to a particular size for the construction industry.

dividend: Number to be divided in the division operation.

dividers: Drafting instrument used to transfer dimensions.

division: Mathematical process of determining the number of times one number is contained in another number.

divisor: Number that a dividend is divided by in the division operation.

door hand: Direction a door swings.

dormer: Projection from a sloping roof that provides additional interior area.

duplex nail: Double-headed nail designed to be pulled out easily to facilitate the stripping of forms.

E

easement: Strip of privately owned land set aside for placement of public utilities.

elastomeric roofing: Composed of continuous sheets of rubberized materials that are rolled out across a flat roof surface.

electric radiant heating system: Radiant heating system in which heat is generated when electricity meets resistance as it flows through embedded heating cables or baseboard units.

elevation: 1. Scaled view looking directly at an object such as a wall. **2.** Vertical measurement above or below the point of beginning.

ellipse: Plane figure generated by the sum of the distances from two fixed points.

engineered lumber: Framing material that is manufactured using solid wood members or veneers; wood strands and fibers; or a combination of solid wood members and wood strand members.

equilateral triangle: Acute triangle that contains three equal sides and three 60° angles.

even number: Number that can be divided by two without a remainder or decimal occurring.

exterior elevation: Scaled view that shows the shape and size of the outside walls of the house and the roof.

exterior insulation and finish system (EIFS): System used to provide exterior building protection through application of exterior insulation, insulation board, reinforcing mesh, a base coat of acrylic copolymers and portland cement, and a finish coat of acrylic resins.

F

fiber-cement siding: Composed of cement, ground sand, and cellulose fiber that are autoclaved (cured with pressurized steam) to increase its strength and dimensional stability.

finger-jointed lumber: Engineered lumber product composed of short pieces of dimension lumber joined end-to-end.

finish grade: Slope of the land after final grading.

fire cut: Angled cut in the end of a wood joist that allows a burnt joist to fall out without disturbing the solid brick wall.

fire protection system: Safety system that detects and suppresses a fire using a system of alarms, sensors, valves, pipes, and delivery devices.

flatwork: Forming, placement, and finishing of concrete slabs such as basements, garages, driveways, walkways, and patios.

floor plan: Scaled view of the various floors in a house looking directly down from a horizontal cutting plane taken 5'-0" above each finished floor.

flush door: Door with flat surfaces with the stiles and rails within the door.

footing: Portion of a foundation that spreads and transmits loads directly to piles or to the soil.

forced warm air heating system: Residential heating system that uses a blower to draw air (return air) from rooms through return air grilles and ductwork.

foundation: Part of a building that rests on and extends into the ground and provides support for the building above it.

full basement foundation: Foundation used in residential structures consisting of 9' high walls to allow space for mechanical systems without sacrificing finished ceiling height.

function key: Key on a keyboard that performs a special task.

furnace: Piece of equipment that heats the air circulating in a forced warm air heating system.

G

gauge: Unit of measurement for identifying sheet steel thickness.

general note: Notation that refers to an entire set of prints.

geothermal heat: Heat derived from heat contained within the earth.

glued laminated (glulam) timber: Engineered lumber product composed of wood laminations (lams) that are bonded together with adhesives.

H

hollow-core door: Flush door with wood surface veneers, a solid wood frame, and a mesh core.

horizontal line: Line that is level or parallel to the horizon.

hot water radiant heating (hydronic) system: Radiant heating system in which water is heated in a boiler at a central location and then distributed to the desired rooms through tubing.

I

improper fraction: Fraction with the numerator larger than the denominator. An improper fraction must be converted to a mixed number.

insulating concrete form (ICF): Type of concrete-forming system that consists of a layer of concrete sandwiched between expanded polystyrene (EPS) foam forms on each side.

insulation: Material used as barrier to inhibit thermal and sound transmission.

interior elevation: Scaled view that shows the shapes, sizes, and finishes of interior walls and partitions of a house.

irregular polygon: Polygon that has unequal sides and unequal angles.

isometric drawing: Pictorial drawing with horizontal lines drawn 30° above (or below) the horizon.

isosceles triangle: Acute triangle that contains two equal sides and two equal angles.

J

job-built form: Foundation wall form constructed piece by piece on top of a footing.

joist: Horizontal framing member that supports a floor.

K

keyboard: Input device containing standard alpha and numeric keys as well as function keys.

keyway: Groove formed in fresh concrete that interlocks the footing with concrete from the foundation wall.

kilogram: Basic unit of weight in the SI metric system.

L

laminated veneer lumber (LVL): Engineered lumber product composed of layered veneers and waterproof adhesive.

light: Pane of glass.

location dimension: Dimension that gives the relationship of a particular component or building feature in relation to another feature.

longitudinal section: Section created by passing a cutting plane through the long dimension of a house.

M

masonry: Form of construction involving the assembly of a structure using individual units such as bricks or blocks bonded with mortar.

masonry construction: System of construction in which masonry units such as brick, concrete masonry units, stone, or structural clay tile are formed into walls to carry the load of floor and roof joists.

mechanical engineer's scale: Drafting scale used when drawing machines and machine parts.

meridian: North-South line that defines a group of townships on a grid.

metal framing: Method of constructing the framework of a building using light-gauge steel framing members.

metal roofing: Roofing made of steel, aluminum, copper, or various metal alloys.

meter: Basic unit of measurement in the SI metric system.

minuend: Total number of units prior to subtraction.

mixed decimal number: Decimal number consisting of a whole number and a decimal number separated by a decimal point.

mixed number: Fraction containing a whole number and a fraction.

model code: National building code developed through conferences between building officials and industry representatives around the country.

modular brick: Brick classified by its actual size and designed so every third horizontal joint falls on a multiple of 4″ (modular measure).

monitor: High-resolution color display screen that allows drawings, data, and text to be displayed.

multiplicand: Number being multiplied in the multiplication operation.

multiplication: Mathematical process of adding a number to itself as many times as there are units indicated by the other number.

multiplier: Number in the multiplication operation that indicates the number of times the addition should occur.

N

natural grade: Slope of the land before rough grading.

nominal size: Size of a piece of wood before it is planed to finished size.

numerator: Part of a fraction that indicates the number of parts included in the fraction.

O

oblique drawing: Pictorial drawing with one surface drawn in true shape and receding lines projecting back from the face.

obtuse triangle: Triangle that includes one angle greater than 90°.

odd number: Number that can be divided by two with a remainder or decimal occurring.

operating controls: Controls that cycle equipment on and off as required.

oriented strand lumber (OSL): Engineered lumber product that is made from flaked wood strands that have a high length-to-thickness ratio.

orthographic projection: Drawing in which each face of an object is projected onto flat planes, generally at 90° to one another.

P

panel door: Door with individual panels between the stiles and rails.

panel form: Prefabricated concrete wall form consisting of a metal frame and metal or wood panel facing or wood studs and plates with wood panel facing.

panned ceiling: Ceiling consisting of two ceiling levels connected by sloped surfaces.

parallel strand lumber (PSL): Engineered lumber product manufactured from strands or elongated flakes of wood that are blended with a waterproof adhesive and cured under pressure.

perspective drawing: Pictorial drawing with all receding lines converging to vanishing points.

photovoltaics: Solar energy technology that uses crystalline silicon wafers that are sensitive to sunlight in order to directly convert solar radiation into electricity.

photovoltaic system: Electrical system consisting of a PV module array and other electrical components needed to convert solar energy into electricity usable by loads.

pictorial drawing: Three-dimensional representation of an object.

piping: Tubing used to distribute hot water from the boiler to terminal devices and return water back to the boiler to be reheated.

pitch: Angle a roof slopes from the roof ridge to the outside walls of the building.

place: Position that a digit occupies; it represents the value of the digit.

plane figure: Geometric shape with a flat surface.

platform framing: System of frame construction in which each story of a building is framed as a unit, with studs being one story in height.

plot plan: Scaled drawing that shows the shape and size of the building lot; location, shape, and overall size of a house on the lot; and the finish floor elevation.

plumbing: System of pipes, fittings, and devices within a building that supplies fresh water and removes waterborne waste and stormwater.

point of beginning (POB): Location point from which horizontal dimensions and vertical elevations are made.

polygon: Many-sided plane figure that is bounded by straight lines.

polyvinyl chloride (PVC): Rigid plastic pipe that is used for water mains and water service lines.

post-and-beam framing: System of frame construction in which posts and beams provide the primary structural support.

potable water: Water free from impurities in amounts that could cause disease or harmful effects.

power controls: Controls located in the electrical conductors leading to the furnace and blower.

prime number: Odd number that can only be divided by 1 or itself without a remainder or decimal occurring.

print: Reproduction of a working drawing.

product: Result of multiplication.

proper decimal number: Decimal number that does not have a whole number, such as 0.9.

Q

quadrant: One-fourth of a circle.

quadrilateral: Four-sided plane figure.

quotient: The result of the division operation.

R

raceway: Enclosed channel designed to protect electrical conductors.

radiant heating system: Series of pipes utilized to transfer heat to the living space by being filled with hot water or a series of electrical cables embedded in the floor or ceiling.

radius: One-half the diameter of a circle.

rebar: Deformed steel bar containing lugs (protrusions) that allow the bars to interlock with concrete.

rectangle: Quadrilateral that contains four 90° angles with opposite sides equal.

regular polygon: Polygon that has equal sides and equal angles.

result: Difference between the minuend and subtrahend in the subtraction operation.

rhomboid: Quadrilateral that has opposite sides equal and opposite angles equal, but does not contain any 90° angles.

rhombus: Quadrilateral that contains four equal sides with opposite angles equal and no 90° angles.

right triangle: Triangle that contains one 90° angle.

riser: Vertical portion of a stair step.

roofing tile: Clay, slate, or lightweight concrete material installed as weather-protective finish on a roof.

rough-in: Installation of pipes and plumbing fittings that will be concealed after construction is complete.

R-value: Measure of the effectiveness of a material to provide thermal insulation.

S

safety controls: Controls that prevent injury to personnel or damage to equipment in the event of equipment malfunction.

scale: Drafting tool used to measure lines and reduce or enlarge them proportionally.

scuttle: Access opening in a ceiling or roof with a removable or movable cover.

section: 1. Scaled view created by passing a cutting plane through a portion of a building. 2. Division of a township and is one mile long on each side.

sector: Pie-shaped segment of a circle.

semicircle: One-half of a circle.

size dimension: Dimension that indicates the length, width, and depth of a particular area or feature.

sketching: Process of drawing without instruments.

slab-at-grade foundation: Ground-supported foundation system that combines short concrete foundation walls or a thickened concrete edge with a concrete floor slab.

slanted line: Inclined line that is neither horizontal nor vertical.

slope: Relationship of unit rise to unit run of a roof.

solar energy: Energy available from the sun in the form of sunlight.

solar thermal energy system: Sustainable energy system that collects and stores solar energy and is used to heat air and water in a residential structure.

solid-core door: Flush door with wood surface veneer and an inner core made of solid wood blocks, engineered wood products, or high-density foam.

specifications: Written supplements to working drawings that provide additional building information.

speculative (spec) house: House built by a contractor on the assumption that a buyer will be found during or after completion of construction.

square: Quadrilateral that contains four equal sides and four 90° angles.

standard brick: Brick classified by its nominal size.

structural insulated panel: Structural member consisting of a thick layer of rigid foam insulation pressed between two OSB or plywood panels.

subtraction: Mathematical process of taking one number away from another number.

subtrahend: Number of units to be removed from the minuend in the subtraction operation.

sum: Total that results from addition.

survey plat: Map showing a division of land, such as a portion of a quarter section of a township, subdivided into streets and lots.

sustainable construction: Construction system that incorporates environmentally sensitive practices and materials into the building process.

symbol: Pictorial representation of a structural or material component used on prints.

T

terminal device: Device that extracts heat from hot water to heat the air in the desired rooms.

T-foundation: Foundation consisting of an independently placed wall above a footing that extends on both sides of the wall.

title block: Area on a working drawing or print that is used to provide written information about the drawing or print.

township: Square area that is 6 miles long on each side, or 36 square miles.

traditional design: Architectural design that reflects long-standing design elements.

transverse section: Section created by passing a cutting plane through the short dimension of a house.

trapezium: Quadrilateral that has no sides parallel.

trapezoid: Quadrilateral that has two sides parallel.

tread: Horizontal portion of a stair step.

triangle: 1. Drafting tool used to draw vertical and inclined lines. 2. Three-sided plane figure that contains 180°.

T-square: Drafting tool used to draw horizontal lines and as a reference base for positioning triangles.

type NM cable: Nonmetallic-sheathed cable where the conductors are enclosed within a nonmetallic jacket, and is the type typically used for dry interior wiring.

type NMC cable: Nonmetallic-sheathed cable where the conductors are enclosed within a corrosion-resistant, nonmetallic jacket that can be used for interior or exterior wiring.

typical note: Notation that refers to all similar items on the prints.

U

unit controls: Set of controls installed on a furnace by the manufacturer or installer to maintain safe and efficient operation of the furnace.

unit rise: Vertical increase in height per foot of run.

unit run: Unit of the total run based on 12″.

V

veneer plaster: Interior wall finish that consists of a fire-resistant gypsum board covered by one or two layers of gypsum plaster measuring ⅟₁₆″ to ⅛″ thick.

vertical line: A line that is plumb or upright.

voice/data/video (VDV) system: Low-voltage electrical system designed for use with various types of information technology equipment, including telephone systems, computer systems and networks, television video systems for cable and/or satellite dish systems, and security and fire alarm systems.

volume: Three-dimensional capacity of a space.

W

walkout basement: Basement with standard-sized windows to provide light and standard-sized doors for entry and exit.

welded wire reinforcement: Heavy-gauge wire joined in a grid and used to increase the tensile strength of concrete and help prevent cracks.

whole-house system approach: System for home building or remodeling used by the homeowner, architect, and builder to optimize home energy efficiency.

whole number: Number that does not have a fractional or decimal part.

wood I-joists: Load-bearing structural members consisting of a web placed between top and bottom flanges.

working drawing: Drawing that contains the graphic information necessary to complete a construction job.

wythe: Single continuous masonry wall, one unit thick.

INDEX

Page numbers in italic refer to figures.